The
KOSHER
CARNIVORE

The
KOSHER
CARNIVORE

The Ultimate Meat and
Poultry Cookbook

JUNE HERSH

ST. MARTIN'S PRESS ❧ NEW YORK

www.stmartins.com

Book design by Jonathan Bennett

ISBN 978-0-312-69942-0

First Edition: September 2011

10 9 8 7 6 5 4 3 2 1

This book is dedicated to my mother,
who taught me to always bring love to the table,
and my father, who taught me to eat with gusto
and cook with abandon. Together you showed me
how to savor life's full flavor.

CONTENTS

ACKNOWLEDGMENTS XII

INTRODUCTION: Meat Me in the Kitchen. 1

COOKING METHODS. 7

BUILDING FLAVOR. 11

READING THE RECIPE. 17

BEEF. Exploring the Neighborhood 19
    Standing Rib Roast 23
    Roasted Beef *and fingerling potatoes in porcini*
        mushroom gravy. 24
    Classic Pot Roast 26
    Steak Pizzaiola 27
    Rib Steak Florentine 28
    Chicken-Fried Steak 30
    Steak and Eggs 31
    Grilled Steak Chimichurri 32
    Coffee-Crusted Hanger Steak 34
    Grilled Steak Salad 35
    Beef Braciole in Sunday Sauce 36
    Crispy Orange Beef and Broccoli 39
    Beef Stew Provençal 41
    Simple Oven-Braised Short Ribs 42
    Simpler BBQ Ribs 44
    Simplest Korean *Kalbi* Ribs 46
    Slow-Day BBQ Brisket 47
    Classic Brisket 49
    New England Boiled Dinner 51
    Corned Beef Hash *with poached egg* 53

Poached Egg 54
The Best Burger 56
Spaghetti Bolognese 56
Spicy Grilled *Mititei* 58
Picadillo 59
Matzo Meat Cakes 60
Pushcart Puppies 63
Sausage and Peppers 64
Breakfast Burrito 66

VEAL 67
Roasted Veal Shoulder *with chicken liver stuffing* 69
Mediterranean Osso Buco *with zesty gremolata* 71
Grilled Veal Chops *and roasted red grapes Syrah* 74
Stuffed Mushroom Caps *with Asian or Italian Filling* . . 75
Veal Meatballs 76
Veal Marengo 78
Veal Milanese *topped with field greens*
    and grape tomato salad 79
Veal Brisket *and cippolini onions and mushrooms* 81
Calf's Liver *and caramelized onions in a*
    balsamic berry glaze 83
Southern Fried Sweatbreads 84

LAMB 87
Herb-Crusted Rib Lamb Chops 89
Mediterranean Rack of Lamb 90
Grilled Lamb Riblets 92
Teriyaki-Glazed Shoulder Lamb Chops 93
Pesto-Crusted Roasted Lamb Shoulder 94
Moroccan Lamb Shanks *with pomegranate sauce* 96
Lamb Tagine 98
Lamb and Spinach Spanakopita 99
Lamb Sliders 102

CHICKEN 103
Simple Spatchcocked Chicken
    and roasted root vegetables 107

Simpler Beer-Basted Chicken 109
Simplest Roast Chicken 111
Roasted Cornish Hen 112
"Bonus" Chicken 114
Topless Chicken Potpie 115
Curried Chicken Salad 117
Chicken Caesar Salad *with garlic croutons* 118
Chicken and Sausage Gumbo 120
Chicken Cacciatore 122
Chicken with Prunes *Tsimmes* 124
Chicken in Red Wine Sauce 125
Crispy Fried Chicken 126
Chicken and Rice 128
Peach and Ginger–Glazed Chicken 129
Moroccan Chicken 131
Skewered Chicken Thighs *with coconut peanut*
    dipping sauce 133
Grilled Spice Rubbed Chicken 135
No-Brainer Wings 136
Chicken Piccata 137
Panko-Crusted Chicken Cutlets 139
Grilled Chicken and Pasta Primavera 140
Pretzel-Crusted chicken *with honey beer mustard sauce*..141
Chicken Lettuce Cups 143
Chicken Croquettes 144
Chicken and Scallion Wontons *with soy dipping sauce*. .145
Chicken Liver Paté *served on crostini 3 ways* 147

TURKEY 149
Turkey with Sauerkraut 149
Oven-Barbecued Turkey 150
Turkey Roulade *with savory stuffing* 152
Country-Style Turkey Meat Loaf 154
Turkey Chili 155
Turkey Sausage *with orecchiette pasta and broccoli rabe*. . 157
Grilled Turkey Paillard
    topped with haricots verts and tomato salad 158

DUCK 161
   Roast Duck *with cherry port sauce* 161
   Pan-Seared Duck Breasts *with fig, apricot, and*
      Madeira sauce 164
   Breast of Duck Salad *with raspberries and candied*
   walnuts 165

SOUP AND STOCK 167
   Homemade Stock 167
   Chicken Stock 169
   Creamy Mushroom Soup 170
   Martha's Excellent Matzo Ball Soup 171
   Abundant Asian Noodle Soup 173
   Tuscan Ribollita Soup *with ground sausage* 174
   Hungarian Bean Soup *with smoked turkey* 176
   Lentil Soup 177
   Beef Stock 178
   Grandma Rose's Cabbage Soup 180
   Beef and Barley Soup 181

GOOD CARBS 183
   Potato and Zucchini Pancakes 183
   Roasted Rosemary Potatoes .185
   Herb Potato Salad 185
   Twice-Fried Potatoes 186
   Creamy Mashed Potatoes 187
   Vegetable Fried Rice 188
   Black Beans and Rice 189
   Porcini Mushroom Risotto 190
   Wild Rice *with dried cranberries* 191
   Basmati Rice 192
   Tomatoey Rice *with zucchini* 193
   Tuscan Beans 194
   Quinoa *with apple cider–braised squash and prunes* 195
   Kasha Varnishkes 196
   Chickpea and White Bean Hummus 197

DOUGH 199
    Egg Barley *with mushrooms and onions* 199
    Israeli Couscous *with mint* 200
    Homemade Egg Noodles 201
    Dumplings and Spaetzle 203
    Yorkshire Pudding 204
    Grilled Pizza Flatbread 205

THE VEGGIES 207
    Roasted Corn on the Cob 207
    Oven-Roasted Plum Tomatoes 208
    Lemon and Garlic Broccoli 209
    Lemony Cauliflower Fritters 210
    Roasted Eggplant and Tomato Salad 211
    Creamed Spinach 212

CHUTNEYS, SALSAS, AND RELISH 215
    Cranberry Raisin Apple Chutney 215
    Pineapple Mango Chutney 216
    Plum Tomato and Tomatillo Salsa 217
    Preserved Lemons 218
    Quick Pickled Cucumber Salad 219
    Celery Root Apple–Slaw 219
    Traditional Guacamole .220

DRESSING UP 223
    Homemade Mayonnaise 223
    Horseradish Cream 224
    Guacamole Cream Aioli 225
    Sofrito 225
    Tomato Jam 226
    Red Pepper Vinaigrette 227

INDEX 229

ACKNOWLEDGMENTS

I cannot begin to thank those who inspired, encouraged, and facilitated my work on this book without thanking the remarkable community of Holocaust survivors who shared with me their cherished food memories for my first book, *Recipes Remembered, A Celebration of Survival*. That rich and rewarding experience taught me so much, not the least of which was how to cook in the kosher tradition.

One of the friendships that developed through *Recipes Remembered* was with Carla Glasser, a wonderful and dedicated literary agent and, more important, a good person. Thank you for recognizing the potential in this idea and knowing that Elizabeth Beier at St. Martin's Press would be the perfect editor for the book. Elizabeth, you brought life and vitality to the subject while inspiring me with your incredible professionalism and broad food knowledge. Your spirit and commitment was unwavering and our having so much fun was an added bonus. Thank you for showing the good judgment to pair me with both Michelle Richter, who chaperoned me through the process, and Ben Fink, who whet our appetites with his beautiful photos. Together they were consummate Sherpas on this satisfying adventure. I remained in the most expert hands, from production to design, PR to marketing, with Elizabeth Curione, Cheryl Mamaril, Steve Snider, Jonathan Bennett, Nadea Mina, and Jeanne-Marie Hudson. Together you served up a delicious book sure to make even the most ardent vegetarian a convert to the carnivorous ways.

A big thank-you goes to my team of mavens: from the butchers behind the counter, to the professionals in all things culinary, you imparted your knowledge and advice patiently, expertly and generously.

At the end of the day, a cookbook is all about the recipes and I had to be certain that the food that I presented tasted good. Thank you to my husband, Ron, who loosened his belt and saddled up to the table nightly to offer his honest critiques. As his meat coma passed, he meticulously cleaned up my mess and then encouraged me to "go write that up." I relied heavily on the objective opinions of my family, who risked rising cholesterol levels and who welcomed every dish with an open mind and a discerning palate. Thank you for intently listening to what I wrote and happily tasting what I prepared.

My final acknowledgment brings us full circle back to my first, and it is to you, the kosher cooks, those who answer to a higher authority and maintain the age-old traditions. My mother grew up in such a home and it helped shape her values and frame her perspective. I have tremendous respect for the choices you have made. For all the readers who are ethically eating, integrating kosher products into your lifestyle, or simply buying with an eye toward quality, I thank you for embracing this book and taking this culinary journey with me.

*If the divine creator has taken pains to give us delicious
and exquisite things to eat, the least we can do is prepare them well
and serve them with ceremony.*

—FERNAND POINT, master restaurateur, chef,
author, and culinary philosopher

INTRODUCTION

Meat Me in the Kitchen

K osher eating is a trend 3,300 years in the making. For thousands of years, observant Jews have "kept kosher" following a code of dietary laws that govern what they can eat as well as how it needs to be slaughtered, butchered, and prepared. These are practices based on the Torah and Talmud and represent a deep spiritual commitment to Judaism and a mindfulness that many find rich and satisfying. Similarly, practicing Muslims follow the laws of Halal, with many of the same guidelines as kosher. For both groups, adherence to these strict laws shows an unwavering acceptance of the written word. It's the ultimate example of "because I said so," with no questions asked and no wiggle room.

However, there is a new wave of consumers who have found ethical arguments and health benefits to support making kosher a part of their life. You might be part of that movement. This book addresses both the new face of kosher as well as the traditional kosher consumer with a focus on meat and poultry. Whether you buy kosher chicken because it is plumper and tastier or kosher steak because you are observant and would not consider eating anything else, this book is an indispensable resource. If you were raised in a kosher home or have kept kosher for some time, then you are familiar with the rules that govern kosher meat and poultry. But, if you are part of this new generation of mindful eaters and conscious cooks, you might need Kosher 101. We'll start at the beginning . . . and I don't mean the book of Genesis.

THE KOSHER CARNIVORE

The Torah identifies as acceptable a variety of animals for human consumption. Among them are antelope, addax, bison, cow, deer, giraffe, goat, gazelle, ibex, and sheep. All these animals chew their cud and have cloven hooves. To be considered kosher, an animal must meet both criteria. I haven't had a hankering for giraffe in quite some time, and I rarely find antelope at my local butcher, so in this book we'll focus on meat from the cow, calf, and lamb. When it comes to fowl, kosher is more about which birds cannot be eaten than which can. There are twenty-four forbidden species, mainly because they are considered to be predators or scavengers. Because the list of acceptable species is not clearly defined, observant Jews use history and tradition to determine if a bird can be eaten. If they cannot find a biblical reference to that bird, then it is considered forbidden. Fortunately there's not much demand for southern fried vulture, which is on the forbidden list, but chicken, turkey, and duck all make the cut.

An animal is not born into a kosher family; it becomes kosher by how it is slaughtered and butchered. The rules governing this aspect are quite strict, and must be adhered to absolutely in order for meat and poultry to be tagged kosher. Kosher slaughtering, while not exempt from controversy, is more humane than non-kosher slaughtering. According to kosher law, the animal must be killed swiftly and as mercifully as possible by a *sochet,* a trained, pious person. The knife must be razor-sharp and smooth to minimize the animal's suffering. After slaughtering, the animal must be drained of blood, rinsed, salted and then rinsed again, as Jewish law forbids the ingestion of blood. Aside from the religious implications of this process, an important health aspect of koshering is that when blood does not circulate, the risk of disease being transmitted throughout the animal is greatly reduced. After slaughtering, the animal undergoes a thorough and meticulous examination. While kosher meat and poultry are not inherently any healthier than non-kosher, the rules overseeing this important stage provide greater assurance that the meat and poultry is "fit and proper," which is the literal translation of the word *kosher.* The animal is checked for more than seventy irregularities and must be disease-free. To be *Glatt* kosher, the highest standard, the animal's lungs must be smooth and there can be no adhesions. Any animal that dies or is killed by any other means is considered *treif,* not kosher. This stringent inspection trumps even USDA standards, and is a compelling reason many consumers choose kosher meat.

Kosher butchering is also guided by very explicit rules. When it comes to butchering, kosher literally kicks butt. Kosher law dictates that certain nerves, fat, and arteries, which are mainly found in the back half of the animal, cannot be eaten. In America, it is difficult and costly to remove those elements as it takes a highly skilled butcher and a time-consuming process, leaving only the front half of the animal deemed kosher. You can find kosher hind portions across the ocean or in the Middle East, but that's a long way to go for a piece of tenderloin.

KOSHER IN THE KITCHEN

After the meat has been *kashered*—made kosher—and makes its way to your market or local meat purveyor, kosher measures don't stop. Dietary laws also govern how to prepare the food. Long before anyone knew the term "lactose intolerant," kosher rules prohibited the mixing of meat and dairy. Cooks have to be clever: there can be no cream, no butter, and *no* exceptions in a dish. Kosher eating does allow meat to mingle with neutral foods, such as oil and eggs, that are termed *pareve* (parve), the dietary equivalent of Switzerland. All recipes in this book will be dairy free. However, because this is a cookbook, not a religious tome, it contains great tips, techniques, and recipes, but no Sunday school lessons, imperatives, or guilt. The kosher spectrum is broad, and your choices need to be compatible with your lifestyle. If you are kosher, you know the rules better than anyone: when in doubt, leave it out.

ETHICAL EATING

Eco-kosher has made its way to the forefront of conscious kosher eating. "Farm to fork" is gaining popularity and large factory production is giving way to organic alternatives and greener pastures. This movement is influencing the way kosher cattle and poultry are raised, slaughtered, and butchered and extends to the treatment of workers, eating local, and a concern for the environment. Kosher consumers now have many more options than they ever did before, including organic, grass-fed, all natural, and pasture raised. I visited a free-range poultry farm when researching this book, and I couldn't help but note that the average chicken had a bigger living space than a typical New York apartment. This ethically humane approach to raising meat and poultry is the tipping point that leads many consumers to choose eco-kosher. While not everyone has access or funds to dabble in this market—the meat is expensive—it is an alternative to mainstream sources and is worth exploring if the philosophy appeals to you.

THE TEAM

I'm a big believer that you don't know what you don't know, and that it's important to ask questions and gather information from reliable, experienced sources. That's why I consulted a team of experts in various food-related fields to gather important tips and techniques that will help me help you. You will find their advice on everything, from which wine goes best with your steak, to which cut of steak is best to pan sear, which pan to sear it in, and which knife to carve it with, throughout this book. Our team members are:

Behind the counter

Butcher:	Omar Valencia *Assistant Butcher* *Sammy's Kosher Market* Bedford Hills, New York
Butcher:	David Perlow *Sammy's Kosher Market* Bedford Hills, New York
Butchers:	Eddie Klarberg and Debbie Bobb *Supersol* Scarsdale, New York
Butchers:	Steven Niederman and Paul Whitman *Fischer Bros. and Leslie* New York City
Butcher:	Michael Kane *Park East Kosher Butchers and Fine Foods* New York City
Butcher:	Irving Diamant *Diamant's Kosher Meat Market* St. Louis, Missouri
Eco-kosher expert:	Ariella Reback, *Green Pastures Poultry* Pepper Pike, Ohio

Eco-kosher experts:	Issac and Rachel Wiesenfeld
	Wise Organic Pastures
	Brooklyn, New York
Venison expert:	Norman Schlaff
	Musicon Farm
	Goshen, New York
Bison expert:	Carl Garber
	Noah's Ark
	Dawson, Minnesota
Sausage expert:	Jeff Rohatiner
	Jeff's Gourmet Kosher Sausage Factory
	Los Angeles, California

In the Kitchen

Culinary professional:	Chef David Kolotkin
	Executive chef
	Prime Grill
	New York City
Knife skills expert:	Norman Weinstein
	Instructor and Author
	Mastering Knife Skills
Cookware & gadget guru:	Norman Kornbleuth
	Broadway Panhandler
	New York City
Wine authority:	Aron Ritter
	The Kosher Wine Society
	New York City
Spice advice:	Kalustyan's
	New York City

COOKING METHODS

Y ou can buy the best meat and poultry and have a precise and professional recipe, but if you don't know about the necessary tools and techniques, your results will be less than stellar. The following information is designed to provide a quick review so you can properly prepare everything from a succulent roast to a perfectly grilled chicken. Use the information to hone your skills, stock your pantry, or show off to your spouse's great aunt at the next holiday dinner.

BRAISING/POT ROASTING/STEWING

Braising, pot roasting, and stewing are designed to tenderize tough cuts of meat by slow cooking with moisture, either on the stove or in the oven. The result is incredibly flavorful food with a fall-apart texture. While all three methods are very similar, stewing generally calls for small cubes of meat and pot roasting usually involves a larger piece of meat cooked in less liquid. To simplify, throughout the book, we'll refer to all three as braising. Many kosher cuts require braising and with the addition of aromatics, stock, wine, root vegetables, or legumes can become a full meal in one pot. Many braised meats will benefit from a night's sleep in their braising liquid, infusing both the sauce and the meat with additional flavor. Also, by cooling the sauce overnight, you will be able to skim off any fat that has risen to the top and solidified. When braising, sear or brown the meat first to seal in the juices and help keep the meat moist. Color equals flavor, so seared meat, even if you are going to slowly braise it, will taste better. That's not opinion, but scientific fact. Meat browns due to a chemical reaction called the Maillard effect. The sugars and carbohydrates contained within meat, when seared, rise to the surface and bring out the meat's full flavor. Even if the meat is going to braise, always sear it first to encourage this browning effect.

Norman Kornbleuth, our cookware and gadget expert, recommends a heavy braising pot with a tight-fitting lid that sits down into the pot, rather than on top, to create a tighter seal. The height of the sidewall should directly relate to the contents, with a minimum of 4 to 5 inches above the food in the pot. The higher the side, the more moisture is retained. For all braising recipes we specify using this type of pot, but you can use a large Dutch oven, or any heavy-bottomed pot with a tight lid.

DRY ROASTING

This is the main method of cooking larger pieces of meat or whole poultry at higher temperatures in an oven, and works well with foods that don't require additional tenderizing. For the best result, you need to have some important items on hand. First, you need the right roasting pan. Norman explains you never want to put a large roast in a small pan where the meat will touch the sides. Conversely, you don't want to put a small roast in a large pan where there is too much room all around, or the meat will dry out. The optimal pan allows for 1 to 1½ inches of space between the food and the side of the pan. When roasting, you should place the meat on either a flat rack or a v-rack that sits in the roasting pan. This allows air to circulate around the meat, providing more even cooking. Norman recommends a roasting pan that has even heat conductive layers, such as All-Clad, so that you can place the roasting pan directly on your stovetop after the roasting period and prepare a sauce right in the pan. Those little brown bits that cling to the bottom of the pan are called "fond" and they result from the juices and proteins being released while the meat roasts. By deglazing the pan—stirring wine or broth into the pan—over heat, you loosen the savory flavor nuggets and encourage them to meld into the sauce. You might need to use two burners to heat and deglaze the entire pan.

To properly roast any meat there are a few gadgets you should not be without. Norman implores you to invest in a good meat thermometer, either one that remains in the meat and alerts you when it has reached its set temperature or an instant-read thermometer with a thin stem so you poke the meat in the least obtrusive way to test doneness. Many recipes will have a suggested internal temperature to measure doneness, but observing and knowing what you're cooking is the best way to judge. When the meat releases less juice into the pan, you know it is drying out and should come out of the oven. The meat should then rest, covered loosely with aluminum foil, for at least 10 and up to 20 minutes; it will actually continue to cook and gain 5 to 10 degrees. Resting will also help the juices to redistribute and keep the meat moist. Never turn the meat with a fork, which will pierce the meat, causing precious juices to escape. Instead, invest in a set of large tongs. For poultry, a large spoon inserted in the cavity of the chicken will help ease the bird over without tearing the skin. Reusable silicone bands to help truss the chicken are available, as is good old kitchen twine. A metal baster is a must for moistening food while it roasts and for extracting fat from a roasting pan. Another great aid is a gravy separator. Pour your drippings in and watch the fat to rise to the top. You can then easily pour the fat off, leaving only the rich drippings for gravy.

BROILING

Let me introduce you to your broiler, that red-hot heat source that floats at the top of your oven. It is used to grill meats quickly and efficiently. It doesn't impart flavor, but it gets the job done with a browned crispy finish. For most broiling, set your broiler rack to the highest position. To achieve the best sear, the meat should optimally be about $1\frac{1}{2}$ inches from the heat source, and no closer than $\frac{1}{2}$ inch. For thicker cuts of meat, first develop a crust, and then lower the rack once the meat is browned to allow it to cook through without burning. Another method would be to turn the oven from broil to bake/roast and cook the meat until it is cooked to your desired doneness. You might remember unpacking your appliance and finding a two-piece pan with a perforated top and a shallow rimmed bottom—that's a broiling pan. It allows the meat to brown, while catching the fat and drippings. If you cannot locate your broiler pan, you can improvise by setting a rack over a shallow rimmed baking sheet or order a replacement metal or porcelain pan. Keep a watchful eye as the fat can catch fire if the meat is placed too close to the heat source, and leave the door ajar if the manufacturer advises you do so.

GRILLING

When warm weather beckons, there's nothing like throwing meat on the grill to bring out the primal pleasure of cooking on an open fire. You can direct-grill foods that you want to cook quickly, or use indirect heat from the grill to slow cook. Meat that can be broiled can also be grilled, and painting a final layer of flavor with a basting sauce or glaze will enhance almost any meat. To prevent sticking, coat the grates with nonstick spray, or oil the meat or poultry. Turn the meat when it releases from the grill: it is the meat's way of saying, "I'm done on this side." It is not always easy to tell when grilled foods are cooked through, as the charred exterior might lead you to think that the inside is cooked when it's not. If you do not have a thermometer, you can check for doneness by poking the meat with your index finger. Norman Schlaff explains it this way: If the meat feels like your cheek, it's rare; like your nose, it's medium to medium rare; and like your forehead it's medium well. For fatty meats, keep a spritz bottle of water nearby to help quench flare-ups. Gas grills are very convenient and user-friendly but do not enhance the flavor of food. For that real outdoor taste, use a charcoal grill. Because every grill differs, preheating and cooking times will depend on your individual grill. The essential tools are a good basting brush, tongs, and spatula, all with extra-long handles.

PAN SEARING

Meat that can be grilled or broiled can usually be pan seared on the stove in either a skillet or stovetop grill pan. The purpose of pan searing is to quickly brown the meat, sealing in the juices. Once seared, the pan can be popped in the oven to finish the cooking, if necessary. Norman Kornbleuth has very definite opinions on the best pans to use on top of the stove. His first choice is a heavy steel pan that is reactive and responsive to the heat source. That means it heats up evenly, conducts the heat across the entire pan, and responds when you lower the heat, thereby not overcooking your food. A steel pan is constructed almost entirely from iron and darkens over time, as compared to stainless steel, which is an alloy and contains iron and usually chromium, which gives it shine and prevents corrosion. Stainless steel is durable but less effective for conducting heat than steel alone. His next choice is a seasoned cast-iron pan, which also conducts heat efficiently, but is less responsive when you lower the heat. A lined copper pan will react similarly to a cast-iron pan, but lined copper pans tend to be very expensive, and do not respond as well to changes in temperature. Norman sees a place for nonstick pans, but remember they will not help you caramelize food or develop that nice crust.

BUILDING FLAVOR

From marinades to rubs, glazes to herbs, this quick overview will help you enhance whatever you cook and help you create your own personal flavor profile.

MARINADES

Marinades are thin liquids that serve double duty with ingredients designed to tenderize as well as flavor meat and vegetables. You will find marinade recipes sprinkled throughout the book, and they can swapped with other proteins for new flavor sensations. Working with marinades is not rocket science, but here are some good things to know:

- When marinating for flavor only, a 1- to 2-hour soak is all you need. When marinating for both flavor and to tenderize, several hours to overnight is recommended. Longer than that, and you run the risk of developing mushy meat. If marinating for under an hour, you can leave the meat out of the fridge.

- Marinades should contain an acid to aid in tenderizing, since acids help break down some of the meat's proteins. Consider red wine for a robust jolt, rice wine vinegar for an Asian flair, apple cider vinegar for a fruity flavor, or balsamic for a bold, sweet taste. Try interesting acidic elements such as lemon juice, orange juice, lime juice, or zested rind. *Fresh* pineapple or papaya are superheroes when it comes to marinating as they contain natural enzymes that can work wonders. Be sure the fruit is fresh, not processed; processing renders their powers useless.

- Some ingredients will need a base, such as oil, to help release their magic. Experiment with bases, such as walnut oil for an earthy flavor, toasted sesame oil for a nutty taste, or chili oil for a touch of heat. Olive oil is effective for marinades that don't require long refrigeration, but it can congeal or solidify in marinades that sit overnight in the fridge. Instead, turn to neutral oils such as vegetable or canola, which impart little taste, but serve as a good foundation and remain liquid when chilled.

- To wake up your marinade, add aromatics and herbs such as finely minced garlic, shallots, or parsley; emulsifiers like grainy or Dijon mustard; and ingredients with *umami* (that savoriness that lingers on your tongue), such as beef stock, soy sauce, tomato paste, hoisin, or Worcestershire sauce. (Some question if Worcestershire is pareve; if you are in doubt, leave it out.)

- Marinades can be prepped by hand, or you can combine all the ingredients in a blender or food processor fitted with the metal blade. Do not overprocess, or they will thicken and become more like a dressing.

- When marinating poultry, if the skin is not an important element in the dish, remove it, as it presents a barrier to the marinade.

- Avoid metal containers. They will react with the acid and could impart a tinny taste to your finished dish. Resealable plastic bags are a better option as you can massage the liquid into the meat and easily turn the meat while taking up little space in your fridge. And cleanup is a snap.

- When you remove meat from a marinade, dry it off with paper towels; wet meat does not brown well.

- Be judicious in your use of sugar or honey, which can clog the meat and prevent the marinade from seeping in. Sweeteners burn quickly when they come in contact with heat, so keep a watchful eye.

- From a safe-handling aspect, once a marinade has been exposed to raw meat, it needs to be treated very carefully. If you thoroughly boil it, you can use it to baste the meat. However, instead of tempting fate, reserve a little marinade at the start and use that as a basting sauce at the end.

- If all else fails, grab a bottle of salad dressing and use it for the soak. It might not be original, but it does have all the elements, and if you tuck the bottle away in the trash, no one will ever know.

RUBS

Another great way to infuse flavor and tenderize meat is to create a dry rub of herbs and spices. The rub adds a layer of spirited flavor and marinates the meat as it sits. You'll find dry rubs paired most often with meats that are being grilled. Most rub recipes can be easily doubled and tripled, so prepare a batch to have on hand whenever you want a jolt of flavor. Use restraint when adding salt to rubs as kosher meat is already salted. It is harder to overcome saltiness than it is to add more salt at the end of the cooking process. Brown sugar, which imparts a deep sweet flavor, is a great addition to a rub and helps the meat caramelize and balances the heat or spice, but be careful when grilling meat coated in a sugary rub, it will burn quickly.

SPICES AND HERBS

Parsley, sage, rosemary, and thyme are more than just brilliant lyrics; they are the four cornerstones of seasoning. Thyme balances and marries with almost everything, adding a subtle herby note that doesn't overshadow the main ingredients' flavor. Its leaves are tiny and can go unchopped. Rosemary can be strong, so use it wisely and with restraint, and be sure to finely chop the leaves; no one likes biting into a whole rosemary needle. Parsley enlivens just about everything, adding color and zing to most dishes. Never substitute dried for fresh parsley: it tastes like cardboard. Sage has a woodsy nuance and pairs especially well with poultry, veal, and lamb. Fresh basil is a beautiful herb to impart a piquant bite; although Simon and Garfunkel ignored it, you shouldn't. Be mindful that woodsy herbs like rosemary can withstand longer cooking times, while soft spring herbs such as parsley or basil should be added at the end of cooking and minced right before using. For a finishing garnish, cut them in chiffonade, by rolling them in a bundle and slicing through them crosswise; you will have ribbonlike pieces to scatter on the platter.

You can't always have fresh herbs on hand, so you need a well-stocked pantry of dried herbs and spices. The words "herb" and "spice" are often confused. An herb is derived from the leaves of a herbaceous plant, while a spice is cultivated from the roots, flowers, fruits, seeds, and bark. Generally herbs add a savory element and spices add the aromatic. Invest in a few blends such as Italian herb, which contains earthy herbs like marjoram, thyme, rosemary, sage, oregano, and basil; *herbes de Provence*, with its combination of floral notes such as chervil, basil, rosemary, tarragon, thyme, marjoram, savory, parsley, and a hint of lavender; yellow curry powder, which is a blend of fragrant spices, such as coriander, cumin, turmeric, cloves, fenugreek, mustard seeds, black peppercorns, and sometimes chili or red peppers; and Chinese five spice powder, with warm aromatic anise, star anise, cinnamon, cloves, and ginger. Additionally, stock several ground peppers, such as ground sweet ancho chili pepper or fiery crushed red pepper flakes. Hungarian paprika, which is derived from red peppers, is the best variety and in many recipes you can choose between sweet or hot, depending on your palate. Most recipes in the book call for kosher salt, which is neither an herb nor a spice, but a mineral. Always sprinkle with a light touch, as kosher meat and poultry is already soaked and salted. But, for finishing a dish you should experiment with specialty salts like sea salt or grey salt for a briny ocean taste. Freshly ground pepper is preferable to already ground, allowing you to adjust the level of coarseness. Sometimes you really want to taste the pepper on your tongue and at other times, it's only needed in the background. However, it's hard to measure, so get to know your pepper mill and understand how much pepper comes from a turn of the grinder. If you don't want to fuss with a grinder, you can use already ground. Dried herbs and spices do have a shelf life, so if you bought that bottle when you first got married and you are about to celebrate your second anniversary, it's time to clean out the pantry. Our spice expert at Kalustyan's says to extend the life of bottled herbs and spices you should keep them in a closed cupboard that is not near a heat source. When substituting dried for fresh, 1 teaspoon of dried equals 1 tablespoon fresh. Give the dried herbs a little rub between your fingers before sprinkling; it helps release their true flavor.

For many, a well-stocked wine cellar is as important as a well-stocked pantry. That's why we consulted Aron Ritter from the Kosher Wine Society. Aron points out that kosher wine is evolving and now comes from every part of the world. He goes on to say, "Pairing food and wine is one of the most exciting and rewarding aspects of planning a meal. When chosen correctly, both the wine and the food work in harmony to emphasize and accentuate each other in such a manner as to make both more enjoyable and memorable. If chosen incorrectly, however, a wine can mask the subtle flavors of a delicate dish, or more commonly, a meal can overpower the finer notes of a complex wine . . . drink what you love and have fun . . . Get out of the normal rules, push the boundaries and always remember how fortunate we are to be enjoying the finer things in life." For more about kosher wine visit:

http://kosherwinesociety.com/NEW/wine_education.php?page=winepairing

. . . or consult Rogov's Guide to Israeli wine.

READING *the* RECIPE

Look for these features in the recipes throughout the book:

Behind the Counter tells you what you need to know about buying the cut of meat tested in the recipe. It will help you engage your butcher in dialogue and make your visit to the market an opportunity to do more than push a cart. Another element in this section will be options for alternate cuts, which although not tested in the recipe, are reasonable substitutions. While prices vary regionally, there is consistency in which cuts are generally more or less expensive. Look for (−$) for cuts that should save you money, (=$) for those that will be a wash, and (+$) for those that will probably cost more. With this information you can make a thoughtful selection not only based on how it will affect your recipe, but how it impacts your wallet.

Side Note will point you to sides, sauces, and more accessories that complement the main dish. Page numbers are provided for easy reference. You should mix and match, but these suggestions are designed to help get your menu started.

Yield and Serving Line offers a general guide as to how much the recipe makes or how many people it can serve. The yield is an accurate number that was measured and carefully calculated. As for serving size, to be honest, I can eat an entire duck by myself, so when I specify how many people can be served by a recipe, know that I err on the side of generous portions.

Start to Finish lets you know before you begin the recipe how long the meat needs to marinate or the stock needs to simmer and factors that in to your total prep and cooking times so you can properly plan ahead. I don't have a sous-chef following me around my kitchen prepping my veggies or preheating my oven. So, when I calculate how long a recipe might take to prepare, I assume you don't either. One thing you can do to stay on track is to have all your ingredients prepped and your cookware and gadgets ready to go when you start the recipe. This culinary concept of "mise en place," which means to "have everything in place," will really be a big help.

Feedback found at the end of many recipes will offer interesting foodie tips and tidbits of information related to the recipe.

NP tells you what non-pareve ingredients we didn't include, but you can if you choose.

Armed with all these tips and techniques you should be able to face the meat counter and your kitchen with confidence. However, a good cook is more than a recipe reader. Invite creativity into your kitchen and make every dish your own. I find that the best food I ever prepared had as much to do with the experience as it did with the ingredients. Trust your instincts, try again if you fail, and be sure to make a food memory every time you cook.

BEEF

Exploring the Neighborhood

For kosher carnivores the world of beef (meat from a domesticated bovine, AKA a cow), is limited to the forequarter, which contains five of the nine primal cuts: chuck, rib, plate, briskets, and foreshank. Primal cuts represent the sections of an animal after it has been butchered and before it reaches the retail level. The names aren't sexy; they are designed to be descriptive of their specific location on the animal. In many cases, once the meat reaches the consumer it has been re-labeled with all sorts of clever names, which can vary from store to store and often sound like cuts of meat in the non-kosher world. It is very confusing as a consumer to know which cut of meat you want when butchers play roulette with the names. Unless you are planning a career in kosher advertising, you won't need to memorize them all. What you do need to know to be a savvier consumer and better cook are the qualities of the five primal kosher cuts. It's easy if you view the forequarter of the cow as a map, and then consider the primal cuts as neighborhoods. Just as every neighborhood has its singular features and distinct flavor, every primal cut has its unique characteristics. To know which cut of meat to buy and how to best prepare it, forget about the inventive names and simply consider location, location, location.

The largest primal cut is the densely populated **chuck,** which includes the neck and shoulder and runs from the first to the fifth rib. The chuck offers the broadest variety of cuts including chuck roasts, shoulder steaks, well-blended ground beef, flavorful stew meat, and savory ribs. Kosher butchers have creatively utilized every portion of the chuck to make the most of this large section. When cooked properly, the chuck is full of complex flavor. But, because much of this region contains cross sections of muscle and connective tissue, it is generally not very tender. To properly prepare it, most meat from this area needs to be braised to break down the collagen and tissue. Some cuts can be dry roasted, grilled, broiled, or pan seared, but a little marinating goes a long way. This is a great neighborhood, if you have a good braising pot and a pair of mighty incisors.

Next door to the chuck, we have the ritzy neighborhood that is the **rib,** which yields rich, savory meat packed with fatty marbleized grains and less muscle and connective tissue. The seven ribs in this section are used to create the glorious standing rib roast, juicy bone-in rib steak, and Flintstonian back ribs. Boneless cuts such as the rib-eye, top

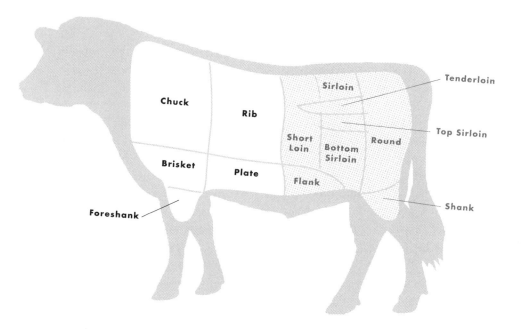

of the rib, and crescent steak are equally delicious. Meat from the rib should be dry roasted, or when cut into steaks, pan seared, grilled, or broiled. The grainy fat gives the meat its buttery texture and melts into the meat as it cooks, moistening and flavoring every morsel. The result is juicy and tender with a beefy flavor and an easy bite. It's a pretty pricey neighborhood, but if succulent and impressive is what you are looking for, this is the place for you.

Below the ribs sits the **plate,** which is the breast of the animal, a large but scarcely populated neighborhood. Fatty plate short ribs cut from the ends of the rib section and salty skirt steak reside there, with intensely meaty hanger steak right around the corner. Meat from the plate can be cooked by most methods. But, because it is close to the exterior of the animal, it absorbs the most salt during the koshering process. For this reason, many butchers feel it's a nice place to visit, but they wouldn't want to spend too much time there.

Down the street from the chuck is the **brisket,** a swanky section known for its most famous cut. While this is a tough neighborhood, you can easily tame it with moist, slow cooking and achieve incredibly flavorful results. The meat ground from the brisket can be added to chuck for an incomparable burger, and this versatile cut can transform into corned beef or pastrami, making the brisket a favorite spot.

The primal cut of **foreshank,** which is actually the arm of the animal, isn't a densely populated neighborhood, but delectable shin meat and rich marrow-filled bones live there. It is no surprise that meat cut from the shank needs slow, moist cooking because the part of the animal closest to the horn or the hoof works the hardest and is the toughest. If you're making a rich stock or want to add depth of flavor to a stew, you'll need to raid this neighborhood.

If lean meat is an important consideration, and your wallet has a deep billfold, then ask your butcher to source grass-fed beef, bison, or venison as an alternative to grain-fed beef. The flavor of each is decidedly different, and can vary from supplier to supplier. Grass-fed beef has the benefit of "good fat," and some describe its flavor as tasting the way meat was meant to taste. Venison is a high-protein, low-fat lean meat with an earthy, rich flavor. Unlike the cow, the entire deer is kosher, so if you have a yen for a top or bottom round, sirloin or tenderloin, then venison is a great choice. Norman Schlaff, our venison expert, suggests you give it a quick marinade, then dry roast, pan sear, grill, or broil. Bison is a great option, with a clean taste and less choles-terol than white meat chicken. Carl Garber, our bison expert, explains that it has less marbling than beef because the animal is so very active. Imagine a cow with a personal trainer, exercising daily and eating right—that's bison, with a lean upper body, tight waist, and low BMI. It can be dry roasted, pan seared, broiled, or grilled, but keep it rare to medium rare to retain moistness. Any of these meats can stand in for beef in almost every recipe where beef is specified, but make sure you adjust the cooking times accordingly.

No matter what type of meat you choose, you shouldn't need a hacksaw to cut it. Norman Weinstein recommends a good 8- or 10-inch carving knife, to slice meat with a bone. A non-serrated scalloped edge curved slicing knife is helpful to get through boneless meat and roasts with a crustier exterior and soft inside. Armed with the right knife, creating picture-perfect presentations is a breeze.

ROASTS, STEAKS, STIR FRY, AND STEW

Large portions of meat cut from any region is considered to be a roast. The cooking method speaks for itself, although tougher roasts will ben-efit from a good braise. A steak is essentially a thinner piece of meat cut from a roast and the quality of the steak will be the same as that of the roast from which it is cut. If you butcher a piece of steak from a rib roast it will have the same marbling and tender bite as that roast; similarly, a steak cut from the tougher chuck roast will need to be tenderized just as the roast does. Roasts can also be cut into very thin pieces that become stir fry or into chunks for stews. You'll want to choose wisely when buy-ing meat for these preparations as a quick stir fry needs to start out with a tender slice of meat while a stew can benefit from low and slow cook-ing. The most important thing to consider when buying a roast, steak, or meat for stir fry and stews is how you want to cook it—choose the right cut for the right preparation and you will not be disappointed.

Standing Rib Roast

There isn't a more impressive or savory main course than a standing rib roast. Its sheer size and presence is awesome, and it requires little attention to achieve greatness. The "standing" comes from the bones that the rib roast rests on, and that serves as a natural rack for the meat while it cooks.

SERVES 6

Start to Finish: Under 2 hours

1 (6-pound) standing rib roast (3 ribs), room temperature

4 tablespoons olive oil

1½ tablespoons kosher salt

½ teaspoon freshly ground black pepper

1 tablespoon chopped fresh rosemary leaves or 1 teaspoon dried rosemary

1 teaspoon chopped fresh thyme leaves or ⅓ teaspoon dried, optional

1 to 2 cups beef stock

Preheat the oven to 450 degrees. Coat the meat in the olive oil and then season with the salt, pepper, rosemary, and thyme, if using. Try to work a little seasoning where the meat is tied to the bones. Place the roast in a roasting pan (no rack needed, the bones provide stability) and roast in the preheated oven for 20 minutes. After that time, **reduce the temperature to 375 degrees** and pour 1 cup of the beef stock into the roasting pan. Baste the meat every 20 minutes with the accumulated drippings, adding water or stock if needed. Continue to roast until an instant-read thermometer inserted into a thick portion of the meat (don't let it touch the bone), reads about 125 to 130 degrees for medium rare. Transfer the finished roast to a platter, cover loosely with foil, and place the roasting pan on the stove. Heat the drippings, scraping up any bits that have collected in the bottom of the pan. Untie the meat from the bones for easier carving, and present the sliced meat with the bones in and the gravy spooned on top.

Feedback

There are other cuts from the standing rib roast that are worth

BEHIND THE COUNTER: For the meatiest piece, have your butcher cut the roast from the short end, where the eye is larger. Not only is there less fat, but the bones are shorter, adding less weight and more bang for your buck. When portioning, figure 1 rib for every 2 people. For easier carving have your butcher separate the meat from the bones, and then tie them back together. Ask the butcher for the weight of the meat alone. You want to calculate cooking time by the weight of the meat only, figuring 15 to 20 minutes per pound for medium rare. You can substitute a boneless rib roast (−$), which gives you more meat for your money, but you'll sacrifice the flavor the bones impart.

SIDE NOTE: For a very proper English approach, serve the roast with a hefty slice of Yorkshire pudding (page 204), and a dollop of horseradish cream (page 224).

noting. The layer of meat that envelops the rib is called crescent steak or butcher's surprise. I was most surprised by the price tag, but have to admit the flavor of the grainy fat and meat is intense and rich. You can buy this separately and roast or cook it in a pan like a steak. Additionally, you shouldn't overlook the "baby back" ribs of medieval proportion, which comprise the rack from a standing rib roast. Irving Diamant, our St. Louis rib man, notes that these are the ribs we watch people gnaw on in fancy restaurants. They can be roasted or grilled and enjoyed as a meal on their own. Have your butcher remove the silver membrane on the back of the rack; this will help your seasoning permeate the ribs, and also makes them easier to cut and eat. Roast them in a hot oven or on the grill until medium rare. You don't want to have your guests fighting over the bones, so plan on at least 1 bone per person.

Roasted Beef
. . . *and fingerling potatoes in porcini mushroom gravy*

If you dream in shades of medium rare, then nothing speaks to you like a good roasted beef. It needs only basic seasonings, and deserves a round of applause when it comes out of the oven.

SERVES 4 TO 6
Start to Finish: Under 1½ hours

BEHIND THE COUNTER: The silver tip makes the best roast beef. It is lean, beefy, and solid (good traits in a mate) and should be roasted to rare or medium rare. Alternate cuts: French or square roast (a little chewier) (=$), Club roast (+$) or boneless rib-eye roast (+$), both tender but pricey.

1 (3-pound) silver tip roast
2 garlic cloves, cut into medium slivers
1 tablespoon kosher salt
1 teaspoon freshly ground black pepper
1 tablespoon Worcestershire sauce
1 (1-ounce) package dried porcini mushrooms, soaked in 1 cup of hot water
1 pound fingerling or small red potatoes, scrubbed clean
2 bay leaves
Olive oil
1 to 2 cups beef stock

With the tip of a very sharp knife, cut about 8 tiny slits into the beef, and insert the garlic slivers into the roast. Place the meat on a sheet of aluminum foil to catch the seasonings and to cover the meat while it sits in the fridge. Season with salt and pepper. Drizzle the Worcestershire sauce on top and work all the seasonings into the meat. Wrap the beef up in the foil and refrigerate until ready to roast. You can do this up to one day in advance.

Preheat the oven to 425 degrees and remove the meat from the fridge. While the oven heats, get the mushrooms ready by soaking them in 1 cup of hot water for about 15 minutes. Remove the mushrooms from the water, squeeze them to release all their liquid, rinse them under cold water to remove any remaining grit, and chop into bite-size pieces. Take the porcini water and strain it through a piece of cheesecloth, a damp paper towel, or a coffee filter. Reserve the mushrooms and their liquid.

When the oven is hot, place the potatoes and bay leaves in the bottom of a roasting pan, then place the beef on a rack placed in the pan. Drizzle olive oil over the meat and potatoes and roast in the preheated oven at 425 degrees for 15 minutes. Pour 1 cup of beef stock into the bottom of the pan and **reduce the temperature to 375 degrees.** Baste the meat every 20 minutes, adding more stock or water if needed. Roast until a meat thermometer inserted into the center of the meat registers 125 to 130 degrees for medium rare; total cooking time is 15 to 20 minutes per pound. Remove the roast and potatoes from the oven, transfer to a platter (to catch the juices), and cover loosely with aluminum foil.

While the roast rests, place the roasting pan on the stovetop, over low heat. Add ¹/₂ cup of the reserved porcini liquid, scraping up the bits from the bottom of the pan. Drop the mushrooms into the pan and cook quickly, stirring. Add any of the beef juices that collected on the platter while the meat rested. To serve, remove the bay leaves and spoon the gravy and mushrooms over the sliced beef and potatoes.

Feedback

A robust meat calls for a full-bodied wine. Aron suggests you try a Barbera, Cabernet Franc, Merlot, or Petite Syrah for beefy dishes.

Classic Pot Roast

Longing for simpler times, when the family came together at the dinner table, no cell phones, texting or BlackBerries? Turn back the clock and prepare a classic succulent pot roast, with a rich beefy gravy, melt-in-your-mouth potatoes, and humble button mushrooms. This recipe features everyone's favorite bona fide shortcut, the tried-and-true packet of Lipton onion-mushroom soup mix. Enjoy it as a family, and be sure to turn the TV off.

SERVES 4 TO 6

Start to Finish: Under 3½ hours

1 (4-pound) chuck roast, tied
1 teaspoon kosher salt
½ teaspoon freshly ground black pepper
1 tablespoon Worcestershire sauce
1 tablespoon olive oil
1 package Lipton onion-mushroom soup mix
1 large onion, sliced
1½ cups beef stock
1 cup water
½ head unpeeled garlic, top cut off
12 whole black peppercorns
12 sprigs fresh thyme leaves
2 bay leaves
3 russet potatoes, peeled and cut into cubes
½ pound white button mushrooms, sliced
1 (9-ounce) package frozen cut green beans, optional

Preheat the oven to 325 degrees. Dry the beef with paper towels, season with salt and pepper, and drizzle with Worcestershire sauce. Heat the olive oil in a braising pot and sear the meat on all sides over medium heat until lightly browned, about 10 minutes. While the meat sears, cut a piece of aluminum foil large enough to hold the meat, and crimp the edges to create a rim. Spread the package of soup mix on the foil. When the meat is finished browning, lay it on top of the soup mix and roll the roast until all sides are covered, manipulating the foil to help you spread the mix evenly.

Lightly brown the sliced onion in the pot, about 5 minutes. Stir in the stock and water, and return the beef to the pot. Wrap the garlic, peppercorns, thyme, and bay leaves in cheesecloth tied together with a piece of kitchen twine, and place in the sauce. Cover and roast in the preheated oven for 1 hour. Turn the meat over and add the potatoes. Cover and continue roasting for another 30 minutes. Turn the meat again, and add the mushrooms. Continue roasting until the meat is very tender, about 1 more hour. If adding the beans, toss them in, frozen, for the last 15 minutes of cooking. To thicken the gravy first remove the meat and veggies from the pot with a slotted spoon and transfer to a bowl. Place the pot directly on the stovetop. Make a slurry by combining 1 tablespoon of cornstarch with 2 tablespoons of cold water, stir back into the pot and bring to a boil. Repeat until desired consistency (see page 79).Slice the roast and spoon the veggies and gravy on top.

Steak Pizzaiola

Steak pizzaiola is what the love child of a perfect slice of Neapolitan pizza and a juicy steak would look like. Laden with fresh oregano and sun-ripened tomatoes, the quickly simmered sauce brings a piquant taste to seared steak or just about any grilled meat.

MAKES 2 HEARTY SERVINGS
Start to Finish: Under 30 minutes

4 tablespoons olive oil

2 garlic cloves, chopped (about 1 tablespoon)

1/8 teaspoon crushed red pepper flakes (more if you like it hot)

1 (28-ounce) can whole tomatoes, drained

2 tablespoons chopped fresh flat-leaf parsley

4 basil leaves, chopped

1 teaspoon dried oregano

2 rib-eye steaks (about 1 pound each)

1/4 cup red wine

BEHIND THE COUNTER: Have your butcher cut boneless rib-eye steaks, about 1 inch thick. Cuts from the small end will have a meatier eye and less excess fat. Alternate cuts: rib steak (=$), club steak (–$), or veal chop center cut (–$) or 1st cut (=$).

> *Seasoned salt for garnish*
> 1 teaspoon sea salt, 1 teaspoon dried rosemary leaves, 1 teaspoon dried oregano, combined

Heat 2 tablespoons of the oil in a medium skillet, add the garlic and red pepper flakes and cook over medium-low heat, stirring, for about 5 minutes; do not let the garlic brown. Place the drained tomatoes in a shallow bowl. Using a serrated knife, cut the tomatoes, while in the bowl, into bite-size pieces. Pour the chopped tomatoes and their juices into the skillet. Add the parsley, basil, and oregano. Raise the heat to medium and cook until the liquid is reduced by half, about 5 minutes. Remove the sauce from the pan and set aside.

Coat the steaks in 1 tablespoon of the olive oil and heat the remaining tablespoon of oil in the skillet. Sear the steaks over medium-high heat until each side is nicely browned, about 5 minutes per side. Transfer the steaks to a plate and cover loosely with aluminum foil. Pour the wine into the skillet and deglaze, scraping up the brown bits that have collected in the bottom of the pan. Pour the tomato sauce into the pan and heat through. Place the steaks in the pan so they absorb some of the sauce's flavor and are cooked to medium rare. Remove the steaks from the pan, sprinkle with the seasoned salt, and serve with the sauce spooned over the top.

Feedback

For a strong wine to stand up to the bold beef taste, Aron suggests a Sangiovese, Nebbiolo, or Zinfandel.

Rib Steak Florentine

This classically prepared *bistecca fiorentina* is named after the ancient city of Firenze (Florence), where the dish originated. On a recent trip, I ate at Buca Lapi, the oldest restaurant in the city, known for their steak Florentine. Luciano Ghinassi, former chef and owner of the restaurant, gave me a tour of the kitchen and some insight into what makes their steak the best. First they use only grass-fed meat from Chianina Tuscan-raised cows. While you probably don't have access to kosher Chianina cows, you can purchase grass-fed beef from most kosher butchers. Second, they cut the steaks into thick slabs, no less than 2 inches thick. Third, they season the meat after it comes off the grill and use cracked sea salt and freshly ground pepper—nothing more, nothing else. This simply divine steak allows the meaty flavor to speak for itself, unadorned.

SERVES 2 (HOW HUNGRY ARE YOU?)

Start to Finish: Under 30 minutes

2 thick-cut rib steaks
Sea salt
Freshly ground black pepper
1 lemon, quartered, optional
Olive oil, optional

Let the steaks come to room temperature at least 30 minutes before grilling. **Heat a stovetop grill pan, or outdoor grill** until smoking hot, and grill the steaks for 5 to 7 minutes per side, turning only once. (If they are too rare for you, you can move them to a cooler spot on your grill until cooked through, or pop them in a 350-degree oven, until desired doneness.) Remove the steaks from the grill and let them rest for 5 to 10 minutes, loosely covered with foil. Sprinkle with sea salt and pepper. If you like, squeeze fresh lemon over each steak and drizzle with a little olive oil just before serving, we won't tell Luciano.

Feedback

If you want to take this steak to the next level, try buying dry aged, which takes 21 days to develop. Chef David explains that the enzyme reaction that occurs in those three weeks tenderizes the meat, while concentrating the proteins and flavor. It costs the steak a little in volume and the consumer a lot in the wallet, but it's a taste worth experiencing.

BEHIND THE COUNTER: Have your butcher cut rib steaks about 2 inches thick. Cuts from the small end will have a meatier eye and less excess fat. Alternate cuts: rib-eye steak (=$), club steak (–$), or veal chop center cut (–$) or 1st cut (=$).

SIDE NOTE: Tuscan beans are a traditional side dish. Why not enjoy the full Firenze experience and prepare a steaming pot. Start them ahead: they take time to prepare (page 194).

Chicken-Fried Steak

If you think this southern specialty is truck-stop fare, you are sorely misguided. This thin slice of steak is coated in a spicy flour blend, quick-fried, and smothered in creamy gravy for a very satisfying and fast steak dinner.

BEHIND THE COUNTER: Have your butcher cut ¼-inch-thick minute or silver tip steak. Alternate cut: Chuck (-$) can be used but will be a little tougher. Rib-eye or club steaks (+$) are overkill for this preparation.

SIDE NOTE: A heaping dollop of creamy mashed potatoes on the side is a beautiful thing (page 187).

SERVES 4

Start to Finish: Under 15 minutes

4 (5- to 6-ounce) thinly sliced steaks
1 cup all-purpose flour
2 teaspoons garlic powder
1 teaspoon onion powder
½ teaspoon kosher salt
1 teaspoon sweet Hungarian paprika
¼ teaspoon freshly ground black pepper
2 eggs, beaten with 1 tablespoon of water and a few dashes of hot sauce
¼ to ⅓ cup vegetable or canola oil
1 to 2 cups chicken stock, warmed

Place the steaks on a chopping block and, using the ridged side of a meat mallet, pound the meat until it is ⅛ inch thick. Be careful not to tear the meat as you pound, and lightly drag the mallet.

In a shallow bowl, combine the flour and all the seasonings. In a separate shallow bowl, beat the eggs with the water and hot sauce. Dip each slice of steak into the flour, then the egg, and then back into the flour. Repeat with the remaining slices. Do not discard the leftover flour.

Heat ¼ cup of oil in a large skillet, shake off the excess flour, and fry each steak over medium-high heat until crisp and golden on each side, 2 to 3 minutes per side. Place the fried steak on a wire rack set on a rimmed baking sheet, and cover loosely with aluminum foil while you finish frying the remaining pieces. Be careful not to burn the residual flour that builds in the skillet, it will be the basis of your gravy. If you do, wipe the pan clean and continue frying using fresh oil.

Reduce the heat to low, and add the reserved dredging flour to the pan a tablespoon at a time. This is not an exact science, so add the flour, whisking vigorously, until a light brown paste (roux) develops in the pan, 5 to 7 minutes; do not let it burn. Once the paste develops, begin whisking in the warm stock. It will quickly bubble up, so proceed slowly and carefully, whisking as you go. Continue adding stock until you have achieved a thick, creamy gravy. Let the gravy cook for a few minutes to get rid of the floury taste. Serve the steaks with the gravy spooned over the top.

Feedback

When creating a dredging station to coat any kind of meat, you should always dip first in flour, then in egg, then in the remaining dry ingredient. The flour at the start gives the egg something to hold on to. If you dunk in the egg first, it would slip right off the meat.

Steak and Eggs

When I was a child one of my favorite meals was breakfast for dinner. My mother would parboil potatoes and pan-fry them till golden brown, then pour beaten eggs over the potatoes and stir them into a scrambled frenzy, picking up the crusty bits of potatoes that clung to the pan. I've combined my mom's signature dish with a lean pan seared steak to create an unbeatable trio: steak, home fries, and eggs, a cowboy-size meal to be enjoyed any time of day. Unless you have short-order cook experience, it's not easy to juggle two pans at once. If you can't juggle two pans at once, why not cook the steaks first and then let them rest, covered loosely with foil, while you fry the potatoes?

BEHIND THE COUNTER: Any tender steak cut from the chuck would work for this dish, such as a good chuck eye or blade steak. Minute steak or silver tip steak (+$) are good options. Have your butcher cut them 1/2 inch thick. Alternate cuts: club steak, rib-eye or rib steak (+$) are very tender, but I think they come with too hefty a price tag for this preparation.

SERVES 2

Start to Finish: Under 1 hour

> 2 russet potatoes (about 1 pound), peeled and diced into bite-
>   size pieces
> Olive oil and vegetable oil for frying

> Kosher salt and freshly ground black pepper
> 2 (5-to 6-ounce) steaks
> 4 eggs, beaten (I use 2 whites and 1 yolk per person)
> Ketchup, seasoned with hot sauce for serving

Add the potatoes to a pot filled with 3 cups of cold water and 1 tea-spoon of salt, bring to a boil and cook about 15 minutes or until a knife can easily slide in and out of the potato. Drain the potatoes and set aside.

Heat a nonstick skillet with enough olive oil to just coat the bottom of the pan. Lightly season the steaks with salt and pepper. Cook the steaks over medium-high heat, 3 to 4 minutes on each side. Transfer the steaks to a plate, cover loosely with aluminum foil, and let them rest while you prepare the potatoes and eggs.

Wipe the pan clean, add about 2 tablespoons olive oil and 1 tablespoon vegetable oil. Cook the potatoes over medium-high heat until brown and crusty, about 10 minutes. Use the two-spoon method of turning the potatoes, one spoon to coax and the other to turn. When the potatoes are crusty on all sides, pour the beaten eggs into the skillet and quickly scramble; it will take just a minute or two. Season to taste with salt and pepper. Serve the eggs and potatoes on the side with the steak and some ketchup kicked up with a few dashes of hot sauce.

Grilled Steak Chimichurri

Argentineans know steak, and when they decide that marinating and smothering their steak in a bright green garlicky sauce is a good idea, it must be true. Fresh herbs such as basil, parsley, and oregano add a fresh touch while lots of garlic adds bite. A soft tortilla makes a great vehicle for wrapping up the sliced steak in a neat package.

SERVES 4

Start to Finish: 2 to 3 hours to marinate; under 30 minutes to grill

For the marinade and dipping sauce

1 cup freshly chopped flat-leaf parsley (cilantro can be substituted)

12 basil leaves, finely chopped

1 tablespoon freshly chopped oregano or 1 teaspoon dried oregano

4 large garlic cloves, finely chopped (about 2 tablespoons)

½ cup extra-virgin olive oil

⅓ cup red wine, sherry, or champagne vinegar

1 teaspoon kosher salt

½ teaspoon freshly ground black pepper

Juice of 1 lemon

Pinch of crushed red pepper flakes

Pinch of ground cumin

1 (1½-to 2-pound) flatiron steak

Combine the marinade ingredients in the bowl of a food processor fitted with the metal blade, and process until the greens are chopped and the ingredients are well combined. If you want to use the marinade to drizzle atop the finished steak, reserve a little at this time. Place the steaks with the marinade in a large resealable plastic bag, seal, and refrigerate for 2 to 3 hours. Most cuts of meat can marinate overnight, but 2 to 3 hours is usually enough to flavor and tenderize without the risk of breaking down the meat too much.

Light the grill, or preheat your broiler or stovetop grill pan. Let the steaks come to room temperature and pat them dry with paper towels. When the pan is sizzling hot, so that a drop of water will dance in the pan, quickly grill the steaks, 5 to 7 minutes per side. Let the meat rest, covered loosely with aluminum foil, before slicing. Serve with ketchup kicked up with a few drops of hot sauce.

Feedback

A dish with this much flavor needs a drink to match. We've paired a Spanish sangria with this delicious steak dinner. Traditionally sangria is made with red or white wine that has been infused with flavor from fruit that macerates (like marinating) in the wine. This version from New York City mixologist Ivan Alvarez of Mañana restaurant gives you all the fruity taste without actually adding any fruit. It's a

BEHIND THE COUNTER: Traditionally, skirt steak is a great cut for this recipe. However, kosher skirt steak is very salty, making it less palatable. You can try to mitigate the saltiness by soaking the steak in cold water. While that does remove some salt, it also takes away some beef flavor. I side with the butchers who avoid this cut. Instead, use a thin cut such as flatiron steak or thinly cut "London broil" from the shoulder. "London broil" is a style of cut, not an actual steak, and usually refers to a lean, thick, solid cut of meat. Alternate cuts: butterflied minute or hanger steak (+$).

SIDE NOTE: Serve guacamole alongside the sliced steak (page 220).

knock-your-socks-off way to wash down this superflavorful steak. For 8 to 10 people, combine and chill: 2 bottles of red table wine (Montepulciano), 1 bottle of white wine (Pinot Grigio), ½ bottle of champagne or Prosecco, 4 ounces St. Germain Elderflower Liqueur, 2 ounces Triple Sec, 1 shot of brandy or cognac, 4 ounces Bacardi or light rum, 4 ounces Peach Schnapps, 1 shot orange juice, 1 shot lemon juice.

Coffee-Crusted Hanger Steak

Why not save time and have your coffee with your dinner rather than after? Freshly ground espresso beans and lots of companion spices combine to give a little jolt to the seared crust of this full-flavored steak.

SERVES 2

Start to Finish: Under 30 minutes

> 2 tablespoons espresso or strong coffee beans, freshly ground
>
> 1 teaspoon ground cumin
>
> 1 teaspoon ground ancho chili pepper
>
> 1 teaspoon Spanish smoked paprika (*pimentón*)
>
> Kosher salt and freshly ground black pepper
>
> 1 (1- to 1¼-pound) hanger steak, halved
>
> Canola oil

Preheat the grill or a stovetop grill pan. Grind the coffee and then the spices in a spice or coffee grinder and pour the ground mixture out onto a large plate. Let the steaks come to room temperature, then coat them in oil and roll in the ground-coffee-and-spice mixture. Grill, about 15 minutes for rare to medium-rare, turning the steaks to brown all sides. Let rest for 10 minutes, loosely covered in foil, then cut into large slices on the diagonal.

Feedback

Did you know that the humble jar of paprika, which many people think is reserved for sprinkling on deviled eggs, not only provides a

BEHIND THE COUNTER: Have your butcher cut the hanger steak, remove the sinewy vein and present two halves; each half makes 1 perfect serving. Alternate cuts: rib eye, rib steak (+$) or a "London broil" cut from the shoulder (−$).

SIDE NOTE: For the complete steakhouse experience, whip up a batch of creamed spinach to serve on the side (page 212).

great splash of color, but also a terrific flavor boost? Your pantry probably holds a jar of sweet supermarket paprika, but let me tempt you to invest in the Hungarian variety, which will wake up most dishes with its earthy and slightly peppery flavor. Paprika was first processed in Hungary and is derived from red peppers, and can have a bit of a bite. For a spicier kick, try using hot paprika, and if you want that mellow smoky taste then reach for Spanish paprika, also known as *pimentón*.

Grilled Steak Salad

Pairing a slightly warm and rare grilled steak with a punchy salad is one of summer's best treats. The choice of add-ins is limited only by your imagination and what's in season.

SERVES 4 TO 6

Start to Finish: 2 hours to marinate, then under 15 minutes to grill

2 pounds silver tip, "London broil" style

For the marinade
1/4 cup low-sodium soy sauce
1 tablespoon honey
Juice of 2 limes (about 2 tablespoons)
1/4 cup rice wine vinegar
1/2 cup orange juice
1 orange, zested (about 2 tablespoons), segments
    removed to garnish the salad (see Feedback)
1/4 cup peanut, canola, or vegetable oil
2 teaspoons hoisin sauce
2 scallions, white and green parts, chopped
Kosher salt and freshly ground black pepper

For the salad
1/2 pound field greens
8 ounces uncooked shelled edamame

BEHIND THE COUNTER: Silver tip "London broil" cut 1/2 inch thick is a lean option, and makes the best choice for this preparation; however, any shoulder steak can be used with the marinade. Alternate cuts: Hanger steak trimmed and butterflied (+$), chicken parts or cubed breast (−$), or lamb cubes (=$).

1 pint cherry tomatoes, halved
2 avocados, peeled and sliced, optional

Place the meat in a resealable plastic bag. In a bowl, combine all the marinade ingredients. Reserve ¾ cup of marinade to use as salad dressing. Pour the rest into the bag with the meat. Marinate in the fridge for at least 2 and up to 4 hours.

Light the grill, or preheat the broiler and remove the meat from the fridge. Dry the meat with paper towels. Grill until medium rare, 5 to 7 minutes per side. Let the meat rest, covered loosely with aluminum foil, before slicing very thinly against the grain.

To compose the salad: Combine the greens, edamame, and tomatoes and toss with the salad dressing, reserving any extra dressing for another use. Lay the sliced beef on top of the greens and fan the avocado slices around the plate. Garnish with the orange segments and drizzle with a little dressing.

Feedback

"Supreming," which is separating fruit segments (*suprêmes*) from the membrane that holds them together, sounds more complicated than it is. Peel the citrus, and be sure to cut away all the rind and bitter white pith. Hold the fruit in one hand, and with a small paring knife begin cutting into the fruit down toward the center, cutting away both sides of the membrane, until the segments release. Continue turning the fruit and cutting in between the membrane so that all the segments fall away from the fruit. If you don't want to supreme the fruit for this recipe, you can just cut the peeled orange into slices or use canned mandarin orange segments.

Beef Braciole in Sunday Sauce

For some, Sunday supper means rolled and stuffed beef simmering away in a big pot of "gravy" (red sauce). For this version, zesty fresh parsley, fiery sun-dried tomatoes, and an obscene amount of garlic wake up the braised meat. To round out the dish, veal meatballs (page 76) can be added to the pot halfway through the cooking time. Invite the entire family over, grab an extra-large bowl, and be sure to have plenty of napkins on hand.

SERVES 6 TO 8

Start to Finish: Under 3 hours

For the sauce

¼ cup olive oil

1 medium onion, chopped

2 garlic cloves, peeled and chopped (about 1 tablespoon)

1½ teaspoons kosher salt

1 teaspoon dried oregano

Pinch of crushed red pepper flakes, optional

1 (28-ounce) can chopped tomatoes, with their juice

1 (8-ounce) can tomato sauce

1 heaping tablespoon tomato paste

Note: 3 cups bottled sauce can be substituted

For the braciole

1 (2-pound) steak or 6 to 8 individual steaks (about 5 to
    6 ounces each), pounded ¼ to ⅛ inch thick

2 teaspoons kosher salt

½ teaspoon freshly ground black pepper

⅓ cup Italian-style bread crumbs

¼ cup finely chopped flat-leaf parsley

¼ cup minced sun-dried tomatoes packed in oil (if dried,
    reconstitute in hot water until soft)

4 to 5 garlic cloves, finely minced (about 2 tablespoons),
    plus 3 garlic cloves, smashed

3 tablespoons olive oil

1 medium onion, diced (about 1 cup)

1 cup beef stock

½ cup red wine

2 bay leaves

1 vine-ripened tomato per person

BEHIND THE COUNTER:

Flatiron steak, cut from the shoulder top blade, makes a great choice for this classic Italian dish. Have your butcher butterfly it and lightly pound it until ½ to ¼ inch thick. Alternate cuts: for individual portions try small thin chuck steaks (–$), minute steaks, or small silver tip steaks (+$).

For the garnish
¼ cup chopped fresh flat-leaf parsley
6 basil leaves, rolled and cut into chiffonade

To make the sauce: Heat the olive oil in a large skillet, add the onions and stir over medium heat until lightly browned, about 10 minutes. Add the garlic and cook several minutes longer. Season with salt, oregano, and red pepper flakes, if using. Add the chopped tomatoes, tomato sauce, and tomato paste and stir to combine. Reduce the heat to low, cover, and cook for at least 30 minutes. If using prepared sauce, heat it in a pot, and keep it warm on a low simmer.

Season the pounded beef with the salt and pepper. Sprinkle one side of the beef with the bread crumbs, parsley, sun-dried tomatoes, and the minced garlic. Use your hands to evenly distribute the filling ingredients over the beef. Starting at the smaller end, roll the beef. Some of the filling might spill out: just tuck it back inside. Tie the beef every 2 to 3 inches with kitchen twine to hold it closed while it cooks. If you don't have kitchen twine, thread wood skewers through the meat or use reusable silicone cooking bands.

Heat the oil in a large braising pot. Sear the meat on all sides, seam side down first, over medium heat, about 5 minutes. Add the onions and the smashed garlic and cook several minutes longer until the beef is browned. Reduce the heat to low and add the tomato sauce, broth, and wine. Stir to combine. Toss in the bay leaves, cover, and cook over low heat for 30 minutes. Turn the braciole over and cook an additional 1½ to 2 hours, turning the meat every 30 minutes.

If adding meatballs, place them in the pot after an hour. For the last 30 minutes, place the whole tomatoes into the pot and allow them to stew along with the meat. If using smaller pieces of steak, you can reduce the cooking time to about an hour, adding the meatballs right from the start, and the tomatoes after the first 30 minutes. When the meat is done, remove the braciole from the pot. Discard the bay leaves. Remove the string (or skewers or bands), slice the braciole, and serve alongside the tomatoes with lots of sauce. Simple spaghetti or orzo makes a great foundation for the dish.

For a non-kosher version, Parmesan cheese (about ¼ cup) can be added as another layer in stuffing the beef.

Feedback

Some versions of braciole add chopped hard-boiled egg to the filling. Feel free to experiment with this traditional variation.

Crispy Orange Beef and Broccoli

This is not your average stir-fry; this one is ready for a Saturday night debut. It has the right balance between spicy and sweet, with both notes partnering perfectly with the beef and broccoli. Successful stir-frying is all about preparation: if you have all your ingredients ready to roll, you will have no problem with this fast cooking method.

SERVES 4 (2 IF YOU ARE SUPERHUNGRY)

Start to Finish: Under 45 minutes

1 pound beef, cut against the grain into strips 1 inch wide and
    2 to 3 inches long
1 large dried poblano chili

For the sauce
2 tablespoons Madeira or dry sherry
2 tablespoons hoisin sauce
2 tablespoons honey
1 tablespoon chili-garlic sauce
2 tablespoons low-sodium soy sauce
Zest and juice from 1 small orange (about 1 tablespoon
    grated zest, ¼ cup juice)
1 tablespoon brown sugar

BEHIND THE COUNTER:

Hanger steak, cut into strips (have your butcher remove the sinewy vein) is very flavorful and tender in this dish. You don't want to use tougher cuts that require braising, as this is a quick stir-fry. Make sure your butcher cuts the beef from a portion meant for stir-fry, not pepper steak. Don't even think about using rib meat for this preparation; it would be like wearing a ball gown to a ball game. Alternate cuts: thin cut minute steak, or thin cuts from the top blade, the silver tip, or the neck portion at the top of the chuck (–$).

For the stir-fry

1 small head broccoli, florets only, blanched

3 tablespoons cornstarch

¼ cup peanut or vegetable oil

1 large garlic clove, minced (about 1½ teaspoons)

1 tablespoon grated fresh ginger

1 scallion, white and green parts, sliced, for garnish

Cooked rice for serving

Spread the beef out on a plate lined with a paper towel and refrigerate, uncovered, for at least 30 minutes or up to 1 hour. Drying the meat will give it a crisper finish when it's fried.

To reconstitute the poblano, cover it in a small bowl with very hot water. When soft, remove the stem and seeds and slice the pepper into thin strips; set aside.

To prepare the sauce: Whisk together the Madeira, hoisin, honey, chili-garlic sauce, soy sauce, orange juice, orange zest, and brown sugar. Set aside.

Bring a large pot of salted water to a boil and blanch the broccoli for 3 to 4 minutes. Drain and place in a bowl filled with ice water to stop the cooking. Set aside.

To stir-fry: Heat half the oil in a large skillet or wok. Remove the meat from the fridge and toss with the cornstarch in a resealable plastic bag. Shake off excess cornstarch and carefully drop the meat into the oil. Cook over medium-high heat until crispy and browned, 5 to 7 minutes. You might need to do this in two batches, so as not to overcrowd the pan. Transfer the finished meat to a plate and set aside. In the same pan, add the remaining oil, only if the pan is dry, and stir-fry the broccoli, garlic, and ginger over medium-high heat for 2 minutes. Add the reserved sauce, poblano chili, and beef. Cook for several minutes until the sauce has thickened and the meat is glossy and coated with sauce. Garnish with the sliced scallions and serve spooned over rice.

Beef Stew Provençal

"Chuck and Stew Get Potted" is not just a good name for a buddy flick, but a way to remember how to best prepare cubed meat from the chuck region. This stew speaks with a French accent and is a take on a classic daube. The full-bodied red wine sauce welcomes chunks of carrots, potatoes, mushrooms, and pearl onions. If you can exhibit some self-control, let the finished dish sit overnight in the fridge, which will intensify the flavor and further thicken the sauce. As for the wine, never cook with anything you wouldn't want to drink; don't skimp.

BEHIND THE COUNTER: Stew meat cut from the neck or shoulder is preferable. Have your butcher cut the meat into 1-inch cubes, trimming excess visible fat. Alternate cuts: Veal or lamb stew meat (+$), bone-in or boneless chuck roast (=$), short ribs (+$).

SERVES 4 TO 6

Start to Finish: Under 5 hours

2 pounds beef stew meat, cut into 1-inch pieces

½ cup all-purpose flour, seasoned with 1 teaspoon kosher salt and
  ¼ teaspoon freshly ground black pepper

4 tablespoons olive oil

2 cups beef stock

2 cups red wine

2 tablespoons Worcestershire sauce

2 tablespoons tomato paste

2 bay leaves

1 teaspoon dried thyme

2 garlic cloves, peeled and chopped (about 1 tablespoon)

1½ cups cleaned baby carrots

2 russet potatoes, peeled and diced into 1-inch pieces

8 ounces small white button mushrooms

2 cups frozen pearl onions, thawed

1 cup frozen peas, thawed, optional

Dry the beef and dredge it lightly in the seasoned flour. Heat 2 tablespoons of oil in a braising pot, and sear the meat until nice and brown, about 5 minutes (you might need to do this in two batches). Add the stock, wine, Worcestershire sauce, tomato paste, bay leaves, and thyme. Bring to a boil, then reduce the heat to low and cook, covered, for about 1½ hours. Add more stock and lower the heat as the sauce is cooking down.

While the meat braises, heat the remaining 2 tablespoons of oil in a skillet. Add the garlic, carrots, potatoes, mushrooms, and onions and cook over medium heat, stirring occasionally, until lightly browned, 10 to 15 minutes. After the stew has cooked for $1^{1}/_{2}$ hours, add the sautéed vegetables and continue cooking, over low heat, for 30 to 45 minutes, or until the meat and vegetables are tender. About 5 minutes before serving, toss in the peas, if using. If the sauce is too thick, add additional stock. If it is too thin, remove the meat and vegetables and create a slurry by whisking together 1 teaspoon of cornstarch or flour with 2 teaspoons of cold water, stir back into the pot, bring to a quick boil, simmer until the sauce has thickened. Repeat until desired consistency. Discard the bay leaves. Serve in shallow bowls with a nice hunk of crusty bread.

Flanken/Short Ribs

For years flanken has been relegated to old-fashioned Eastern European preparations, braising for hours in well-seasoned pots while its more fashionable twin, the short rib, has graced the menus of trendy restaurants. What many people don't realize is flanken and short ribs are the very same meat and it is only the stroke of a butcher's knife that distinguishes these two savory cuts. Flanken is crosscut, yielding strips of meat interlaced between small sawed-off bones. Short ribs are cut parallel to the bone, revealing large chunks of meat perched atop a single long bone. They both come from the chuck section and are preferable to short ribs cut from the plate. Those are fine to flavor stews or sauces, but the meat is fatty and less choice. Flanken and short ribs work well in almost every braising recipe, and will yield succulent, fall-apart tender meat when cooked low and slow. Here are three variations from simple to simplest using three different cuts of flanken short rib.

Simple Oven-Braised Short Ribs

These savory ribs are comforting and nourishing on a cold winter's day when the intoxicating aroma will fill your home, and these meaty ribs will fill your belly.

SERVES 4

Start to Finish: Under 3 hours

4 pounds beef short ribs

1 tablespoon kosher salt

1 teaspoon freshly ground black pepper

2 tablespoons vegetable oil

2 medium onions, sliced

2 cups beef stock

1 (28-ounce) can whole tomatoes, juices reserved

1 cup red wine

1 bouquet garni: several sprigs of parsley, thyme, and bay leaves wrapped in a piece of cheesecloth, or just tied tied together with kitchen twine

1 tablespoon olive oil

1 pound peeled and cleaned baby carrots (about 3 cups)

2 parsnips, peeled and cut into 1-inch chunks

Preheat the oven to 325 degrees. Dry the short ribs with paper towels and season them with the salt and pepper. On the stovetop, heat the vegetable oil in a large braising pot and brown the meat on all sides (even the bone), about 10 minutes. Don't rush this step; remember that color equals flavor. You will probably need to brown the meat in two batches. Remove the short ribs from the pot and set aside. In the same pot, brown the onions over medium heat, about 10 minutes. Add the beef stock, tomatoes (crush them into the pot with your hands), and add 1 cup of the reserved juices, and the wine. Bring to a boil, scraping the little brown bits from the bottom of the pot. Add the short ribs to the pot along with the bouquet garni. Cover and roast in the preheated oven for 1½ hours, turning the ribs every 30 minutes.

While the ribs are braising, heat 1 tablespoon of olive oil in a skillet, add the carrots and parsnips, and cook over medium heat, stirring

BEHIND THE COUNTER: Have your butcher cut the short ribs into 2- to 3-inch pieces. Alternate cuts: 2nd cut brisket (+$), deckle (−$), or veal osso buco (+$).

SIDE NOTE: To capture the luscious sauce you could boil up a box of broad egg noodles or try your hand at authentic dumplings (page 203).

occasionally, until lightly browned, about 10 minutes. Set aside. After 1½ hours of cooking, add the carrots and parsnips to the pot of ribs, cover, and continue to cook until the meat and vegetables are very tender, 45 to 60 minutes longer.

When the meat and vegetables are done, season to taste with salt and pepper. Discard the bouquet garni. If the sauce is thin, remove the ribs and vegetables from the pot, skim off most of the fat. Create a slurry by mixing 1 tablespoon of cornstarch with 2 tablespoons of water, stir back into the pot, bring to a boil, then simmer. Repeat until desired consistency. To serve, you can present the rib on the bone, but chances are the meat has already fallen off. Try to cut away any remaining fat. Serve the short ribs with the gravy and vegetables spooned on top.

Feedback

Here's the rundown on carrots. The ones you see in the market with their fresh "Bugs Bunny" green tops are the freshest, possibly locally grown, and sent to your market in a matter of days. They will have real depth of carroty flavor. Bagged carrots may have sat around for weeks or months in their plastic packaging. Sounds like a no-brainer. However, if you are looking for the sweetest carrots, chances are they will be found in the dreaded bag, because as the carrot sits and waits, the starch is converted to sugar, making the carrot sweeter.

Simpler BBQ Ribs

When the summer comes and the BBQ beckons, you want to treat your short ribs with a different approach. A quick sprinkling with a sweet-heat rub flavors and tenderizes the meat and gets it ready for the grill. Irving Diamant, our butcher from St. Louis, where ribs are iconic, implores you "not to torture your ribs". Eating beef ribs involves a little wrestling, and a fair amount of chewing, but that's half the fun. Slather on your favorite bottled sauce or one of our quick-fix basting sauces during the last few minutes to achieve that "I need a wet nap," picnic table, backyard barbecue effect.

SERVES 4 (3 TO 4 RIBS PER PERSON)

Start to Finish: At least 2 hours or up to overnight to marinate; under 30 minutes to grill

For basting

Traditional quick BBQ sauce:

½ cup ketchup

¼ cup low-sodium soy sauce

1 tablespoon honey

1 tablespoon Worcestershire sauce

OR

Oaky Bourbon glaze:

¼ cup bourbon

⅓ cup molasses

¼ cup orange juice

1 tablespoon grainy mustard

For the rub

¼ cup brown sugar

1 tablespoon hot or sweet paprika, to taste

1 tablespoon kosher salt

2 teaspoons chili powder

1½ teaspoons freshly ground black pepper

¼ teaspoon cayenne pepper

1 teaspoon garlic powder

1 teaspoon Worcestershire sauce

1 teaspoon liquid smoke

3 to 4 pounds BBQ-style flanken/short ribs

BEHIND THE COUNTER:
Irving recommends your butcher cut the flanken "sparerib-style for the BBQ," ¾ inch thick and 4 to 6 inches long. Alternate cut: When pressed, Irving prefers back ribs from the rib section. Those have a layer of fat that lubricate the meat, and in between the bones, there's plenty to gnaw on. If using back ribs, watch them carefully as the fat can ignite and char quickly. Cook them to medium rare (=$).

SIDE NOTE: No barbecue is complete without potato salad. Ours is a cross between a German vinegar and American mayonnaise-based salad. Fresh herbs wake it all up (page 185).

To prepare the traditional BBQ sauce: Mix all the ingredients together in a bowl.

To prepare the Oaky Bourbon glaze: Put all the ingredients in a small saucepan and cook over low heat until syrupy.

To prepare the ribs: Combine all the ingredients for the rub in a blender or food processor. Pulse until mixed.

Place the ribs in a shallow dish and generously sprinkle the ribs with the rub. Cover tightly and refrigerate for 2 hours or up to overnight. Take the meat out of the fridge about 30 minutes prior to grilling. Grill the ribs for about 7 minutes. Turn them over, slather on some sauce, and cook an additional 7 minutes. Turn them again, give them another coating in sauce, and cook for just another minute or two. Ribs can be served medium rare.

Feedback

If you prefer fall-off-the-bone ribs, braise them first for 45 minutes to 1 hour and then grill, but I feel you sacrifice some of the beefy goodness with this method. You can also grill them low and slow, with the grill cover closed, using indirect heat, for at least 1½ hours.

Simplest Korean *Kalbi* Ribs

Beef flanken is the meat of choice for traditional Korean barbecue, also called *kalbi* (*Galbi*), which is Korean for rib. The thinly sliced flanken is marinated in an authentic Asian sauce and finished with a sprinkling of sliced scallions to add color and a crisp oniony bite.

SERVES 4

Start to Finish: 4 hours or up to overnight to marinate; under 15 minutes to grill

BEHIND THE COUNTER: Have your butcher cut flanken from the chuck, ½ to ¼ inch thick. Alternate cut: flanken from the short plate tip of the rib section is not preferred but can be used (–$).

SIDE NOTE: Step up your presentation with a bountiful vegetable fried rice (page 188).

For the marinade

¼ cup mirin

2 tablespoons low-sodium soy sauce

¼ teaspoon ground ginger

2 garlic cloves, peeled and chopped (about 1 tablespoon)

2 teaspoons sesame oil

1 tablespoon hoisin sauce

2 teaspoons brown sugar

2 scallions, white and green parts, chopped (reserve half for garnish)

¼ teaspoon kosher salt

⅛ teaspoon freshly ground black pepper

1½ pounds flanken

Combine the marinade ingredients in a bowl. Place the ribs in a shallow pan or large resealable plastic bag. Pour three-quarters of the marinade over the ribs and refrigerate for 4 hours or overnight. Reserve the remaining marinade for basting. **Light the grill or broiler** and remove the ribs from the marinade. Grill over medium-high heat for 7 to 10 minutes, turning the meat often to prevent it from burning, and basting each time you turn. Sprinkle with the reserved chopped scallion and serve with any remaining basting sauce on the side.

Brisket

Brisket is one of the most flavorful and versatile cuts from the breast of the animal. It can be braised, smoked, barbecued, pickled, or boiled. Brisket is a workhorse and holds up to bold sauces and robust combinations of vegetables. It is the foundation for the classic triumvirate of Jewish soul food: brisket, corned beef, and pastrami. Leftover "bonus" brisket can be shredded for sloppy sandwiches, and is a great add-in for chili or meat loaf.

There are two cuts of brisket. 1st cut, also called flat cut, is very lean and can be a bit dry. It weighs between 5 and 7 pounds and is the best choice if you want less fat and if size matters. 2nd cut is fattier and smaller, weighing in at 2 to 3½ pounds. The fat melts into the meat as it slow cooks and creates a very juicy, flavorful result.

Slow-Day BBQ Brisket

Pick a quiet weekend to prepare this dish because it is two days in the making, and worth every minute. First the meat is lacquered with a piquant rub as it sleeps the night away. The next day it is slow roasted and infused with the tangy barbecue sauce. This recipe is based on one given to me by my friend Karen Banschik, who developed her version after tasting a pricey sandwich from one of New York's premier butchers. Determined to re-create the flavor, Karen found the right balance

BEHIND THE COUNTER:
You can use either 1st (+$) or
2nd cut brisket (−$).
Alternate cuts: top of the rib,
while not cut from the
brisket, comes from the
uppermost portion of the rib
section and braises quite well.
It has more fat than the 1st
cut, but is leaner than the 2nd
cut, so many find it a happy
medium. It generally weighs
3½ to 4 pounds and costs
about the same as 2nd cut
(=$).

SIDE NOTE: Celery root–
apple slaw makes a great
accompaniment. Its sweet
flavor and crisp texture
balances the sharp tones of
the BBQ sauce (page 219).

between heat and sweet. This recipe feeds an army, but you can easily
cut it down for a smaller brisket.

SERVES 10 TO 12

*Start to Finish: Under 30 minutes to prep; 6 to 8 hours or overnight to rest;
5 to 7 hours to slow roast*

For the rub
3 teaspoons liquid smoke
⅓ cup lightly packed brown sugar
⅓ cup minced garlic
2 tablespoons kosher salt
3 tablespoons freshly ground black pepper, or more to taste
1 tablespoon cayenne pepper

For the meat
8 to 9 pounds brisket

For the sauce
1 cup tomato sauce
¾ cup honey
¾ cup low-sodium soy sauce
6 tablespoons distilled white vinegar
¼ cup light or dark corn syrup
3 tablespoons Worcestershire sauce
2 tablespoons hoisin sauce
½ teaspoon cayenne pepper
Kosher salt and freshly ground black pepper

To prepare the rub: Combine all the rub ingredients in a blender or
food processor. Pulse until thoroughly mixed. Place the meat in a large
roasting pan and rub all sides with the mixture. Cover tightly and refrigerate 6 to 8 hours, or overnight.

To prepare the BBQ sauce: Mix all the ingredients in a saucepan and stir
over medium heat until combined. Lower the heat, cover, and cook for
30 minutes or until the sauce is thick and syrupy enough to coat the back
of a spoon. Season to taste with salt and pepper. Let the sauce cool and
refrigerate until needed. The sauce can be prepared several days ahead.

When ready to roast, **preheat the oven to 250 degrees** and remove the meat from the refrigerator. You should never put a cold piece of meat in a warm oven; it will reduce the oven temperature dramatically and throw off your cooking time. Cover the roasting pan tightly and bake 5 to 7 hours, basting every 2 hours with the juices that collect in the pan. If covering with aluminum foil, don't let the foil touch the meat; it can impart a tinny taste. Try laying a piece of parchment paper over the meat and then cover with the foil. When the brisket is fork-tender but not falling apart (after 4 to 5 hours), uncover the pan. Remove about 2 cups of the collected juice and discard. Pour the BBQ sauce over the brisket, using enough to cover but not drown the meat; you will have sauce left over. Cover the meat and continue cooking for 1 hour. When done, transfer the meat to a cutting board and cut the brisket against the grain with a nonserrated knife. Serve with the sauce on the side. (See Feedback for cutting against the grain.)

Feedback

When a recipe calls for slicing against the grain, look carefully and follow the long strands that run the length of the meat. If you slice parallel to those strands, you will get chewy, stringy slices of meat. Rather, make your cuts perpendicular to them, going against the grain; that will yield the most attractive and tender pieces.

Classic Brisket

This brisket braises to fall-apart tenderness and can be served in two distinctive ways. Classic juicy slices can enjoy the company of the rich vegetable-laden gravy, or you can shake things up by shredding the brisket for a more rustic ragout. Anyway you slice it, it's mouth-wateringly good.

SERVES 4 TO 6

Start to Finish: Under 4 hours

1 (2½ to 3-pound) brisket
2 teaspoons kosher salt

BEHIND THE COUNTER: 2nd cut brisket is perfect for this dish as it imparts the most flavor to the sauce, shreds easily, and stays juicy while cooking. Alternate cuts: 1st cut brisket (+$), short ribs (=$), which would shred well or present perfectly served on the bone, cubed chunks of lamb or veal shoulder (+$), which would braise beautifully with the vegetables and make a wonderful stew.

SIDE NOTE: Nothing could be more iconic than nestling the sliced brisket in a big bowl of kasha varnishkes generously smothered with gravy (page 196).

1 teaspoon freshly ground black pepper, slightly coarse

Olive oil

2 carrots, cut into 1-inch pieces

3 celery stalks, cut into 1-inch pieces

2 medium onions, sliced

4 garlic cloves, peeled and chopped (about 2 tablespoons)

$^1\!/_2$ cup red wine

1 (28-ounce) can whole tomatoes, drained

2 bay leaves

2 cups beef stock

Preheat the oven to 350 degrees. Pat the meat dry with paper towels and season both sides with 1 teaspoon of the salt and $^1\!/_2$ teaspoon of slightly coarse pepper. Lightly coat the bottom of a braising pot with olive oil, and brown the brisket over medium heat until a nice crust begins to form, about 10 minutes. The meat will tell you when it's time to turn it by easily releasing from the bottom of the pot. Remove the meat to a plate and reserve.

Add a coating of oil to the pot. Add the carrots, celery, and onions and cook over medium heat, stirring occasionally, until they are soft and lightly browned, about 10 minutes. Add the garlic and give it all a quick stir. Pour in the wine and the remaining salt and pepper and cook for just a minute or two. Carefully crush the tomatoes with your hands as you add them to the pot. Lay the brisket over the vegetables, add the bay leaves, and pour in the stock. You want the top third of the brisket to be above the liquid, so it develops a brown, flavorful crust while it roasts. You might need to add a little more or less stock. Cover the pot and place it in the preheated oven. Roast in the preheated oven for 2 to 3 hours, or until the meat is fall apart tender. When the brisket is done, remove it from the sauce and remove and discard the bay leaves. At serving time, slice the brisket against the grain and serve family style by spooning the vegetables and gravy on top. (See Feedback page 49)

Feedback

For a yummy ragout, shred the slightly cooled brisket and puree all the vegetables with the gravy. The vegetables and gravy can be pureed using an immersion blender right in the pot, or use a standard blender. To shred the brisket, use two large forks to pull it apart. Spoon the shredded beef and veggies over pappardelle noodles, whose broad and thick character really stand up to the bold ragout. If you can't find pappardelle noodles, cut cooked lasagna noodles into 3-inch pieces for the same effect. A seasoned bread-crumb mixture can be easily prepared to top the dish by combining 1 cup Panko (seasoned bread crumbs can be substituted), 3 garlic cloves, finely minced, and 1 teaspoon dried Italian herbs. Quickly fry the seasoned crumbs in a skillet with a little olive oil until toasty, about 5 minutes, shaking the pan to prevent them from burning. Sprinkle over the ragout before serving.

New England Boiled Dinner

This classic dish of corned beef and cabbage will undoubtedly make your house smell like your local deli, but that's not a bad thing! Corned beef is brisket that has been cured with large kernels of salt that resemble corn; hence, corned beef. Because it is salted, while corned beef cooks it releases its liquid and will shrink considerably, so buy a larger piece than you feel you need. Additionally, the "bonus" meat is great the next day (hash recipe follows). For a traditional New England boiled dinner you'll want to boil vegetables to serve alongside the beef. Be creative in your mix, adding your favorites from small red potatoes to cubed turnips and parsnips. The corned beef water will be salty and fatty, so I recommend cooking the vegetables in a separate pot. You'll lose a bit of the authentic flavor, but your veggies will be fat free. The key is to baby the corned beef before cooking, and be patient while it slowly simmers. It takes a little extra time and attention, but the end result is well worth it.

SERVES 4 TO 6 (THE RECIPE CAN BE EASILY DOUBLED IF PREPARING A LARGE CORNED BEEF)
Start to Finish: 12 to 24 hours to soak the beef and change the water; about 1½ hours to cook

BEHIND THE COUNTER: Ask your butcher for a whole corned beef, with the fatty top layer. You can trim the fat after cooking, but it adds moistness and flavor. Alternate cuts: lean flat cut; same as a 1st cut brisket, will not be as tender (+$). Here's a good preparation in which to try pickled tongue (=$).

1 (3-pound) corned beef

1 medium onion, quartered

4 garlic cloves, smashed

2 tablespoons pickling spice or 12 whole black peppercorns, 4 bay leaves,
  and any of the following: allspice, coriander seeds, mustard seeds,
  cardamom, cloves, mace, cinnamon, ginger to equal 2 tablespoons

4 carrots, peeled and cut into 1-inch pieces

1½ to 2 pounds small red new potatoes, scrubbed clean
  (If planning on "bonus" corned beef hash, add 8 extra new potatoes)

1 small head green cabbage, quartered

2 turnips, peeled, optional

2 parsnips, peeled, optional

If boiling the vegetables separately you'll need

1 tablespoon pickling spice or 2 bay leaves and 12 peppercorns, 1 onion
  halved, and 3 garlic cloves to add to the water

Rinse the meat under cold water. To remove the intense saltiness and help tenderize the meat, soak the corned beef in cold water for at least 12 hours or up to 1 day. Place the corned beef in a large resealable plastic bag and fill with cold water. Place the bag in a pot or shallow dish to prevent leakage and place in the fridge. Change the water every several hours, more frequently in the beginning, less frequently as the day goes on. When ready to cook, remove the corned beef from the bag, rinse, and pat dry with paper towels.

Place the beef in a heavy braising pot with a tight-fitting lid with the onion, garlic, and pickling spice or assorted spices. Cover the meat with fresh cold water (about 2 quarts) and bring to a boil. Skim and discard any foam that rises to the top. Reduce the heat to a gentle simmer and cook, covered, skimming the foam that collects on the surface as needed, until a knife inserted in the center comes out easily, 50 to 60 minutes per pound. If you are cooking the vegetables with the corned beef, add them (except the cabbage) during the last 30 minutes of cooking and add the cabbage for the last 15 minutes.

If preparing the vegetables separately: Bring a large pot of salted water to a boil. Be sure the pot is large enough to hold all your veggies once they displace the water in the pot. Add all the vegetables except the cabbage. Cook, uncovered, about 15 minutes, then add the cabbage. Continue cooking an additional 15 minutes, or until all the vegetables are tender.

When the meat and veggies are fork-tender, slice the beef against the grain, using your knife to trim the layer of fat that sits on top of the beef. Delis charge extra for lean corned beef; at home it's free. Save some of the liquid to pour over the "bonus" meat so it does not dry out, then reheat the beef in the original cooking liquid. If you plan on using some of the beef for hash, refrigerate a portion and carve it when it is cold.

Feedback

Pickling spice is an interesting flavor combination hitting both sweet and spicy notes. It infuses the cooking liquid with an array of spices ranging from cinnamon to cardamom and often overlooked spices such as mace and clove. The flavors dance on your tongue. For a more traditional corned beef taste, you can rely on the standbys of bay leaves and peppercorns, but for a more adventurous result give pickling spice a try.

Corned Beef Hash
. . . with poached egg

The morning bonus of last night's corned beef dinner is undoubtedly waking up to a steaming skillet of freshly slung hash. You don't need to be a short-order cook to prepare this simple, satisfying, hearty breakfast. While your local coffee shop might top the hash with a fried egg, a perfectly poached egg adds an elegant element to the dish and is a true upscale way to serve the hash.

SERVES 4

Start to Finish: Under 15 minutes

6 to 8 new potatoes, skin on, or 2 russet potatoes, peeled
   (If using leftover potatoes from the corned beef, simply dice them;
   you'll need about 2 cups)
2 tablespoons vegetable oil

1 large onion, chopped (about 1½ cups)
2 garlic cloves, chopped (about 1 tablespoon)
½ cup diced green or red bell pepper, seeded and cored, optional
2 cups roughly chopped corned beef
Kosher salt and freshly ground black pepper
Fried or poached egg, optional

Bring a large pot of salted water to a boil and cook the potatoes until fork-tender, 15 to 20 minutes. Drain, dice, and reserve. If using leftover potatoes, skip to the next step.

Heat the oil in a 12-inch skillet. Add the onions and garlic and cook, stirring occasionally, for about 3 minutes, then add the diced potatoes and peppers, if using. Let the potatoes cook over medium-high heat without disturbing until they begin to develop a crust, 5 to 7 minutes.

When the potatoes are crusty, add the corned beef and stir until the ingredients are well combined. Continue to cook until the beef has begun to brown. Season to taste with salt and pepper. Serve as a side dish or topped with a fried or poached egg (recipe follows).

Poached Egg

There are a few tricks to making a perfectly poached egg. It might take a practice run or two—that's why they put a dozen eggs in the box.

1. The water needs to be at a strong simmer, but not boiling.
2. Add white vinegar to the water to help stabilize the egg white.
3. Swirl the water when adding the egg. It creates a tornado effect and bundles the white strands.
4. Cook exactly 3 minutes for soft, $3^1/2$ for medium, and 4 for a hard center.

Bring a wide shallow pot of water to a strong simmer, filling the pot two-thirds full. Add 1 tablespoon of vinegar to the water. If you have a poaching tool (a tool that resembles a ladle), it works best. If not, crack your egg into a ladle. This method will allow you to crack the egg in the same vessel you'll use to lower it into the water. If you can't manage holding the ladle and the cracking, place the round portion of the ladle in the mouth of a drinking glass, resting the handle against something solid. This will free your hands. Now crack the egg into the free-standing ladle. If you break the yolk, reserve that egg for a scramble, and start again.

When bubbles fill the bottom of the pot, it is time to lower the egg into the water. Take a wooden spoon and swirl the water to create a whirl-pool effect. Lower the ladle with the egg into the water. Set your timer as directed above. Remove the egg with a slotted spoon and drain on a waiting paper towel. Dab the top of the egg so it is not watery. Place on top of the prepared hash.

Ground Beef

Commonly called chopped meat, ground beef is created when the butcher grinds any meat from the cow. Which part of the animal the ground beef comes from distinguishes the flavor, fat content, and texture. Often butchers will use scraps from various cuts to create a ground beef blend. When you buy ground beef, keep your recipe in mind and what percentage of fat content will work best in it. Where the meat will be crumbled, and you will be able to pour off the drippings, you can use meat with a lean to fat ratio of 70:30. The fat will add flavor and moistness, but not stay with the final dish. For meatballs or meat loaf where you want a firmer texture, and the fat becomes integrated in the final product, ask for ground beef that has a lean to fat ratio of 80:20. And if you want the leanest ground beef, which tends to be drier, look for an 85:15 or 90:10 lean to fat ratio. It's fun to try ground beef from various parts of the animal and see if you can tell the difference. You can also incorporate other ground meats, such as lamb or veal, to mix in with beef to change the taste and texture.

Whatever the fat content or recipe, there are a few hard-and-fast rules when dealing with ground beef. Do not overwork the meat or it will become tough. Use a light hand when adding salt as ground kosher beef tends to hold the salt from the koshering process. Cook the beef to a higher temperature than you would a roast: 160 degrees is the USDA recommended internal temperature. Ground beef has a shorter shelf life than solid meat such as roasts or steaks, so use it within 2 days of purchasing, or freeze it tightly wrapped to prevent freezer burn.

BEHIND THE COUNTER: I set out to find the secret to the juiciest, most flavorful burger by speaking to New York's "burger kings" at Pat LaFrieda Meat Purveyors. I know they're not kosher, but they know burgers. Mark Pastore, who is the COO of the company and has been in the business for two decades, shared this advice. "The best burger is something that gets created by grinding your own meat." If you have a KitchenAid stand mixer, or a Hobart, they can both do the job. Mark advises using a medium grind, and suggests you freeze the meat, or make sure it is really cold before grinding. You'll want a mix of cuts. Mark prefers 30 percent brisket with 70 percent chuck from the shoulder (collicle). You can, of course, ask your butcher to grind the meat to your specifications for you. Once you have the beef ground, you want to handle it as little as possible. Although Mark defers to personal preference, he feels all a burger needs is some salt and pepper to bring out its natural flavor. When it comes to cooking your burger, he suggests you get your grill or stovetop grill pan nice and hot, and cook that burger once on each side. When the burger is cooked halfway, flip it, never push it flat, and then grill on the second side. For a change, ask your butcher to grind bison. It makes a great burger, but needs less cooking time (+$).

The Best Burger

If you view the drippings that land on your shirt when you bite into a burger as a badge of honor, then this recipe is for you. The toppings are a real matter of personal taste, but we can suggest some quick-fried pastrami or turkey bacon. Make sure the bun is fresh and that you have plenty of napkins handy.

MAKES 4 BURGERS
Start to Finish: Under 15 minutes

> 1½ pounds freshly ground beef
> Kosher salt and freshly ground black pepper

Divide the beef into 4 equal parts and shape into burgers, about ½ to ¾ inch thick. Season with salt and pepper at this time, or wait until the burgers have finished cooking and season with salt and pepper to taste. Grill, broil, or pan sear to desired doneness, 4 to 5 minutes per side for rare to medium rare, 6 to 7 minutes per side for medium. Serve with your choice of toppings.

Feedback

Our wine expert, Aron, recommends pairing your burger with any hearty and robust red wine that you would enjoy with a steak. Cabernet and French wines such as Côtes du Rhone are a good choice.

Spaghetti Bolognese

Spaghetti Bolognese is all about the meat. The stock, sautéed aromatics, touch of tomato sauce, and pinch of oregano are all designed to support the main focus: slow simmered ground beef. Together they produce a robust and full-bodied sauce that screams to be scooped up with crusty bread and twirled onto pasta-laden forks.

SERVES 4
Start to Finish: Under 2 hours

3 tablespoons olive oil
1 medium onion, chopped (about 1 cup)
1 carrot, peeled and finely minced (about ½ cup)
1 celery stalk, finely minced (about ½ cup)
2 large garlic cloves, finely minced (about 2 tablespoons)
Pinch of crushed red pepper flakes (or more to taste)
1½ pounds lean ground beef
1 cup red wine
1 cup beef stock
1 cup tomato sauce
1 tablespoon tomato paste
1 teaspoon dried oregano
Kosher salt and freshly ground black pepper
1 pound spaghetti

SIDE NOTE: Tomato jam is a concentrated kick of tomatoey taste, and makes a great condiment for these burgers (page 226). For the total experience, a big batch of twice-fried potatoes is a must. Start them first; they take more time than the burger (page 186).

BEHIND THE COUNTER: Lean, but not extra-lean ground beef works well, as does a combination of ground beef and ground veal (+$).

Heat the oil in a large skillet, add the onions, carrots, celery, garlic, and red pepper flakes and sauté over medium heat, about 10 minutes. Crumble and add the ground beef to the skillet, using the back of a spoon or a potato masher to gently break up any clumps of meat. You want the texture to be coarse, not clunky. Cook over medium heat just until the meat is no longer pink, about 10 minutes. Add the red wine and ½ cup of the stock. Reduce the heat to low, cover, and cook for 30 minutes. Add the remaining ½ cup of stock, cover, and continue cooking for 30 minutes longer. After an hour, stir in the tomato sauce, tomato paste, and oregano and season to taste with salt and pepper. Cover and continue cooking until ready to serve. It can be as little as 15 minutes more or hours longer, just keep the heat low enough that the sauce barely simmers.

While the sauce cooks, bring a large pot of salted water to a rapid boil. Cook the spaghetti according to package directions, until al dente; it will cook a little more in the sauce. Reserve a cup of pasta water, then drain. Stir the spaghetti into the skillet and cook for a few minutes, stirring, adding a little pasta water, if needed, to loosen the sauce.

Feedback

Rather than buying tomato paste in the can, keep a tube of tomato paste in the fridge, simply squeezing what you need. If you do use canned paste, you can dollop what remains onto wax paper, wrap it tightly and freeze, or freeze the tomato paste in ice cube trays and pop out a cube as needed. Anchovy paste can also be bought in a tube and makes adding anchovy flavor to a dish easy and economical. The jury is out on whether or not anchovy paste is pareve—so when in doubt, leave it out.

Spicy Grilled *Mititei*

These garlicky little bites of ground meat are Romania's answer to trendy street food. They are crowd-pleasers hot off the grill and served on long bamboo skewers with dipping sauce or simple grainy mustard. The texture of these little sausages can vary from dense and meatball-like to authentic and spongy when seltzer and baking soda are added.

BEHIND THE COUNTER: Lean ground beef works best. Alternate cuts: ground lamb, chicken, or turkey (+$).

SIDE NOTE: To complete the Romanian theme, serve with a spicy eggplant and tomato salad (page 211).

MAKES 12 PIECES

Start to Finish: 15 minutes to prepare the meat; at least 4 or up to 24 hours to rest in the fridge; under 15 minutes to grill

1 pound ground beef
4 to 5 garlic cloves
1 teaspoon kosher salt
1 teaspoon sweet or hot Hungarian paprika
1/2 teaspoon freshly ground black pepper
Generous splash of Worcestershire sauce
1 tablespoon ketchup
1/4 cup finely chopped flat-leaf parsley
2 tablespoons seltzer or club soda, optional
2 teaspoons baking soda, optional

For the dipping sauce
4 tablespoons ketchup
2 tablespoons Dijon mustard
1/4 teaspoon ground cumin
Splash of Worcestershire sauce

Put the ground beef in a medium bowl. Grate the garlic using a Microplane over the meat so the garlic juice is included; you want about 2 tablespoons total. Add the salt, paprika, pepper, Worcestershire sauce, ketchup, and parsley. For a more authentic spongy texture add the seltzer and baking soda. Use your hands to thoroughly blend the spices into the meat. Cover and refrigerate at least 4 hours or up to 1 day. Combine the dipping sauce ingredients and refrigerate until ready to use.

When ready to cook, **light the grill or preheat the broiler** and take the meat out of the fridge. Wet your hands and form the meat into rounds the size of a golf ball, then elongate them into 3-inch thumb-like shapes. Grill or broil for 4 to 5 minutes, turn them over, and continue to cook for 3 to 4 minutes longer. Serve with the dipping sauce or mustard on the side.

Picadillo

My friend Patricia Pita, who is Cuban American, happily offered me her family recipe for a very Cuban savory ground beef dish called *Picadillo*. Patricia explains, "Every Cuban cook has a special way to make picadillo. Some omit the capers, others add fried potatoes or top each serving with a fried egg. There are those who claim the picadillo must simmer for an hour for optimal taste and still others who say one need only make a quick *sofrito*, toss in the rest of the ingredients, and cook it for a few minutes."

SERVES 4
Start to Finish: Under 30 minutes

1 tablespoon vegetable oil
1 medium onion, chopped (about 1 cup)
1 large green bell pepper, cored, seeded, and chopped
3 garlic cloves, minced (about 1½ tablespoons)
1 pound extra-lean ground beef
½ cup tomato sauce
¼ cup sliced green pimento-stuffed olives

BEHIND THE COUNTER: Lean ground beef is recommended. Alternate cut: lean ground turkey (+$).

SIDE NOTE: For a real Cuban feast you can add fried potatoes, black beans, or platters of ripe plantains. Try our black beans and rice (page 189) and whip up a batch of homemade sofrito to really bring the flavor home. (page 225).

¼ cup raisins

1 tablespoon capers

2 tablespoons white vinegar

¼ teaspoon granulated sugar

1 teaspoon kosher salt

½ teaspoon freshly ground black pepper

2 to 3 tablespoons sofrito, homemade (page 225) or store-bought can
  be found in the specialty food aisle

Heat the oil in a large skillet over medium heat. Add the onion and
bell pepper and cook, stirring occasionally, until the onion is translucent, about 3 minutes. Add the garlic and cook 2 minutes longer.
Add the beef, breaking it up with the back of a spoon or a fork. Stir
in the tomato sauce, olives, raisins, capers, vinegar, sugar, salt, and
pepper. Reduce the heat to low, cover, and simmer for 20 minutes, or
until the consistency is like that of a "sloppy Joe." See Side Note for
serving suggestions.

Feedback

Picadillo can be the basis for many other Latin favorites. Try using
the meat as a filling for a layered lasagna or for empanadas. Most
markets sell empanada dough already prepared and ready to fill.

Matzo Meat Cakes

BEHIND THE COUNTER: Lean ground beef is traditional. Alternate cuts: ground veal or lamb (+$).

In my home, where there were Sephardic influences from my father's side of the family, we always enjoyed traditional Greek dishes.
None were more important at our Passover table than what we call
matzo meat cakes. There are Egyptian and Turkish versions, some
layered like lasagna, others topped with mashed potatoes like Shep-
herds' pie. My great grandmother's version, with its roots from the
Isle of Rhodes, is slow-simmered ground beef, sandwiched between
softened matzo, and baked to a crisp golden brown. These meat
cakes are great hot or cold, as a terrific lunch, satisfying dinner, or
midnight snack.

Start to Finish: Under 4 hours

½ cup olive oil, plus 2 tablespoons for the pans

3 pounds ground beef

10 large onions, chopped

10 ounces chicken stock

Kosher salt and freshly ground black pepper

6 (7-inch) square aluminum disposable pans

9 eggs (5 eggs for the cakes, 4 eggs for the coating)

Matzo meal

1 box Streit's unsalted matzo (have an extra box standing by)

Heat 2 tablespoons of olive oil in a large skillet. Add the ground beef and cook, stirring over medium heat until completely browned, about 7 minutes. Remove the meat with a slotted spoon and set aside. Pour off the fat from the skillet. Add ¼ cup of the oil to the skillet, add the onions and cook, stirring, over medium heat until soft and golden, 10 to 15 minutes. If your skillet cannot hold all the onions, cook them in batches, adding additional oil if needed. When the onions are lightly browned, return the meat to the skillet. Pour one-third of the stock into the meat and onion mixture. Reduce the heat to low, cover, and cook 1½ to 2 hours, adding a little stock every 30 minutes or so until all the stock has been incorporated. Season generously to taste with salt and pepper. Spoon the meat mixture into a bowl and allow it to cool (you can cover and refrigerate overnight, but be sure to bring the meat and onions back to room temperature before proceeding to the next step).

Preheat the oven to 350 degrees, and pour a little olive oil into the bottom of each aluminum pan. When the oven is hot, place the pans in the oven to heat the oil; this will prevent the meat cakes from sticking to the pan and helps the bottoms crisp up. Beat 5 of the eggs and add to the meat mixture. Slowly add matzo meal until the mixture is thickened and a little gummy and all the liquid has been absorbed.

In a separate bowl, beat the remaining 4 eggs with 3 tablespoons of the olive oil. Lay a damp cloth on your countertop and dampen a second cloth. Now comes the only delicate portion of the recipe. It takes a little practice to get it just right; hang in there, it will be worth it. Hold 1 piece of matzo under warm running water until it is pliable, like a piece of wet cardboard. Place the matzo on the damp towel and repeat with a second piece of matzo, placing it to the side of the first piece. Cover both pieces with the second damp towel and lightly press down.

Remove one pan from the oven and swirl the oil to make sure it is evenly distributed. Hold one softened piece of matzo in your hand, and dip your other hand into the egg and oil. Coat the matzo on both sides with the egg and oil (you can use a pastry brush, but it's much less fun). Place the matzo in the pan. Spoon one-sixth of the meat mixture onto the matzo. Generously coat both sides of the second piece of softened matzo with the egg and oil and place on top of the meat mixture. Lightly press down to evenly distribute the meat between the two pieces of matzo. Using the tip of a very sharp knife, gently score the cake into 4 pieces, being sure not to pierce the bottom of the pan. Bake for 60 minutes. Repeat with the remaining five pans.

When done, the meat cakes should be brown on top. Remove the pans from the oven and let the cakes cool slightly before removing from the pan. (I find cutting away the sides of the aluminum pan with a scissor helps release the cakes easily.) Flip the cakes over, allowing the bottoms to cool and become a little crisper. You can leave the cakes in large squares, or cut the squares on the diagonal.

Sausage

Take ground beef, combine it with herbs and spices and then cure it, smoke it, or enclose it in an edible collagen casing and you've got sausage. Sausages are a versatile, economical, and delicious way to make the most of ground beef. To some, sausage seems like a non-kosher food, but almost every kosher butcher now features a variety of sausages. Mine made the transcontinental trek from California's premier sausage maker, Jeff Rohatiner. They arrived special delivery, ready to take the plunge into sauces, soups, and a variety of dishes. The ubiquitous hot dog that "answers to a higher authority" is at every market and is technically sausage. Whether you slice them, crumble them, or wrap them in a blanket, sausages enliven many dishes, and are just plain fun to eat.

Pushcart Puppies

The pushcarts of New York are famous for their soft salted pretzels and steaming franks. By combining the two, right in your kitchen, you create sidewalk paradise. When filled with plump beef franks, these are terrific for Sunday game day, or to make any time with children as fun pick-up food.

MAKES 10 PUSHCART PUPPIES
Start to Finish: Under 2 hours

For the dough
1 cup lukewarm water (about 110 to 115 degrees)
1 tablespoon brown sugar
1 tablespoon active dry yeast
1 teaspoon salt
3 cups all-purpose flour
2 tablespoons margarine, melted

For the hot dogs
10 fat (knockwurst or dinner-size) beef, chicken, or turkey hot dogs
8 cups water
1/2 cup baking soda

For the egg wash
1 egg, beaten with 1 teaspoon water
Coarse salt

Spicy brown mustard for serving

Combine the water, sugar, and yeast in the bowl of a standing mixer. Gently stir and let the yeast bubble for 10 minutes (if it doesn't, the yeast isn't fresh). After 10 minutes, add the salt, flour, and margarine. Place the bowl on the mixer, and with the dough hook attachment, combine the ingredients on low speed, then increase to medium speed and continue to mix the all the ingredients are well combined and the dough completely pulls away from the sides of the bowl, 2 to 3 minutes. Turn the dough out onto a clean work surface and knead with your hands for just a minute. If the dough is sticky, add a little more flour, as needed, and up to $\frac{1}{4}$ cup. Place the dough in a large bowl that has been lightly greased with vegetable oil. Cover with plastic wrap and let the dough rise in a warm spot for about 1 hour, until roughly doubled in size.

When the dough has doubled in size, turn it out onto a lightly floured work surface. Fill a shallow pot with 8 cups of water and the baking soda and bring to a boil. **Preheat the oven to 450 degrees** and line a baking sheet with parchment paper.

Divide the dough into 10 pieces. Dry the hot dogs with paper towels; you don't want them to make the dough soggy. Take a piece of dough and gently roll or pull it into a 4- to 5-inch circle. Roll the hot dog up in the dough, just like a blanket; you can tuck in the ends as you roll or let the ends of the hot dog peek out. Continue until you have prepared all 10 pieces.

Drop the wrapped hot dogs, one at a time, into the boiling water, and allow them to boil for 40 to 50 seconds each. Remove them with a slotted spoon, shake off the water, and place on the lined baking sheet. Brush each hot dog with the egg wash and sprinkle with coarse kosher salt. Bake at 450 degrees, for 12 minutes, or until the blankets are a golden brown. Serve whole, cut in half, or sliced on the diagonal for smaller bites. Dunk liberally in spicy brown mustard.

Sausage and Peppers

BEHIND THE COUNTER:
Sweet Italian sausage was used for this preparation, but the same dish can be prepared with any type of sausage (=$).

You've got to love a dish where every ingredient speaks volumes. From the well-seasoned Italian sausage to the medley of peppers, there are no shy fellows here. The beauty of sausage and peppers is the versatility of the finished dish. Serve as is, toss the combo with pasta for a fiery main course, or spoon generously into soft baked rolls for a classic hero sandwich. Raise or lower the spice and heat; it's a classic however it's served.

SERVES 4

Start to Finish: Under 1 hour

2 tablespoons olive oil

1 pound beef sausage, cut into 1-inch chunks

1 medium red onion, sliced

3 garlic cloves, crushed

1½ to 2 pounds assorted peppers, cored, seeded, and cut into chunks.
   (red and green bell peppers and Italian frying peppers [cubanelle]
   all work well)

1 teaspoon smoked paprika (*pimentón*)

Pinch of crushed red pepper flakes (more or less to taste)

1 teaspoon dried oregano

1 (28-ounce) can whole tomatoes, with their juice

1 pound rigatoni pasta, cooked

Kosher salt and freshly ground black pepper

Fresh basil, for garnish

Heat the oil in a large skillet, add the sausage, and stir over medium heat until lightly browned (they'll cook through at the final step). Remove with a slotted spoon and set aside. Add the onions and cook in the fat left in the pan, about 5 minutes. Add the garlic, peppers, paprika, red pepper, and oregano and cook over medium heat, stirring occasionally, until lightly browned, 10 to 15 minutes. Stir in the tomatoes, crushing them gently with the back of a spoon, reduce the heat to a gentle simmer, cover, and cook for 15 minutes.

Bring a large pot of salted water to a rapid boil. Cook the pasta according to the package directions. Reserve 1 cup of the pasta water and drain.

After the sauce has cooked down, toss the sausage back into the pan, cover, and cook 10 to 15 minutes longer. Add the cooked pasta, combine and heat through, adding a little of the reserved pasta water to smooth or loosen the sauce if needed. Season to taste with salt and pepper and garnish with fresh basil leaves.

Feedback

Another great combination is sausage, peppers, and potatoes. Feel free to stir in some diced parboiled potatoes along with the onions, and let them get crispy and golden brown in the pan, then prepare as described above.

Breakfast Burrito

BEHIND THE COUNTER: Buy
sausage that easily crumbles
and has a slight kick, such as
chorizo.

SIDE NOTE: Homemade salsa
is fast and easy and oh-so-
delicious spooned over this
burrito. By making it yourself,
you control the heat and the
chunk factor (page 217).

Nothing says good morning like starting your day with skillet-seared
spicy sausage, freshly scrambled eggs, and authentic refried beans all
wrapped up in a flour tortilla blanket.

MAKES 1 BREAKFAST BURRITO
Start to Finish: Under 15 minutes

¼ pound chorizo sausage
2 eggs, beaten
Kosher salt and freshly ground pepper
1 medium 10-inch flour tortilla
¼ cup canned refried beans, seasoned with a pinch of cumin
    and a pinch of smoked paprika (*pimentón*)
Salsa, store-bought or homemade, optional
Chopped fresh cilantro leaves for garnish, optional

In a small skillet, cook the crumbled sausage, stirring over medium
heat for 3 to 5 minutes or until it lightly browns and renders its fat.
Don't overcook; you don't want to dry it out. Remove the sausage
with a slotted spoon and set aside. Scramble the eggs in the same
pan, without draining or wiping it out. Season the eggs with salt and
pepper. Set aside. Wipe the pan clean and quickly heat the tortilla,
about 15 seconds on each side.

Spread a thin layer of the beans on the tortilla, top with the scrambled
eggs, and then scatter the crumbled sausage on top. Roll the tortilla
and cut in half on the diagonal. Serve with the salsa on the side, garnished with chopped cilantro.

NP

For a non-pareve presentation, add your favorite cheese either to the
eggs, or sprinkled on top of the finished tortilla. Queso fresco is a good
match for the burrito.

VEAL

Veal is delicate meat that comes from a calf, a cow between 6 weeks and 3 months old. Because the calf is young, its meat is quite tender with subtle flavor and little fat. In a calf, the forequarter is referred to as the foresaddle and comprises the **shoulder, rib** (rack), **breast,** and **foreshank.** Because a calf is smaller than a cow, the cuts of meat are also relative in size. When buying veal, look for a light pink color with very little or no grainy fat or sinewy tissue and you'll be rewarded with lovely flavor, supple texture, and infinite possibilities.

Veal **shoulder,** which is the neck and chuck region, yields elegant roasts, savory stew, delicate ground meat, or thin slices for veal scallopini. The roasts can be braised or dry roasted, while the thin slices are perfect for pan searing. The stew, of course, needs to be braised and the ground meat is so versatile you can use it in many preparations. The **breast** and **foreshank,** which on the calf is considered one cut, yields the yummy breast of veal which can be prepared on or off the bone—with or without a pocket for stuffing— and takes well to dry roasting. It can also be trimmed to reveal a small brisket, which can be braised to savory goodness. The breast ribs are fatty but delectably delicious and can be grilled, braised, or roasted. The foreshank gives us the famous osso buco: round shin bones with a meaty exterior and a soft marrow-rich center. The gelatinous nature of veal bones makes them a natural to add to stews, soups, and stock. The **rib** section, also known as the **rack,** is the prime area of the calf, where meaty rib chops and crown roasts are built. The most expensive cuts come from the rib, where the meat presents beautifully with juicy flavor and tender texture.

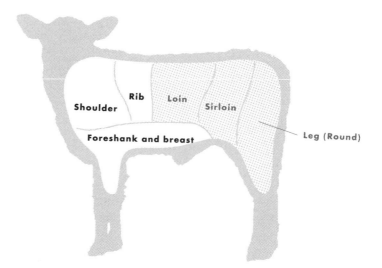

Roasted Veal Shoulder
. . . *with chicken liver stuffing*

Veal shoulder is a versatile cut, that can be roasted or braised, simply seasoned or embellished with stuffing. For this recipe a savory stuffing featuring rich porcini mushrooms, assertive chicken livers, and sweet red onions brings an exquisite balance to the dish, while herbs and dry vermouth add depth of flavor. If you are not a liver fan, leave them out, and if you don't want to fuss with stuffing the veal itself, you can cook this stuffing in a casserole alongside the roast.

SERVES 4 TO 6

Start to Finish: Under 2 hours

For the stuffing

1 (1-ounce) package dried porcini mushrooms
2 tablespoons chicken fat, duck fat, or olive oil
¾ pound chicken livers, optional
1 medium red onion, chopped (about ¾ cup)
1 cup chicken stock
½ teaspoon poultry seasoning or ½ teaspoon ground sage
3 cups (1 5.25-ounce package) croutons, plain or seasoned
Kosher salt and freshly ground black pepper

For the veal

1 (3½-pound) veal shoulder
1½ teaspoons kosher salt
½ teaspoon freshly ground black pepper
1 teaspoon poultry seasoning or ½ teaspoon ground sage and ½
    teaspoon ground thyme leaves
1 tablespoon chicken fat, duck fat, or olive oil
1 cup chicken stock
½ cup dry white vermouth or white wine
½ cup strained porcini liquid, optional (you'll have this if making the
    stuffing or risotto)
1 bay leaf

BEHIND THE COUNTER: Have your butcher trim and cut a veal shoulder. There are two options for stuffing the shoulder. The butcher can create a pocket to stuff, or pound the shoulder thin so you can roll the shoulder around the stuffing. Have your butcher show you how to roll and tie the shoulder after it is stuffed. There is a technique to this process, and a quick how-to would be helpful. Alternate cut: breast of veal (with or without a pocket for stuffing, on or off the bone) costs less overall, but it also presents less edible meat (-$).

SIDE NOTE: A beautiful alternative to the stuffing is a porcini-studded risotto, which can be served as an elegant side dish (page 190). The porcini liquid from the risotto can be incorporated into the gravy for added flavor.

To prepare the stuffing: Soak the porcini mushrooms in 1 cup of hot water (you can actually soak them right in the glass measuring cup). While the mushrooms are soaking, heat 1 tablespoon of fat in a skillet and cook the livers over medium-high heat, about 5 minutes. Cover the pan and cook several minutes longer until the livers are no longer red inside. Transfer them to a bowl, using a slotted spoon. When cool, cut them into small pieces, about the size of raisins. (If *kashering* the livers in the broiler, join us at the next step.) Wipe the skillet clean and heat the remaining tablespoon of fat. Add the onions and cook over medium heat, stirring occasionally, until lightly browned, about 10 minutes. Spoon the onions into the bowl with the cut-up chicken livers.

By now the mushrooms should have softened and released their flavor into the soaking water. Remove the mushrooms from the water, squeeze them to release all their liquid, rinse them under cold water to remove any grit, and chop into bite-size pieces. Take the porcini water and strain it through a piece of cheesecloth, a damp paper towel, or a coffee filter. Reserve the mushrooms and their liquid (about 1 cup). Pour half of the strained liquid into the bowl with the livers; reserve the rest for the sauce. To the bowl, add the chicken stock, poultry seasoning, croutons, and salt and pepper to taste and stir to combine, being sure the croutons soak up all the liquid and become spongy. If they feel dry, add more stock. Let the stuffing come to room temperature before filling the pocket or layering the stuffing on top of the roast.

Preheat the oven to 350 degrees and set a rack in a roasting pan. Season the veal with salt, pepper, and the dried herbs. If stuffing the veal, fill the pocket with the stuffing, or spread a thin layer of stuffing on one side. Roll and tie the veal, securing it every 2 inches using kitchen twine or reusable cooking bands. If cooking the stuffing alongside the roast, grease a casserole and spoon in the stuffing. Set it aside: you'll add the casserole to the oven after the roast has cooked 30 minutes.

Heat the fat in a large skillet and sear the veal over medium-high heat for just a few minutes on each side, until a light brown crust develops. Carefully transfer the veal to the roasting pan. Pour in the chicken stock, vermouth, any remaining porcini liquid, and bay leaf. Roast the veal in the preheated oven for 30 minutes, basting with the accumulated drippings. After the 30 minutes, place the casserole with the stuffing in the oven and continue roasting and basting the veal, adding water or broth to the pan if beginning to dry out. Roast about 1 to 1¼ hours longer, or until an instant-read thermometer inserted in the center of the breast registers about 150 degrees. Remove the roast from the pan, and let it rest covered loosely with aluminum foil. Place the roasting pan directly on the stovetop and heat the juices to create a gravy, scraping up the bits that are clinging to the bottom of the pan. Slice the roast and serve with the stuffing and gravy spooned on top.

Feedback

Vermouth is a fortified wine blended with herbs and botanicals, and was widely popular in the '60s. It lost favor when vodka supplanted it as a must-have in the perfect martini. And while that's always been vermouth's principle function, it also makes a great alternative to dry white wine for cooking. It has a longer shelf life and lower initial cost per ounce while adding a subtle floral note and herbaceous flavor to sauces. After you've given cooking with it a whirl, why not create the classic gin and vermouth martini? Recipes and tastes vary, but anywhere from a 3:1 ratio of gin to vermouth to a 5:1 ratio makes a balanced blend. Shake or stir with lots of ice. Add a twist of lemon, a cocktail onion, or a green olive (with some of its juice for a dirty martini) and you have a James Bond–worthy drink.

Mediterranean Osso Buco
. . . with zesty gremolata

This veal dish, which has its roots in Milan, is braised in wine and aromatics and served over saffron-scented rice. *Osso Buco* means "hole bone" in Italian, alluding to the rich, melt-in-your-mouth marrow contained in the center of this cut of meat. Be sure to provide small forks or tiny or narrow spoons to coax out the soft, custardy delicacy. This recipe calls for a dash of balsamic vinegar and offers the option of adding olives and anchovies to give the dish a little extra intrigue. The gremolata is a classic accompaniment that lends a vibrant note when spooned over the veal.

BEHIND THE COUNTER: Have your butcher cut the shanks into 2½- to 3-inch pieces (about 10 ounces each), and tie kitchen twine around the outside of the meat, as if cinching the shank with a belt at the waist, so the shank pieces do not fall off the bone when cooking. Alternate cuts: there is no other cut that will produce the same dish, but you can use the same ingredients and method to prepare veal spareribs (–$) or lamb shanks (–$).

SERVES 4

Start to Finish: Under 2½ hours

3 tablespoons olive oil

4 veal shanks, cut osso buco style

¼ cup flour for dredging, seasoned with 1 teaspoon kosher salt, ½ teaspoon freshly ground black pepper, and 1 teaspoon sweet Hungarian paprika

2 carrots, peeled and cut into 1-inch pieces (about 1 cup)

1 large onion, diced (about 1 cup)

2 celery stalks, cut into 1-inch pieces (about 1 cup)

4 garlic cloves, smashed

1 cup pitted and halved Kalamata olives, optional

2 to 3 small anchovy filets, finely minced or 1 tablespoon anchovy paste, optional

¾ cup white wine

2 tablespoons balsamic vinegar

1 cup diced tomatoes, drained

2 cups chicken stock

1 bouquet garni: 1 bay leaf, 4 sprigs thyme, wrapped and tied in cheese cloth, pouch, or just tied with kitchen twine. If you are not preparing the gremolata, then add 6 sprigs of parsley to the bouquet.

For the gremolata

½ cup minced fresh flat-leaf parsley

1 lemon peel, zested (about 1 tablespoon)

1 tablespoon finely minced garlic

Preheat the oven to 325 degrees. Heat the oil in a heavy braising pot with a tight-fitting lid. Pat the veal dry with paper towels, and dredge them in the seasoned flour. Brown the veal on both sides, over medium-high heat, until a nice brown crust forms on each piece. Transfer the veal to a plate. In the same pot, cook the carrots, onions, and celery over medium heat until lightly brown, about 5 minutes. Add the smashed garlic, the olives, and the anchovies, if using, and cook 5 minutes longer. Pour the wine and vinegar into the pot, scraping up any bits that have collected on the bottom, and cook until the liquid is reduced by half, about 10 minutes. Place the veal back in the pot, along with any liquid that collected on the plate. Add the tomatoes and stock. The liquids shouldn't drown the meat; the top portion of each shank should show. Nestle the bouquet garni in the sauce. Place in the preheated oven and cook, covered, for 1¹⁄₂ to 2 hours, until the meat is very tender.

Prepare the gremolata right before you plan on serving the meat by combining all the ingredients, and set aside. When the meat has finished cooking, carefully remove the shanks from the pot with a slotted spoon. Remove and discard the bouquet garni, and bring the sauce to a slow boil. To thicken the sauce you can puree it right in the pot using an immersion blender, or ladle it (allowing it to cool for several minutes), into a standard blender. For a chunky sauce, leave some of the vegetables whole and puree only half. Or you can thicken the sauce by creating a slurry with 2 teaspoons of cornstarch mixed with 4 teaspoons of cold water. Bring to a boil, and reduce to a simmer. Repeat until desired consistency. Season to taste with salt and pepper.

Before serving, remove the string from the veal and generously spoon the sauce over each serving. Top with a tablespoon of gremolata to garnish.

Feedback

Osso Buco and rice Milanese have enjoyed a long marriage. Preparing rice Milanese is as easy as making boiled rice, with the addition of golden saffron threads, which add mellow yellow color and a burst of flavor. This precious spice comes from the dried stigma of a saffron crocus and by weight is the most expensive spice in the world. You only need a pinch to impart its distinctive taste and distinguishing color. Prepare white rice as directed on the package and add a pinch of saffron to the cooking liquid. If you replace the water with chicken or vegetable stock, the flavor will be even more amplified.

Grilled Veal Chops

. . . and roasted red grapes Syrah

Veal chops are the premier cut from the rack of veal, with a meaty center and a thin layer of fat that helps keep the chops juicy and flavorful. This simple preparation showcases the chops and surrounds them with a delicate sweetness from the roasted red grapes and fruity yet peppery Syrah (Shiraz) wine.

BEHIND THE COUNTER: You have three choices when buying veal chops. 1st cut is the most expensive and features the least fat and meatiest eye. Choose it if cost is not an issue and you want to present the most perfect chop (+$). Center cut has a good balance of meat to fat, and presents beautifully; it's the most popular cut (−$). 2nd cut, your most cost-efficient, is the least impressive in appearance, taste, and texture, and does best when breaded (−$). Have your butcher french the bone for the nicest presentation and least amount of fat. Alternate cuts: rib lamb chops (=$) or shoulder chops (−$).

SERVES 2

Start to Finish: Under 30 minutes

2 tablespoons olive oil

2 (8- to 10-ounce) veal chops

½ pound seedless red grapes

¼ cup red wine (Syrah/Shiraz works well)

2 teaspoons sea salt combined with 1 teaspoon chopped fresh
   rosemary, 1 teaspoon dried oregano, 1 teaspoon chopped fresh
   thyme for garnish

Preheat the oven to 350 degrees. Heat 1 tablespoon of olive oil in a skillet large enough to hold both chops. Coat the chops in the remaining tablespoon of olive oil, and sear in the heated skillet over medium-high heat until each side is nicely browned, about 5 minutes per side. Toss the grapes into the skillet with the chops and add the red wine. Pop the skillet in the oven so the chops can finish cooking, about 10 minutes, or until your desired doneness or an instant-read thermometer reads about 140 to 145 degrees. Sprinkle a little of the seasoned sea salt over the veal and let it rest covered with foil for about 5 minutes. Serve with the sauce and grapes spooned on top.

Feedback

Aron from the Kosher Wine Society suggests Pinotage or Tempranillo as alternatives to the Syrah.

Stuffed Mushroom Caps
with Asian or Italian Filling

These perfect little bites speak with an Asian or Italian accent, making them a wonderful appetizer. They take little time to prepare— and less time to eat!

MAKES 2 DOZEN BITES

Start to Finish: Under 45 minutes

BEHIND THE COUNTER: This recipe utilizes lean ground veal. Alternate cuts: ground chicken, turkey, lamb (=$), or lean ground beef (~$).

24 small to medium-size white button mushrooms, stems removed
Olive oil

Asian filling
1/2 pound ground veal
1 teaspoon grated fresh ginger
1 scallion, minced (about 1 tablespoon)
1/2 teaspoon kosher salt
1/4 teaspoon freshly ground black pepper
1 teaspoon cornstarch
1 garlic clove, minced (about 1 teaspoon)
Panko bread crumbs for dredging

Italian filling
1/2 pound ground veal
1 teaspoon dried oregano
1 shallot, minced (about 1 tablespoon)
1/2 teaspoon kosher salt
1/4 teaspoon freshly ground black pepper
1 teaspoon Italian-style bread crumbs, additional for dredging
2 garlic cloves, minced (about 2 teaspoons)
1/2 teaspoon hot sauce

Preheat the oven to 350 degrees. Remove the stems from the mushrooms and save for soup or stock. Wipe the mushrooms clean with a damp cloth or paper towel. Slice the stem side edge off the mushroom so the cap is flatter and the ragged edges are gone. Use a teaspoon to lightly scoop out any fibers in the cap. Place the caps, hollow side down, on a baking sheet and drizzle lightly with olive oil. Bake for 10 minutes. While the caps bake, prepare your filling by combining all the filling ingredients. Remove the tray from the oven and allow the caps to cool hollow side down.

Raise the oven temperature to 400 degrees. Use a paper towel to dry any liquid that puddles in the caps as they cool. Loosely fill each cap with enough stuffing to create a small mound. The amount will vary depending on the size of the cap. Let them sit for a few minutes while you heat the oil in a medium skillet. Dunk the meat side of the caps in the Panko or bread crumbs. Fry the caps, crumb side down, for 2 to 3 minutes. Use a spoon to coax them over and brown for 1 to 2 minutes on the other side. Place the mushrooms, crumb side up, on the baking sheet and finish cooking in the oven until the tops are crusty, about 7 minutes.

Veal Meatballs

BEHIND THE COUNTER:
Ground veal is recommended. Alternate cut: lean ground beef (-$) or a blend of both meats works well.

Veal's sweet, delicate flavor and leanness makes it a perfect choice for savory meatballs. The trick is to handle the meat as little as possible to retain the light, open texture and create a moist meatball. The Sunday sauce (pages 36-38) calls for these veal meatballs. However, they can stand alone simmered in your favorite sauce and served with a big bowl of pasta or orzo.

MAKES ABOUT 16 MEATBALLS
Start to Finish: Under 1½ hours

> 3 to 4 cups tomato sauce (for homemade see pages 37–38),
>   heated in a large pot
> 1 pound pasta, cooked according to package directions
> 1 cup chicken stock
> ¼ cup finely minced flat-leaf parsley (you'll need a good handful to start)
> 1 (7-ounce) loaf Italian-style bread, crust removed, torn into small
>   pieces
> 1 egg, beaten

1 teaspoon dried oregano
½ teaspoon garlic powder
½ teaspoon kosher salt
¼ teaspoon freshly ground black pepper
1 pound ground veal
¼ cup olive oil
¼ cup Italian-style bread crumbs, for dredging

Heat the sauce in a large pot, cover, and simmer until you are ready to cook the meatballs.

Combine the chicken stock and minced parsley in a bowl. Tear the bread into very small pieces, add to the stock and parsley, and let it stand until the bread absorbs most of the liquid.

In a separate bowl, beat the egg and add the oregano, garlic powder, salt, and pepper. Stir to combine. Add the veal to the egg mixture and, with clean hands, work lightly to incorporate all the ingredients. Refrigerate for 15 minutes, to help the mixture bind. Remove the veal mixture from the fridge. Using your two best tools—clean hands— lightly squeeze the liquid from the bread and combine with the veal. Discard the remaining liquid.

Heat ¼ cup olive oil in a large skillet and pour the bread crumbs onto a plate. Wet your hands and roll the meatballs into 1-inch rounds and then in the bread crumbs. When the oil is shimmering (drop a few bread crumbs in the pan: if they sizzle and brown the oil is ready), fry the meatballs until nicely browned on all sides, about 10 minutes. An easy way to turn them is to use the two-spoon method to coax them to roll over in the pan. When the meatballs are browned, remove them with a slotted spoon and plop them in the simmering sauce. (If adding them to Sunday sauce, follow the instructions on page 38). Cover and cook on gentle simmer for 30 minutes. Right before serving, add the chopped parsley and basil leaves. Spoon over your favorite pasta.

Veal Marengo

This traditional veal dish, which originated in the Piedmont region of Italy, is a variation on a classic stew. It is flavored with crisp white wine, earthy mushrooms, and savory herbs. Sicilian green olives add a briny brightness to balance the sweet tomatoes and sautéed onions and peppers.

BEHIND THE COUNTER: Have your butcher cut veal from the shoulder into 1- to 2-inch cubes, trimmed of excess fat. Alternate cut: lamb stew meat (+$)

SIDE NOTE: The robust sauce is wonderful when served over broad egg noodles. While it's easier to open a box, it's infinitely more fun to make them yourself (page 201).

SERVES 4

Start to Finish: Under 1½ hours

2 pounds veal stew meat

½ cup flour for dredging, seasoned with 2 teaspoons kosher salt

½ teaspoon freshly ground black pepper

¼ cup olive oil

2 green bell peppers, or (1-pound) Italian frying peppers [cubanelles], seeded, cored and cut into 1-inch pieces

1 medium onion, coarsely chopped (about ¾ cup)

4 garlic cloves, finely chopped (about 2 tablespoons)

1 cup semidry white wine or vermouth

2 cups chicken stock

1 (28-ounce) can whole tomatoes, drained

½ teaspoon kosher salt

¼ teaspoon freshly ground black pepper

½ teaspoon chopped fresh thyme leaves or ¼ teaspoon dried thyme

½ teaspoon dried oregano

2 bay leaves

1 pound cremini mushrooms, wiped clean and quartered

½ cup green Sicilian olives, pitted and halved, optional

Pat the veal dry with paper towels. Heat half the olive oil in a braising pot. Dredge the veal in the seasoned flour and cook over medium heat, turning the veal as needed until brown on all sides, 5 to 7 minutes. You might need to do this in batches to avoid overcrowding the pan. Transfer the veal to a plate with a slotted spoon and set aside. In the same pan, heat the remaining oil, add the peppers and onions, and cook over medium heat, stirring occasionally, for 5 minutes. Add the garlic and cook an additional 5 minutes until everything is golden but not brown.

Gradually add the wine and stock to the pot, and cook over medium heat for about 10 minutes. Add the veal and any juices that have collected on the plate, the whole tomatoes, salt, pepper, thyme, oregano, and bay leaves. Reduce the heat to a simmer, cover, and cook for about 1 hour. Stir the mushrooms and olives into the pot, and continue to cook, uncovered, until the veal is fork-tender. With the cover off, the sauce will thicken on its own, but you can also make a slurry (see Feedback) and stir it back into the pot if you prefer a thicker gravy. Remove the bay leaves before serving.

Feedback

A slurry is a quick thickener that imparts no flavor. Mix one part flour, corn, or potato starch (thickener) with two parts cold water, until it resembles the consistency of thin Elmer's Glue. Then stir it back into the pot and bring to a boil. Repeat as necessary. Cornstarch thickens and glosses the sauce the most efficiently and quickly while flour or potato starch are half as effective and take a little longer. 1 tablespoon of cornstarch mixed with about 2 tablespoons of liquid will thicken $1\frac{1}{2}$ to 2 cups of sauce.

Veal Milanese
. . . topped with field greens and grape tomato salad

This dish is Italy's answer to Austria's schnitzel. Paper-thin slices of veal cutlet are dipped in a coating of egg and seasoned bread crumbs, fried quickly, and served simply. This recipe features field greens and grape tomato salad, which top the finished cutlet.

SERVES 4

Start to Finish: Under 15 minutes

> *For the veal*
> 1 cup vegetable oil or solid vegatable shortening
> 2 eggs
> 2 tablespoons water
> $1\frac{1}{2}$ cups Italian-style bread crumbs or plain bread crumbs,

BEHIND THE COUNTER: Have your butcher cut the veal scallopini style into paper-thin slices. When pounded they should almost be transparent. Alternate cuts: chicken or turkey cutlets (−$). For a dramatic presentation, use center cut (+$) or 2nd cut (−$) veal chops, pounded to $\frac{1}{4}$ inch thickness. Have your butcher french the bone for a more elegant finish.

seasoned with 1 teaspoon dried basil, 1 teaspoon dried thyme,
and 1 teaspoon dried oregano, or 1 tablespoon dried Italian herb
seasoning blend
1 cup all-purpose flour, for dredging
4 (5 - to 6-ounce) veal cutlets, pounded paper thin
Kosher salt and freshly ground black pepper

For the salad
¼ cup red wine vinegar
¼ cup olive oil
2 tablespoons water
1 teaspoon dried oregano or Italian herb seasoning blend
1 teaspoon kosher salt
¼ teaspoon freshly ground black pepper
1 cup halved grape tomatoes
¾ pound mesclun (field greens)

Heat about ½ inch of the vegetable oil in a large skillet and place a wire
rack on a rimmed baking sheet to hold the cooked veal when you are
finished frying.

In a shallow bowl beat the eggs with the water. Pour the bread crumbs
onto a plate large enough to dredge the veal cutlet and pour the flour onto
a second plate. Lightly season the veal with salt and pepper. Dip the veal
into the flour, then the egg, and then coat with the seasoned bread
crumbs, pressing the crumbs lightly into the cutlet so they adhere.

When the oil is shimmering (you can test it by dropping a few bread
crumbs into the pan and see if they sizzle and fry quickly), carefully place
1 cutlet in the pan and cook over medium-high heat until the underside
is golden brown, 2 to 3 minutes. Turn the cutlet over and continue to
cook until the other side is crisp and brown, 2 to 3 minutes more. Carefully remove the veal to the rack. Repeat with the remaining cutlets.

To prepare the salad: Combine all the dressing ingredients in a large
bowl. Toss in the tomatoes and let them marinate for about 5 minutes
so they pick up the dressing's flavor. When you are ready to serve, toss
the lettuce into the bowl and coat with the dressing. To serve place one
cutlet on each plate and top each with one-fourth of the salad.

Standing Rib Roast (page 23) *photo by Ben Fink*

Coffee–Crusted Hanger Steak (page 34) *photo by Ben Fink*

Classic Brisket (page 49) *photo by Ben Fink*

Veal Milanese (page 79) *photo by Ben Fink*

Pushcart Puppies (page 63) **and Lamb Sliders** (page 102) *photo by Ben Fink*

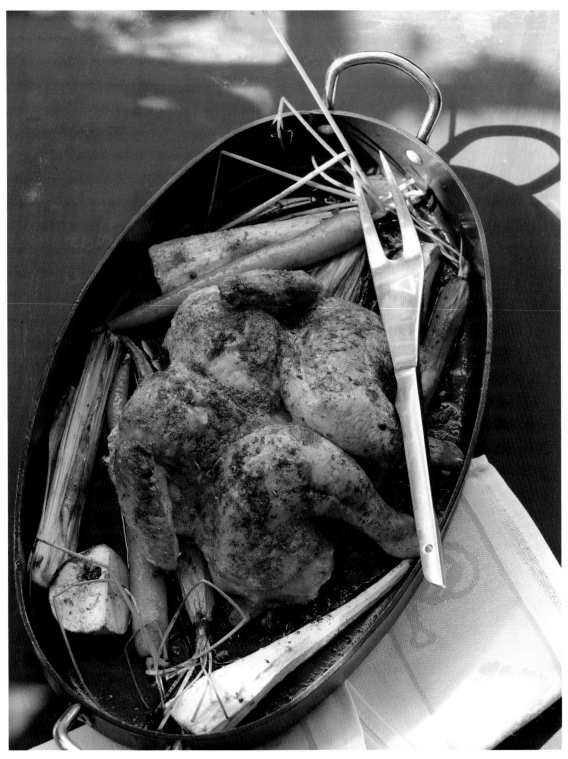

Simple Spatchcocked Chicken (page 107) *photo by Ben Fink*

Turkey Sausage with orecchiette pasta and broccoli rabe (page 157) *photo by Ben Fink*

Abundant Asian Noodle Soup (page 173) *photo by Ben Fink*

Feedback

Wiener schnitzel and veal Milanese are very similar dishes, but a few small changes in preparation make a world of difference. For schnitzel you do not want to press the bread crumbs into the veal, rather just lightly dredge the cutlets. When ready to fry, try solid vegetable shortening, rather than liquid oil. To create the subtle ripples that appear on the surface of the fried cutlet, gently swirl the pan when frying, allowing air to circulate under the breading, causing little hills and valleys in the coating. Serve schnitzel simply with a wedge of lemon and boiled new potatoes dressed with chopped flat-leaf parsley for a true Austrian finish.

Veal Brisket
. . . *and cippolini onions and mushrooms*

Lean and delicate veal brisket is a delicious alternative to the more common beef brisket. Its subtle flavor marries well with a crisp white wine sauce fragranced with sweet cippolini onions and earthy mushrooms.

SERVES 4

Start to Finish: Under 2½ hours

3 tablespoons olive oil

1 pound cippolini onions, roots and ends trimmed, peeled
    (small white onions or pearl onions can be substituted)

1 pound white button and cremini mushrooms, cut in half,
    caps only

1 teaspoon *herbes de Provence*

1 (2½- to 3-pound) veal brisket

1 teaspoon kosher salt

1 teaspoon freshly ground black pepper

½ cup dry white wine or dry vermouth

1 cup chicken stock

1 bay leaf

A few sprigs fresh thyme, optional

BEHIND THE COUNTER: Have your butcher cut a brisket from the breast, trimmed of all fat and bones. Alternate cuts: veal or lamb stew meat (−$).

SIDE NOTE: This spirited gravy can be spooned over simple broad noodles or homemade spaetzle (page 203).

Heat 2 tablespoons of the olive oil in a braising pot. Add the onions and cook, stirring, over medium heat until they begin to turn medium brown, about 5 minutes. Add the mushrooms and sprinkle with the *herbes de Provence.* Cook, stirring, until the mushrooms brown, about 10 minutes. Transfer the onions and mushrooms to a plate, using a slotted spoon, and set aside.

Season the veal with salt and pepper. Add the remaining tablespoon of oil to the same pot that you used for the onions and mushrooms, raise the heat to medium-high, and sear the veal on both sides, about 5 minutes. Transfer the veal to a plate.

Pour the wine and stock into the pot and deglaze, scraping up the brown bits from the bottom of the pot. Cook for several minutes, then return the veal and its collected juices to the pot. Toss in the bay leaf and fresh thyme, if using, cover, and simmer for 1 hour. Add the reserved onions and mushrooms and continue cooking for 30 to 45 minutes, or until the veal is fork-tender. Remove and discard the bay leaf and thyme twigs; they'll be easy to pick out. Place the veal on a plate and cover loosely with aluminum foil.

To thicken the sauce, create a slurry by mixing 1 tablespoon of cornstarch with 2 tablespoons of cold water. Stir back into the pot, bring to a boil, and repeat if necessary. If you are not serving the veal at once, refrigerate it overnight. The veal will develop additional flavor and be even better the next day. It is easier to slice the veal when it is cold, and then reheat in the sauce over low heat until warmed through.

Feedback

Mushrooms are funny little fungi sponges that soak up anything they mingle with, including liquid and flavor. To achieve browned mushrooms, you need high heat, a pan large enough to hold them so they can touch the bottom of the pan, and less liquid. That's why you should not salt the mushrooms while sautéing: that will encourage them to release water and create mushy mushrooms. To clean mushrooms use a lightly dampened paper towel to wipe away any dirt. White cultivated mushrooms are usually pretty clean; cremini (mini portobello) mushrooms tend to be dirtier. You can rinse them under cold running water just before using and then quickly dry them.

Calf's Liver

. . . and caramelized onions in a balsamic berry glaze

Crisp sautéed calf's liver is fashionable bistro fare at its best. Here it is dressed in caramelized onions and a balsamic reduction, a rich sauce that brings a sweet note to the dish. The addition of fresh berries adds a vibrant and colorful finish.

SERVES 4

Start to Finish: Under 45 minutes

¼ cup olive oil

2 medium yellow onions, sliced into ¼-inch-thick slices

1 teaspoon fresh thyme leaves

1½ pounds calf's liver, patted dry with paper towels

½ cup all-purpose flour, seasoned with 1 teaspoon kosher salt and
     ¼ teaspoon freshly ground black pepper

½ cup balsamic vinegar

¼ cup red wine (water or beef stock can be substituted)

1 teaspoon honey

½ cup sliced strawberries, raspberries, or blueberries, optional

Heat 3 tablespoons of the olive oil in a large skillet, add the onions, and cook over medium heat, stirring occasionally, until golden brown and very soft, 20 to 25 minutes. Don't rush this step: it is what caramelizes the onions and sweetens the dish. Sprinkle the onions with the thyme and cook 5 minutes longer. Remove the onions from the pan and cover to keep warm.

In the same skillet, heat the remaining oil. Lightly dredge the calf's liver in the seasoned flour on both sides. Cook the liver over medium-high heat until both sides are golden and crusty, 3 to 4 minutes per side for medium, 5 to 7 minutes for medium well. Transfer the liver to a plate and cover loosely with aluminum foil. If you need to *kasher* the liver, broil it, and join us at the next step.

In the same skillet, add the vinegar, red wine, and honey. Cook over medium heat until the vinegar is syrupy and reduced by half, 5 to 10 minutes. Toss in the berries, if using, and cook an addi-

BEHIND THE COUNTER: Have your butcher trim, clean, and slice the liver about ⅓ to ½ inch thick. While calf's liver is the only choice for this recipe, you could create a similar flavor using chicken livers, sautéing them (or broiling first to be *kashered*) and then serving with the balsamic reduction and onions (–$).

tional minute or two. Pour the vinegar reduction into a small bowl, cover, and keep warm. Quickly toss the onions into the pan to reheat, then spoon the onions over the liver. Drizzle the vinegar-berry reduction on top.

Feedback

Ever wonder how restaurant chefs create that amazing blur of sauce painted onto your plate? Well, you just made that same magical reduction. A *gastrique* is reduced and concentrated vinegar, wine, and sugar (and often fruit) that's drizzled on for a sweet and tart finish to a dish. Want to get fancy? Puddle a little of the sauce from this recipe on your plate, then take a spoon and quickly drag it through the sauce. The result will resemble an exclamation point, certain to elicit oohs! And aahs!

Southern-Fried Sweetbreads

BEHIND THE COUNTER: Ask your butcher for sweetbreads from the thymus, which Chef Kolotkin prefers.

While some might find the work involved in preparing sweetbreads a little daunting, Chef Kolotkin has certainly demystified them with one of his signature recipes. Is the allure of sweetbreads their creamy texture or their sublime flavor? Try this recipe that appears daily on Chef Kolotkin's restaurant menu, and you decide.

SERVES 4

Start to Finish: 6 to 12 hours to soak the sweetbreads; under 30 minutes to prepare

1½ pounds raw sweetbreads
Canola or vegetable oil for frying

For the court bouillon (can be made ahead, strain and refrigerate until needed, can be stored up to 1 week)
2 quarts water
1 cup dry white wine
½ cup white vinegar
1 carrot, peeled, tops removed, roughly cut
1 onion, roughly cut
1 celery stalk, washed, roughly cut

2 bay leaves

1 teaspoon whole white peppercorns

1 tablespoon finely chopped fresh tarragon or 1 teaspoon dried tarragon

For the southern seasoning dredge

1 cup all-purpose flour

1 tablespoon garlic powder

1½ tablespoons butchers' black pepper or coarsely ground black pepper

For the egg wash

4 whole eggs

3 tablespoons Frank's Red Hot Sauce

For the horseradish sauce

3 tablespoons Hellman's mayonnaise

1 tablespoon prepared white horseradish

Soak the sweetbreads for 6 to 12 hours in cold water, changing the water every 2 hours. This is a crucial step that pulls out any extra salt left from the koshering process. The sweetbreads do not need any additional salt for seasoning.

When ready to cook, bring all the ingredients for the court bouillon to a boil, then reduce the heat to a simmer for 30 minutes. Place the sweetbreads in the simmering court bouillon and bring back to a simmer; this should take 6 to 10 minutes. Place the entire pot into an ice bath and cool the sweetbreads in their cooking liquid. When cool, peel the thin membrane gently and remove, along with any veins that are present. With a sharp knife, slice the sweetbread into ¼-inch-thick medallions. Lay the cut sweetbreads on a clean, dry dishtowel and dry on both sides. Keep refrigerated for up to 3 days, or until ready to prepare.

When ready to fry, heat enough oil to cover the sweetbreads by about one-third. Dredge them in the southern seasoning dredge. Shake off all excess flour. Dip in the egg wash mixture, coat evenly, and shake off any excess egg wash. Dredge again and then pan fry in the oil, over high heat, on both sides until brown and crisp, 1 to 2 minutes per side. Drain the sweetbreads on paper towels and quickly whip up the sauce by combining the mayonnaise and horseradish. Serve hot with the horseradish sauce on the side.

LAMB

Although sheep and calves do not speak the same language, they have more in common with each other than either has with its more prolific barnyard neighbor, the cow. The forequarter of a sheep is often referred to as the foresaddle, and the primal kosher cuts are the same: **shoulder** (chuck, neck), **rib** (rack), **breast** and **foreshank**. Like veal, lamb is derived from a young animal, less than one year old. Therefore, its meat is tender, delicate, and has less fat and marbling than beef. Lamb has a distinctive gamy flavor and aroma, and does best when cooked at lower temperatures. This helps keep the lean meat moist and prevents gaminess from defining the dish. Here's a quick guide to the primal cuts of lamb.

The **shoulder** yields two types of chops, which are economical and have great flavor, but a somewhat chewy texture. One features a long bone and comes from the blade and the other has a round pinbone and comes from the portion closer to the shank. They taste essentially the same, though the long bone is slightly moister and more tender. They can be braised, grilled, or broiled and both do well when marinated before cooking. There is a bone-in shoulder roast and the more popular boneless roast, which is rolled and tied. The neck and shoulder yield flavorful and sweet cuts for lamb stew, and the juiciest ground meat. The **breast and foreshank** gives us lamb riblets, which although not very meaty are very tasty. Lamb also yields a breast that can be trimmed and stuffed. Because it is very small, it is not very popular. The **foreshank,** which is actually the arm of the lamb, probably provides the most succulent meat that slow braises to melting tenderness or can be ground or cubed and braised. That leaves the **rib,** also called the rack, considered the crowning glory of the lamb. There you will find superior rib chops, tasty rib bites, and elegant rack of lamb. Meat from the rib is tender enough to dry roast, grill, broil, or pan sear.

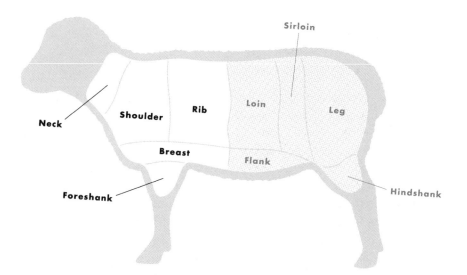

Herb-Crusted Rib Lamb Chops

To take these succulent chops to the next level, we've invited lemon and rosemary, lamb's two best friends, to the party. They lend a vibrant note when hidden in the crust. You can easily prepare these premier chops without the topping, using only a sprinkling of salt and pepper, or with the lemony marinade found on page 91.

SERVES 2

Start to Finish: Under 30 minutes

> *For the crust*
> 2 heaping tablespoons plain bread crumbs (Panko can be substituted)
> 2 teaspoons minced fresh herbs, such as thyme, parsley, or sage, or
> ⅓ teaspoon dried herbs
> Zest of ½ lemon
> 2 garlic cloves, finely minced (about 1 tablespoon)
> Pinch of kosher salt and freshly ground black pepper
>
> *For the chops*
> 6 single rib chops
> Olive oil to brush on the chops and for drizzling (about 2 tablespoons)
> ¼ teaspoon kosher salt
> Pinch of freshly ground black pepper
> 1 teaspoon chopped fresh rosemary leaves or ⅓ teaspoon dried rosemary
> 2 tablespoons Dijon mustard

Preheat the broiler and heat a stovetop grill pan over medium-high heat. Prepare the crust by combining the bread crumbs, herbs, grated lemon zest, garlic, salt, and pepper in a shallow bowl; set aside.

Dry the chops with paper towels. Brush the chops with olive oil and then season both sides with the salt, pepper, and rosemary. Grill the chops for about 3 minutes on each side until nicely charred and still very pink inside. You will be able to judge the doneness by pressing into

BEHIND THE COUNTER:
Have your butcher cut single or double thick rib chops. Your butcher can trim the fat from the bone (referred to as frenching), but the fat does impart flavor. It can also flare up when cooking, so keep a watchful eye. If cooking on the stovetop, use a ridged grill pan so the chops don't sit in their own fat while searing. Alternate cuts: shoulder lamb chops, either long bone or round bone (–$), center cut or 1st cut veal chops (=$).

the meaty portion of the chop. If it is spongy, it is just right. Transfer them to a plate.

Pour the prepared bread crumbs on one half of a small plate and the mustard on the other half. Using tongs to lift the chops, dip one side of the meaty portion in the mustard and then press into the crumbs. Drizzle a little olive oil on top of the breading. Place the chops, breaded side up, on a broiler pan and broil for just a minute or two until the crumbs lightly brown. If the chops are too rare for you, lower the oven rack and continue broiling, or turn the oven temperature to 350 degrees and cook until the chops are cooked to your desired doneness.

Feedback

Lemon zest is an amazing ingredient. If I could carry it around in my pocketbook to brighten up everything I come in contact with, I would. At the urging of my sister, who is an accomplished home cook, I am going to give you a little advice about lemon zest. While dried zest can be purchased in a store, you won't find fresh lemon zest in the spice aisle. Lemon zest is the grated or zested peel of a lemon. Cold lemons—or any citrus—zests better than warm, but warm yields more juice. Invest in a Microplane grater, which provides a finely grated zest, or a zester, which produces thin strands of zest that you can chop. Whichever you choose, be sure to grate only the peel, which contains the aromatic oils and flavor. The white pith beneath is bitter and should never be used. And be sure to rinse the fruit and remove the little grocery label. I cannot tell you how many times I've found tiny shreds of a sticker mingled in my zest!

Mediterranean Rack of Lamb

This recipe is from Flatiron Kitchen, a charming and innovative catering firm in Manhattan. While all their dishes are not strictly kosher, they are experts in preparing kosher food for many of their clients. This lamb is one of their signature dishes.

SERVES 4

Start to Finish: At least 2 hours to marinate; under 30 minutes to cook

For the marinade

½ large onion

6 to 8 garlic cloves

Zest and juice of 2 lemons

1 cup extra-virgin olive oil

½ bunch mint

¼ bunch flat-leaf parsley

2 teaspoons kosher salt

½ teaspoon freshly ground black pepper

2 (14- to 16-ounce) frenched racks of lamb (about 12 to 16 chops)

Oil for searing

Combine all the ingredients for the marinade in a blender and pulse until liquefied, but still somewhat coarse. Score the fatty side of the rack of lamb with a sharp knife to allow the marinade to penetrate the meat. Pour most of the marinade over the lamb, reserving some to use as a sauce when serving. Cover and refrigerate the lamb. Leave it to marinate for at least 2 hours, or up to overnight. Bring the lamb to room temperature 1 hour before cooking.

Preheat the oven to 425 degrees. Remove the lamb racks from the marinade, scraping them almost clean. Sear the lamb racks in a hot skillet with a small amount of oil, just to brown them, and then transfer the lamb to a roasting pan. Cover the bones with aluminum foil so they do not burn, brush the meat lightly with olive oil, and place the racks flesh side down in the pan. Roast in the preheated oven for 8 to 10 minutes, then turn and roast for another 8 to 10 minutes on the other side. Transfer the lamb to a carving board and let rest, covered loosely with foil, for 10 minutes. Slice the rack between each bone for serving.

BEHIND THE COUNTER: Have your butcher prepare the racks of lamb frenched, with the fat removed from the bones. The same prep can be used for a crown roast; have your butcher tie two or three racks together to form the circular crown. Alternate cut: rack of veal (=$).

SIDE NOTE: The chef recommends their Israeli mint couscous as the perfect side (page 200).

Grilled Lamb Riblets

BEHIND THE COUNTER: Have your butcher cut the tips from the rib chop, about 1 inch long or a small rack from the lamb breast. Alternate cuts: shoulder or rib lamb chops or veal chops (+$) would make a nice main dish rather than a small bite.

SIDE NOTE: Especially if traveling the Middle Eastern route, you might want to pair the riblets with some freshly made hummus (page 197) and warm grilled flatbread (page 205).

A favorite among the butchers I consulted were the tiny ribs from either the breast of lamb or the tips of the rib lamb chops. Seasoned butcher Eddie Klarberg called riblets "more of a nosh than a meal," but what a nosh it is! The fat crisps up and lubricates the small morsels of meat hidden beneath with the guava glaze adding a peppery sweetness. For a quick trip to the Middle East, you can simply grill these ribs with salt, pepper, and a dash of *za'atar,* an intriguing spice blend. Either way, they make great small bites to serve as a winter starter or to whet appetites at your next summer barbecue.

MAKES ABOUT 15 RIBLETS
Start to Finish: Under 1 hour

For the glaze
1 Granny Smith apple, peeled, cored, and grated
½ cup guava jelly
2 pieces star anise
1 cinnamon stick
1 tablespoon honey
2 teaspoons molasses

1 pound lamb riblets

Combine all ingredients for the glaze in a saucepan and bring to a boil. Reduce the heat, cover, and cook for 15 minutes. Mash, or blend with immersion blender. Remove from the heat and let the glaze cool in a bowl, removing a small amount to use as a basting sauce. When the glaze comes to room temperature, toss the riblets in the bowl and let them marinate for about 15 minutes. Preheat the broiler or light the grill while the riblets marinate.

Broil the riblets, turning them so all sides brown evenly, 10 to 12 minutes, brushing them with the glaze each time you turn them. Serve as soon as they come off the grill or out of the broiler.

Feedback

Za'atar is a spice, which blends sumac, sesame seeds, thyme, savory, oregano, and often hyssop, an herb mentioned several times in the Bible. Its flavor ranges from nutty and salty to minty and lemony depending on the blend you find. The intense herbal essence balances the gamy flavor of lamb and is wonderful when sprinkled on warm flatbread or added to salads and spreads for a Middle Eastern flavor.

Teriyaki-Glazed Shoulder Lamb Chops

This teriyaki marinade works especially well with shoulder lamb chops, which, cut from the muscular region of the lamb, can be a bit chewy. Its symphony of ingredients, with fresh pineapple juice leading the way, are naturally tenderizing and enhance but don't overwhelm the meat.

SERVES 4

Start to Finish: 1 hour to marinate; 15 minutes to grill or broil

For the marinade

½ cup fresh (not canned) pineapple juice

½ cup honey

½ cup low-sodium soy sauce

1 teaspoon kosher salt

½ teaspoon ground ginger

½ teaspoon dry mustard

2 tablespoons rice wine vinegar

2 tablespoons brown sugar

4 (8-ounce) shoulder lamb chops

Combine all the ingredients for the marinade, reserving ½ cup for basting. Place the chops in the marinade (a resealable plastic bag works well), seal, and leave out on your counter for 30 to 60 minutes. If it will be longer than that, refrigerate.

Pour the reserved marinade in a deep saucepan. In testing this recipe, I burnt the sauce, sacrificing my little saucepan, when the

BEHIND THE COUNTER: Have your butcher cut shoulder chops ½ to ¾ inch thick. Alternate cuts: rib lamb chops or veal chops (+$) (because they are naturally more tender they don't need to marinate as long), chicken cutlets or chicken parts (−$), or why not try a mixed grill?

SIDE NOTE: An intriguing fruit chutney with spicy pineapple and sweet mango works well with this dish (page 216).

burnt-on glaze wouldn't budge from the pan. My sacrifice is your salvation: watch that pot carefully and cook the marinade slow and low until reduced by half. Reserve to baste the chops. **Preheat the broiler, stovetop grill pan, or outdoor grill.**

Dry the chops with a paper towel, and discard the marinade. Broil or grill the chops 3 to 4 inches from the heat source, until browned, 5 to 7 minutes for the first side, 3 to 5 minutes for the second, brushing with reserved marinade. Cook until the lamb is pink inside. Remove from the heat, cover loosely with aluminum foil for 5 minutes, then serve with any additional glaze drizzled on top.

Pesto-Crusted Roasted Lamb Shoulder

Lamb shoulder is full of flavor, and when dressed in an herb-infused pesto; the outside develops a delicious crust that elevates the taste and locks in the moisture. Fresh zingy mint, grassy basil, pungent garlic, creamy pine nuts, and zesty lemon build character and boost the lamb's natural taste.

SERVES 4 TO 6
Start to Finish: 1 hour to marinate; under 3 hours to roast

For the pesto
1/4 cup pine nuts
1 cup loosely packed basil leaves
1/2 cup loosely packed mint leaves
4 garlic cloves (2 cloves chopped, 2 cloves cut into slivers)
Zest and juice of 1 lemon
1/4 cup olive oil
Kosher salt and freshly ground black pepper

For the lamb
1 (3½-pound) rolled and tied lamb shoulder
1 cup beef stock
1/2 cup red wine

BEHIND THE COUNTER:
Lamb shoulder roast does not start out as a solid piece of meat. Because the shoulder portion of the lamb is relatively small, your butcher will form a roast by piecing together several smaller cuts from the shoulder, and then roll and tie them. When sliced, you can see the patchwork quality of the meat, so it doesn't present as elegantly as other roasts. Alternate cut: rolled veal shoulder roast (=$) will appear less "piecey" when carved because it comes from a larger animal.

In a small skillet, lightly toast the pine nuts over medium heat for 2 minutes. In the bowl of a food processor, fitted with the metal blade, combine the pine nuts with the basil, mint, chopped garlic, and lemon zest and juice. Process until smooth, scraping down the sides of the bowl to incorporate all the ingredients. With the motor running, slowly drizzle in the olive oil until the mixture resembles a grainy soft paste. You might need to add a little more olive oil if the mixture is too thick. Season with salt and pepper to taste.

Place the lamb on a large sheet of aluminum foil. With the tip of a very sharp knife, cut small slits into the meat, and insert the slivers of garlic into the slits. Slather the pesto all over the meat, and loosely seal with the foil. Reserve any remaining pesto to serve alongside the meat. Marinate the lamb for 1 hour on the countertop or up to several hours in the fridge.

When ready to roast, **preheat the oven to 325 degrees** and remove the lamb from the fridge. Place the lamb on a rack set in a roasting pan. Roast in the preheated oven for 2 hours. At that time, add ½ cup of the stock and ¼ cup of the wine, baste the meat with the liquids and continue roasting until a meat thermometer inserted into the lamb reads 145 to 150 degrees (medium rare), 30 to 45 minutes longer. Check the pan periodically to baste the meat and add more water or stock if needed.

When the lamb is done, transfer it to a plate and cover loosely with aluminum foil. Place the roasting pan directly on the stovetop and heat the pan juices over low heat. Add the remaining ½ cup of stock and ¼ cup of wine, scraping up any bits that have collected at the bottom of the pan. To thicken the gravy, make a slurry by mixing 1 tablespoon of cornstarch with 2 tablespoons of cold water, stir into the pan, and heat to a boil. Repeat if necessary. Remove the string, and slice the roast. Serve with the gravy spooned over the meat and the pesto on the side.

Feedback
Pesto originated in the Genoa area of Italy and derives its name

from the word meaning to pound or crush. Traditionally, basil leaves are crushed with a mortar and pestle, and then combined with pine nuts, garlic, olive oil, and Parmesan cheese (which in this book is a definite no-no, because cheese with meat is not kosher). With so many wonderful fresh herbs available, pesto has taken on new character and amplifies the most humble greens such as mint, dandelion leaves, and arugula. Pine nuts (*pignoli*) are commonly added, but they are expensive, so you can substitute blanched almonds. Toasting them adds to their nuttiness and releases their natural oils and the warmth helps create a creamier finish. As for the mortar and pestle, if you received one as an engagement gift, go ahead and pound away; otherwise a food processor fitted with a metal blade is infinitely easier.

Moroccan Lamb Shanks
. . . with pomegranate sauce

Lamb shanks are rich, meaty, and succulent, with a layer of fat enveloping each shank and basting it while it cooks. This Moroccan version features aromatic spices, which blend to give the shanks a punchy taste while never overpowering their natural flavor. The pomegranate juice brings a subtle sweet and tart flavor to the sauce.

BEHIND THE COUNTER: The taste of lamb shanks really has no equal. Alternate cuts: short ribs (+$) or osso buco (+$) or even turkey drumsticks cut osso buco style (−$).

SERVES 4

Start to Finish: Under 3 hours

4 (12- to 16-ounce) lamb shanks
Kosher salt and freshly ground black pepper
2 tablespoons olive oil
1 large onion, sliced
6 garlic cloves, smashed
1 teaspoon ground cinnamon
1 teaspoon ground coriander
½ teaspoon ground ginger
1 teaspoon ground cumin
1 teaspoon kosher salt

2 dozen juniper berries

2 tablespoons tomato paste

1 cup sweet red wine

2 cups beef stock

1 cup fresh pomegranate juice from 1 large or 2 medium pomegranates, or 1 cup bottled juice

Preheat the oven to 350 degrees. Season the shanks with kosher salt and pepper. Heat the olive oil in a braising pot and brown the shanks, over medium to high heat, on all sides, about 10 minutes. Be sure to stand the shanks up to brown the ends. Transfer the shanks to a platter or rimmed baking sheet. Add the onion and garlic to the pot and cook, over medium heat, stirring occasionally until lightly softened, about 5 minutes. Add the spices, tomato paste, wine, and stock. Stir and cook over medium heat for 5 minutes. Return the shanks to the pot, cover, and braise in the preheated oven for 2 hours. Check the shanks every 30 minutes, turning them over in the sauce each time you check and admire them. While the lamb cooks, process the pomegranate seeds if using fresh pomegranates (see Feedback).

When the lamb is nearly cooked, after about 1½ hours, add the pomegranate juice. Continue cooking 30 minutes longer, or until the meat on the shank is buttery soft and nearly falling off the bone. When finished, the sauce will be thick and concentrated (you can thin it with a little water or beef stock if needed). Spoon the sauce over the shanks and serve alongside rice, noodles, or couscous.

Feedback

While pomegranates are loaded with antioxidants, their real power is to stain anything porous they come in contact with. If you are working with fresh pomegranates, I applaud your initiative. Late fall—October and November—is the best time to buy fresh pomegranates, when they are bursting with ripe seeds. Here are some tips for handling this persnickety fruit.

1. Wear something that can take a joke when you work with pomegranates or their juice. You could end up looking like a victim from *Law & Order*, stained with red splatters.

2. Halve, then squeeze the pomegranates over a bowl so you don't lose any of the precious juice. There is additional juice in the tiny seeds. To juice them, fill a bowl with water, and gently loosen the seeds with your fingers over the bowl, separating the seeds from the papery membrane. The seeds will fall to the bottom of the bowl, while the thin fiber will float. Strain the water, reserving the seeds.

3. Pulverize most of the seeds in a blender (reserve a few for garnish). Strain the liquid, pressing on the solids to extract all the juice. Discard the solids. Between the squeezed juice and the pureed seeds, you should get $3/4$ to 1 cup of fresh juice from 1 large or 2 medium pomegranates. You can also buy bottled pomegranate juice. It's cleaner and easier than the fresh fruit, but not nearly as much fun!

Lamb Tagine

Shallots Bistro in Chicago is known for their inventive kosher cuisine. This dish is Chef Carlos' signature recipe. It contains the best cuts of lamb to braise: both the shoulder and the shanks. I wouldn't change a thing.

SERVES 4

Start to Finish: Under 2 hours

2 tablespoons vegetable oil
2 pounds lamb shoulder, cut into 1-inch pieces
1 small lamb shank
1 large Spanish onion, chopped
4 cups water
1 pinch saffron
2 cinnamon sticks
1 small sweet potato, peeled and cut into $3/4$-inch pieces

¾ cup pitted prunes

½ cup Turkish dried apricots

2 teaspoons honey

Kosher salt and freshly ground black pepper

Pinch of freshly grated nutmeg or already ground nutmeg

Toasted slivered almonds

Heat 1 tablespoon of the oil in a wide, shallow casserole pot over moderately high heat until hot. Brown the lamb shoulder and shank on all sides in 2 batches, transferring to a dish as browned. Add the remaining tablespoon of oil to the pot and cook the onion, stirring, until softened. Return shoulder meat and shank to pan.

Stir in the water, saffron, and cinnamon sticks and bring to a boil. Reduce the heat and simmer, covered, stirring occasionally, until the lamb is tender, about 1½ hours. Remove lamb pieces from sauce to a separate dish, leaving the shank in the pot.

Add the sweet potato to sauce and return it to a simmer. Cover and cook, stirring occasionally, until barely tender, about 8 minutes. Add the prunes and apricots and simmer, covered, stirring occasionally, until the vegetables and fruits are tender, about 5 minutes.

Return the lamb pieces to the stew and stir in the honey. Season with salt, pepper, and nutmeg and simmer uncovered, stirring occasionally, 5 minutes. Turn off heat and let it rest for an additional 5 minutes. Serve the tagine over couscous garnished with slivered toasted almonds and the shank.

Lamb and Spinach Spanakopita

In this version of the beloved Greek spinach dish, ground lamb scented with cumin, dill, parsley, and oregano are encased in phyllo and baked to golden flaky perfection. The spanakopita makes a light meal or, cut into smaller pieces, a savory small bite. For an interesting twist, use this same lamb filling as the basis of a shepherd's pie, baked

BEHIND THE COUNTER: Lamb marries particularly well with the other ingredients in this dish, and will prove to be the best choice. Alternate cuts: ground turkey (=$), chicken (=$), or beef (–$).

in a casserole and topped with creamy mashed potatoes (page 187) served with peas and carrots on the side.

YIELDS ABOUT 14 TRIANGLES, OR 2 TO 3 DOZEN
ROLLED "CIGARS"
Start to Finish: Under 1 hour, plus time to thaw the phyllo

1 package (½ box) phyllo sheets, 20 (9 x 14) sheets
    (about 8 ounces) thawed according to manufacturer's instructions
1 (10-ounce) box frozen chopped spinach, thawed and thoroughly
    drained
1 tablespoon olive oil, plus about ½ cup for the phyllo
1 large shallot, minced (about 2 tablespoons)
2 garlic cloves, minced (about 1 tablespoon)
1 pound ground lamb
¼ teaspoon dried oregano
½ teaspoon kosher salt
⅛ teaspoon freshly ground black pepper
¼ cup loosely packed fresh dill leaves, finely chopped
¼ cup loosely packed flat-leaf parsley, finely chopped
3 scallions, white and half the green parts, finely chopped
⅛ teaspoon ground cumin
Zest of ½ lemon
1 egg, beaten
1 tomato, halved and thinly sliced (you'll need about 14 pieces)

Thaw the phyllo sheets and spinach. Do not open the phyllo package until ready to use or it will dry out. When the spinach has thawed, squeeze it with your hands or place it in a towel you don't mind getting stained, and wring out all the liquid.

Preheat the oven to 350 degrees and have a large baking sheet handy. Heat 1 tablespoon of olive oil in a skillet, add the shallots and garlic, and cook over medium heat, stirring occasionally, until soft, about 5 minutes. Add the ground lamb, increase the heat to medium-high, and cook until it is no longer pink. The lamb will release some fat. You can drain the fat off, but for additional flavor and moistness, I like to keep it and let it be reabsorbed by the meat. Spoon the lamb mixture into a large bowl and set aside to cool. Add the oregano, salt, pepper, dill, parsley, scallions, cumin, and lemon zest. Taste and adjust the seasonings if necessary. Add the beaten egg and combine until all the ingredients are well incorporated.

Unroll the thawed phyllo dough on a clean work surface or large baking sheet, placing a barely damp towel on top of the sheets to prevent them from drying out. Have the remaining $1/2$ cup of olive oil ready in a small bowl. Locate a pastry brush or a sponge (see Feedback below). To assemble the triangles (directions for rolling "cigars" follow), move one sheet of phyllo to your work surface. You will be cutting the dough, so it needs to be a large cutting board, baking sheet, or a scratch-resistant countertop. Use your brush or sponge to lightly dab the sheet with oil. You don't want to saturate the sheets, merely dampen them with oil to help the next sheet adhere. The first sheet almost always tears, but don't worry, there will be several layers. Lay a second sheet on top, repeat the oiling process, lay a third, and repeat again.

Using a sharp knife or pizza cutter, slice through all the layers of the sheets in half lengthwise. With the small end facing you, place a generous tablespoon of filling in the bottom left corner of one of the halves. Top with a piece of tomato. Bring the bottom left corner to the right side, forming a triangle. Continue rolling, alternating sides, to maintain that shape. When you are through folding, you should have one unfolded corner on the top right side. Brush that with a little oil and fold to close. Brush the entire triangle with oil and place on an ungreased baking sheet. Repeat until you have used all the filling and dough.

For a cigar-style roll, follow the layering directions above, cutting the phyllo sheets in half lengthwise, then cut each half in half again (this will yield 4 medium pieces) or cut in thirds (this will yield 6 smaller pieces). These will make up your cigars. Place a teaspoon of filling on the phyllo sheet and roll into a thin tight package (do not add the tomato). You can tuck in the ends or pinch them closed as you roll; either way the firm filling will not ooze out while baking. Bake the triangles or cigars in the preheated oven for 15 minutes. Drain on paper towels.

Feedback

If necessity is the mother of invention, then I stumbled onto a very easy technique to oil the phyllo sheets. I could not find my pastry brush.

I did, however, find a bag of triangular makeup sponges that I normally use to apply foundation. I figured I would give one a whirl. I was pleasantly surprised. I found the makeup sponges infinitely easier to use than the brush. I dipped the sponge into the oil and was able to lightly dab the sheets as though I were sponge painting a wall. Squeeze out excess oil from the sponge to dab on the sheets, and then discard the sponge after it's used. I highly recommend this resourceful alternative.

NP

For a non-pareve version, you could add ¼ cup crumbled feta, goat, or grated Parmesan cheese to the lamb mixture. You could also create a dipping sauce with sour cream, dill, lemon, and parsley or a yogurt-based cucumber tzatziki sauce.

Lamb Sliders

When making a big burger, nothing beats ground beef, but for these small sliders, where you want a savory punch of flavor, nothing comes close to the taste of lamb. Most markets now sell tiny buns to house sliders, but mini pocket pitas work too. Top the sliders with a schmeer of scallion mayonnaise and the usual suspects, such as sliced tomatoes or peppery arugula.

BEHIND THE COUNTER: Have your butcher grind the lamb for you. It can come from the shoulder, neck, breast, or shank—or a combination.

SIDE NOTE: Cold chilled pickled cucumber salad can be served as an accompaniment or drained and used as a topping (page 219).

YIELDS: ABOUT 1 DOZEN SLIDERS OR
4 FULL-SIZE BURGERS
Start to Finish: Under 15 minutes

For the sliders
1½ pounds ground lamb
3 garlic cloves, grated on a Microplane
1 teaspoon dried oregano
1 teaspoon kosher salt
½ teaspoon freshly ground black pepper
1 tablespoons finely chopped flat leaf parsley
¼ teaspoon ground cumin

1 scallion, finely chopped (about 2 tablespoons), white and green parts

For the scallion mayonnaise
2 tablespoons mayonnaise
1 teaspoon finely chopped scallion
1 teaspoon finely minced flat leaf parsley
Dash of Worcestershire sauce
Pinch of ground cumin
Squeeze of a lemon

Gently combine all the slider ingredients and form the ground lamb into small patties, about 3 inches in diameter. Press your thumb into the top of the burger: this will prevent it from puffing up while cooking. **Light the broiler or grill,** heat until nice and hot, and cook the burgers just until they are pink, several minutes on each side. Combine all of the ingredients for the scallion mayonnaise in a small bowl. Serve with the scallion mayonnaise and your favorite toppings.

Feedback

Italian and Greek Oregano is a principle flavor in Mediterranean cooking and are the most common oreganos on the market. Italian oregano has a slightly sweet taste derived from the marjoram that is part of the herbaceous mix. You can also look for Greek oregano, which can be found in specialty stores, and imparts a stronger flavor and pairs well with hot and spicy cooking. Oregano is one herb that I prefer dried rather than fresh. The drying mellows the intense flavor and prevents the oregano from overpowering the dish. By adding oregano at the start of the cooking process, the pungent flavor becomes subtler and melds with the dish.

CHICKEN

Kosher Poultry Rules the Roost

Unlike their four-legged barnyard neighbors, every part of the bird is kosher, from the wing to the drumstick and every delectable morsel in between. Whether you choose whole birds or itty-bitty Cornish hens, chicken parts, cutlets, or ground meat, kosher poultry is readily available and easy on the wallet.

When choosing kosher chicken, you now have more choices than ever. A recent addition to poultry farming is the concept of pasture-raised poultry, part of the eco-kosher movement. Pasture-raised poultry live a "free-as-a-bird" lifestyle without cramped quarters or artificial feed, so their skin is white and unbruised. A member of the Wise poultry family, who raise organic birds, explained, "They are happier chickens." Ariella Reback of Green Pasture Poultry describes the cage-free philosophy: "Pastured poultry is part of a cycle in which the sun feeds the grasses, the grasses feed the poultry, and the poultry fertilizes and renews the land." Pasture-raised poultry costs more, but if you respect the philosophy and appreciate the taste, then it is worth the extra expense.

Safe handling is always an issue with poultry. Be sure to clean all sufaces and utensils raw chicken comes in contact with, and thoroughly wash your hands before handling other items in the kitchen.

Chicken: Whole birds

Kosher chickens are the most delicious—and that's not just my opinion.

After a careful comparison of nine major brands of whole birds, America's Test Kitchen concluded "...that the only kosher chicken in our tasting was also the best tasting.... If you are looking for advice on purchasing a high-quality chicken, we recommend kosher." The kosher method of handling poultry is the reason it earns such high marks for flavor and texture. The process mandates a cold-water dunk followed by an hour of salting, then a second cold-water rinse. This brining technique, coveted by five-star chefs, firms both the skin and the fatty layer that lies beneath, in turn plumping the bird. I have to add that these steps are less efficient for removing feathers, so your kosher chicken might look like it needs electrolysis. When you get it home, plucking with a good pair of tweezers will go a long way. When buying a whole bird, be sure it does not emanate an odor and look for the tip of the drumstick to be light pink; these are signs of a fresh chicken. If time allows, let the chicken sit on a paper towel–lined plate, uncovered in the fridge for about an hour. This will help the chicken dry out even more and encourage crisp skin when the chicken is roasted. If it will be longer than an hour, loosely cover it and always be careful not to let the chicken touch other items in your fridge.

Most kosher birds are fresh, not frozen, but in the rare case yours is not, never thaw it on the counter; rather, let it defrost in the fridge. Generally there is no packaging inside the cavity, but some butchers do tuck the livers in there, so remember to remove them.

When it comes to whole chickens, size matters. There was a time chickens were labeled fryer, broiler, or roaster and that would help indicate its usage. Now they are simply called whole chickens, so the size and weight is what should guide you. For most recipes, look for a bird that tips the scales at 3½ to 4 pounds, a perfect size for two hungry eaters or four with average appetites. Not a good sharer? Choose a whole chicken weighing between 5 and 7 pounds, which will feed four and hopefully yield leftovers, or what I term "bonus" meat. If your mission is to find the largest chicken, choose a capon, which is a castrated rooster. Out of sheer frustration, he lets himself go, weighing in at 7 to 10 pounds. I recommend roasting two smaller (younger) birds as opposed to one roaster or capon when you need to feed a crowd. The younger birds are often more tender, as opposed to the larger "old bird," which, as the expression would indicate, can be pretty tough. Reserve that mature chicken—sometimes called a stewing hen or pullet—for making a hearty stock or stew.

Now, let's roast some chicken worth crossing the road for.

If there's one dish everyone should master, it's a whole roasted chicken. It's comforting, satisfying, and goes from weeknight to Saturday night in a snap. Here are three variations, from simple to simplest, building on different flavors and featuring various techniques to elevate the bird and take you from beginner to expert.

Simple Spatchcocked Chicken
. . . and roasted root vegetables

Grab your dictionary and you'll find that spatchcock is a method of splitting (butterflying) a chicken. It's a fun word, which you can use to impress your friends or win at Scrabble. If time is of the essence, but you want to make a crispy, flavorful roast chicken, spatchcocking is a great option.

BEHIND THE COUNTER: Have your butcher butterfly the chicken. You can do this yourself by removing the backbone and pressing down on the breast until flat. Alternate cut: turkey parts (=$).

SERVES 2 TO 4

Start to Finish: Under 1 1/2 hours

1 (3 1/2- to 4-pound) chicken, butterflied and pressed flat

1 to 2 tablespoons olive oil

1 teaspoon kosher salt

1/2 teaspoon freshly ground black pepper

1/2 teaspoon sweet Hungarian paprika

2 carrots

1 parsnip

1 medium celery root

1 medium leek

4 sprigs rosemary

4 sprigs thyme

1/2 head garlic, unpeeled, with the top cut off to expose the cloves

1 to 2 cups chicken stock

1/2 cup white wine

Juice of 1/2 lemon

1 teaspoon cornstarch

Dry the chicken and place the bird on a paper towel–lined plate, refrigerate uncovered for 1 hour. This can be done earlier in the day, cover the chicken if it sits longer than an hour. When ready to roast, **preheat the oven to 425 degrees,** and take the chicken out of the fridge. Drizzle olive oil over the chicken and season both sides with salt, pepper, and paprika.

Prepare the veggies by cutting the carrots, parsnips, and celery root into 1-inch thick pieces. For the celery root, remove the Medusa-looking end and stand the celery root on the flat side. Using a wide knife, cut around the root, holding one hand on top of the celery root and turning it as you go. Cut off the remaining end. Cut the celery root into rounds, then into a small dice.

For the leek, remove the tough green end. Split the leek down the middle lengthwise, and then cut them lengthwise again. Rinse it thoroughly under cold running water to remove sand, pat dry. Do not separate the leeks into strands: they roast better when they are left intact.

Place the leek, rosemary, and thyme in the center of a roasting pan. Lay the chicken, breast side down, on top of the leeks. Sprinkle the carrots, parsnips, garlic, and celery root around the chicken. Drizzle a little olive oil over the vegetables and season with salt and pepper. Pour 1 cup of stock into the pan.

Roast in the preheated oven, uncovered, for 20 minutes. Using tongs, turn the chicken over and continue roasting for 20 minutes longer. Position the legs so they slightly cover the breast, or truss to help the legs brown while preventing the breast from overcooking. Baste the chicken with the collected juices, and roast until a meat thermometer inserted in the thigh reads 160 to 165 degrees. Transfer the chicken to a plate, and cover loosely with aluminum foil. The internal temperature will rise 5 to 10 degrees while the chicken rests.

Remove the vegetables from the pan with a slotted spoon and transfer to a bowl. Cover with foil to keep warm. Remove the head of garlic and squeeze each clove into the roasting pan, discarding the outer skins.

Place the roasting pan on the stovetop. Skim off some of the fat, and then add the remaining stock, wine, lemon juice, and cornstarch. Whisk to pick up any brown bits stuck to the bottom of the pan and incorporate the ingredients, being sure to mash the garlic into the sauce. Heat the sauce until it thickens. Spoon the sauce over the chicken and vegetables and serve.

Simpler Beer-Basted Chicken

Basting is a great way to ensure a juicy chicken, but every time you open the oven, you let precious heat escape. A better method is to baste the chicken from the inside out. There's no delicate way to explain this process. Take a can of beer, be sure to pop the top, and then push the can into the cavity of the chicken so that the bird is perched upright with the can of beer in its "tush." The beer infuses the cavity with constant moisture, and the metal can helps conduct the heat consistently from the inside out. The result is an incredibly moist chicken that roasts very quickly. If your chicken is on the wagon, try filling the can with chicken stock, herbs, and freshly squeezed lemon juice or any flavorful liquid such as cola or ginger ale.

SIDE NOTE: While the chicken roasts, you can easily prepare roasted rosemary potatoes whose herbs and flavor partner perfectly with the chicken (page 185).

SERVES 4

Start to Finish: Under 1½ hours

> 1 (3½- to 4-pound) chicken
> 1½ teaspoons kosher salt
> ½ teaspoon freshly ground black pepper
> 1 teaspoon garlic powder
> 1 teaspoon sweet Hungarian paprika
> 1 teaspoon freshly chopped rosemary leaves or ⅓ teaspoon chopped dried rosemary
> 1 to 2 tablespoons olive oil
> 1 *open* can of beer
> 2 bay leaves and fresh herbs, optional
> 1 large onion, quartered

6 unpeeled garlic cloves, optional
1 to 2 cups chicken stock

Pat the chicken dry inside and out, and remove any packaging hidden in the cavity. If time allows, place the chicken on a paper towel–lined plate and let it hang out in the fridge for an hour. When ready to roast, **preheat the oven to 450 degrees** and lower your oven rack to its lowest position. Take the chicken out of the fridge.

Combine the seasonings in a small bowl (this helps prevent cross contaminating your seasonings while working with the chicken). Take a pinch of seasoning and rub it inside the cavity. Drizzle the oil over the entire bird and then sprinkle the outside with the seasonings. Pop the top of the beer can (toss in some fresh herbs or bay leaves if you like for added flavor) and carefully place the chicken upright on the can. Jiggle the legs in position so the chicken appears to be sitting and does not topple over. Place the bird, upright, in a shallow roasting pan and **lower the oven temperature to 425 degrees**. Scatter the bay leaves, onions, and garlic, if using, and add ½ cup of the stock. After 30 minutes, add ½ cup more stock and continue roasting, until an instant-read thermometer registers 160 to 165 degrees when inserted in the thigh, about 30 minutes more. Transfer the chicken to a carving board and cover with a piece of aluminum foil; the internal temperature will rise 5 to 10 degrees while the chicken rests and the juices will redistribute throughout the bird. Do not handle the can—it will be very hot!

Place the roasting pan directly on the stove, skim off some of the fat, and add more stock if needed to create the gravy. If you roasted the garlic cloves, squeeze them to extract the roasted garlic and mash it into the sauce. Discard the skins. Let the gravy simmer until heated through. If you prefer a thicker gravy, make a slurry by mixing 1 teaspoon of cornstarch with 2 teaspoons of cold water, stir back into the pan, bring to a boil, and repeat if necessary. When ready to carve, using an oven mitt, carefully remove the beer can from the chicken. Carve the chicken and serve with the gravy drizzled on top.

Simplest Roast Chicken

Kosher salt and pepper are a roast chicken's best friends. You could truly stop there, pop the bird in the oven, and have a great meal. I've added a few simple ingredients to elevate the flavors, but if you opt for only salt and pepper, you will not be disappointed. I also suggest turning the chicken, but if you want a set-it-and-forget-it meal, skip that step.

SERVES 4

Start to Finish: Under 1½ hours

1 (3½- to 4-pound) chicken
1½ teaspoons kosher salt
½ teaspoon freshly ground black pepper
1 to 2 tablespoons olive oil
1 teaspoon sweet Hungarian paprika
1 lemon, halved, optional
A few sprigs of fresh herbs such as parsley, rosemary, or thyme, optional
1 onion, peeled and quartered, optional
1 to 1½ cups chicken stock

Pat the chicken dry and if time allows, let it sit uncovered in the fridge, on a paper towel–lined plate so it thoroughly dries out. The drier the chicken goes in, the crisper the skin comes out.

When ready to roast, preheat the oven to 425 degrees.

Combine the salt and pepper in a small bowl (this helps prevent cross contaminating your seasonings while working with the chicken). Take several pinches of seasoning and rub it thoroughly in the cavity. Pour the oil into your hand, and spread it all over the outside of the bird. This does two things: it helps the seasoning stick to the chicken and helps the bird develop a nice brown crispy skin. Season the outside of the bird with the remaining salt and pepper and then sprinkle the chicken with the paprika. This will help develop color and add flavor while roasting. If using, place the halved

SIDE NOTE: Consider lemon and garlic broccoli (page 209) as an easy side to mirror the lemon and herb flavors in the chicken, or a simple potato pancake for a traditional accompaniment (page 183).

lemon in the cavity along with any fresh herbs. Scatter the onions in the roasting pan. Place the chicken on a rack set in the roasting pan and pour $1/2$ cup of stock into the bottom of the pan.

Roast the chicken in the preheated oven for about 20 minutes, then turn the chicken over so the underside has a chance to develop a crisp skin and the juices can flow back into the breast. To turn the chicken, push a large spoon into the cavity of the bird and use it to flip the bird over. This prevents you from tearing the skin or piercing the chicken. After 20 minutes, turn the chicken again, add another $1/2$ cup of stock, and continue roasting until an instant-read thermometer inserted in the meaty portion of the thigh reads about 160 to 165 degrees, about 20 minutes longer. When done, the juices should run clear and the thighs should jiggle in their sockets. Remove from the oven, cover the chicken with aluminum foil, and let the chicken rest for at least 10 minutes before carving. The internal temperature will rise 5 to 10 degrees while the chicken rests, and the juices will redistribute throughout the bird.

While the chicken rests, place the roasting pan directly on the stovetop, and skim off some of the fat. Scrape up the brown bits that collected on the bottom of the pan, and add a little more stock, if needed, to create a gravy. To thicken the sauce, make a slurry by mixing 1 teaspoon of cornstarch with 2 teaspoons of cold water, stir back into the pan, bring to a boil, and repeat if necessary. Carve the chicken and serve with the gravy spooned on top and the roasted onion quarters scattered on the plate.

Roasted Cornish Hen

BEHIND THE COUNTER: A Cornish hen's tiny frame feeds one hungry person, as the bird weighs in at only 1 to 2 pounds. Alternate cuts: duck (+$) or chicken (−$) can be prepared in a similar method.

One of the first fancy dinners I made for my husband was on our first New Year's Eve. I roasted Cornish hens—an elegant name for itty, bitty chickens—not fully knowing how long to cook them. I brought them to the table, beaming at my accomplishment, only to find that when we cut into them, they were nearly raw. My new husband didn't flinch and was about to eat his raw hen so that I wouldn't feel badly. I learned two things that night, the most important that my husband of now thirty-five years was definitely a keeper, and the second was how to properly time a roasted Cornish hen. The hens in this recipe are glazed in a cherry-tinged sauce that is drizzled over the birds as they emerge from the oven. They roast beautifully and make a serious impression when served.

SIDE NOTE: Wild rice with dried cranberries provides a tart backdrop for the salty, sweet sauce and can be used as a side dish or a stuffing (page 191).

MAKES 2 GENEROUS SERVINGS

Start to Finish: 1 hour for the hens to rest uncovered in the fridge; under 1½ hours to roast

2 (2-pound) Cornish hens
1 cup chicken stock
1½ teaspoons kosher salt
½ teaspoon freshly ground black pepper
6 sprigs flat-leaf parsley
1 to 2 tablespoons olive oil

For the glaze
¼ cup low-sodium soy sauce
¼ cup white wine
¼ cup cherry preserves
¼ cup chicken stock
2 tablespoons honey
2 tablespoons orange juice
1 cinnamon stick
Freshly ground black pepper

To prepare the hens, remove any packaging from the cavity, and dry the hens with a paper towel. Place on a plate and if time allows, refrigerate, uncovered, for 1 hour to help draw out any residual moisture. This can be done earlier in the day: cover if sitting in the fridge longer than 1 hour. When ready to roast, **preheat the oven to 425 degrees,** and take the hens out of the fridge. Place the hens on a rack in a shallow roasting pan. Pour 1 cup of stock into the bottom of the pan. Season the cavity with salt and pepper and place the parsley sprigs inside. Drizzle a little olive oil over the hens and season with salt and pepper. Place the hens, breast side down, on the rack, and roast in the preheated oven for 30 minutes. Turn them over and continue roasting until an instant-read thermometer inserted in the thigh portion registers 160 to 165 degrees, about 30 minutes longer.

While the hens roast, make the glaze by stirring all the ingredients for the glaze in a small saucepan until they are well combined. Cook over low heat until the the glaze is thick and syrupy. Remove the cinnamon stick and set aside.

When the birds are done, remove them from the oven and baste with the glaze. Let the birds rest, loosely covered with aluminum foil, for 10 minutes before carving. While the hens rest, add the juices that collected in the bottom of the roasting pan to the glaze and heat through. Serve the hens drizzled with the glaze.

Feedback

You can stuff the birds with wild rice or bread stuffing, but you need to keep several important safe-handling considerations in mind. Do not stuff the bird until ready to roast. Have the stuffing at room temperature, but not cold, which can cause contamination because the internal temperature of the stuffing may not be able to reach safe levels. Pack the stuffing in loosely; it will expand while roasting. You can use kitchen twine or roasting bands to truss the bird; this will help keep the stuffing inside the cavity. Roast as directed above, but add at least 30 minutes to the cooking time, and be sure the internal temperature of both the bird and the center of the stuffing is at least 160 to 165 degrees.

"Bonus" Chicken

The following recipes rely on "bonus" chicken, which you ought to have after roasting one or two birds. "Bonus" chicken sounds so much more refined than calling these delicious holdouts leftovers. However, if you don't have any, it is so simple to roast a couple of breasts to yield juicy white meat for the recipes that follow. You can take a shortcut and buy an already-cooked rotisserie chicken; just be sure to stash the trash so no one knows.

YEILDS 2 BREASTS (1 WHOLE BREAST, HALVED),
ABOUT 2 TO 3 CUPS OF CUBED OR SHREDDED CHICKEN

Start to Finish: Under 1 hour

Preheat the oven to 375 degrees. Season the breasts with salt and pepper and a drizzle of olive oil. Roast in a baking sheet for 30 to 45 minutes, until done. An instant-read thermometer should register 160 degrees. Cover loosely with aluminum foil and let them rest for 5 to 10 minutes. Remove the skin and take the meat off the bone. If using the meat in a salad, it is always best to dress the chicken while it is still warm: it will absorb the dressing and flavors better. Save the flavorful drippings to add to a sauce or stock. And, be sure to trim away any excess fat; it will congeal as the meat cools.

BEHIND THE COUNTER: In butcher-speak, a chicken breast is a whole breast which when split yields two halves. Be sure you are clear with your butcher when ordering chicken breasts so you don't end up with twice as much as you need. Alternate cuts: duck breasts (+$) or a turkey breast(=$).

Topless Chicken Potpie

If you find eating chicken potpie a religious experience but you just can't bear to make a pie crust or don't have a set of those cute little ramekins, then you are in luck. This topless chicken potpie makes six single bundles of chicken and vegetable goodness without the crust *or* bowls and is a great way to use "bonus" chicken. These individual potpies can be personalized by adding spices and herbs such as curry, cumin, or chili pepper.

SERVES 6

Start to Finish: Under 30 minutes

1 box frozen puff pastry shells
2 small russet potatoes, peeled and diced into ½-inch cubes
    (about 2 cups)
1 (1-pound) bag frozen mixed vegetables: carrots, peas, corn, and
    green beans
1 cup frozen pearl onions, thawed
2 to 3 cups chicken stock
¼ cup all-purpose flour
¼ cup vegetable oil
¼ cup dry white wine
1 tablespoon chopped fresh thyme leaves or 1 teaspoon dried thyme
1 teaspoon chopped fresh rosemary leaves or ⅓ teaspoon dried rosemary

2 tablespoons chopped fresh dill leaves

½ teaspoon sweet Hungarian paprika

2 to 3 cups diced "bonus" chicken (turkey or duck can
    be substituted)

Kosher salt and freshly ground black pepper

To prepare the pastry shells: Bake the pastry shells as directed. Keep them warm while you prepare the filling, or time them so they emerge from the oven hot and crusty just before you are ready to serve.

To prepare the filling: Fill a medium pot with 3 cups of cold water and a teaspoon of salt. Add the diced potatoes and bring to a boil. Cook 15 to 20 minutes or until the potatoes are tender. Test them by piercing a potato with a paring knife; it should slide out easily. Drain and set aside. Thaw the bag of frozen vegetables and pearl onions and drain in a colander. Heat the stock in a saucepan or in the microwave.

In a separate 3- or 4-quart saucepan, add the oil then the flour, and cook, stirring constantly over medium-low heat until it forms a light blonde roux (see Feedback), 5 to 10 minutes. Let the roux cool just a bit and slowly whisk in 2 cups of the warm stock. The roux will immediately change its texture and loosen; don't worry, it will smooth out as you whisk and turn it into gravy. Stir in the wine, thyme, rosemary, dill, and paprika, thawed mixed vegetables, diced cooked potatoes, and chicken (if you just roasted the chicken, add the pan drippings at this time). Stir and heat until everything is well combined and bubbling hot, about 10 minutes, adding more warm broth if the gravy is too thick. Season to taste with salt and pepper.

When the pastry shells are done baking, remove each small pastry lid and spoon a generous amount of chicken filling into each shell, let the filling spill over onto the plate, set the top askew and use it as a scooper for the runaway filling.

Feedback

A roux is a classic thickening and flavor agent comprised of equal parts fat and all-purpose flour. To create a roux, you whisk flour into heated fat, stirring continuously over medium-low heat until the fat and flour combine and begin to change color. The roux goes through almost every shade of brown found in a box of crayons. The flavor and thickening power of a roux directly relates to its color; the lighter the roux, the less it flavors but the better it thickens. You can easily make a big batch of roux and freeze or refrigerate it, so you always have some on hand. Be sure you let it come to room temperature before using. You should never add hot liquid to a cold roux or vice versa.

Curried Chicken Salad

Many people avoid curry, feeling it must be too spicy. While some curry blends can be hot, sweet yellow curry, with its distinctive color derived from turmeric, has a gentle warmth. This chicken salad is a good opportunity to explore the flavor of curry and a range of companion tastes and textures, from plump raisins to crisp grapes, buttery almonds to crunchy celery. Feel free to be playful and substitute your favorite fruits or vegetables. You really can't go wrong.

SIDE NOTE: To make this dish a bit more special, try making your own mayonnaise; it's fast and easy and will enrich the taste of your chicken salad (see page 223).

MAKES 2 CUPS

Start to Finish: Under 15 minutes

½ cup good-quality store-bought or homemade mayonnaise
  (page 223)
½ to 1 teaspoon sweet yellow curry powder
2 celery ribs, diced (you can include some of the sweet leaves)
½ cup golden raisins
½ cup green or red seedless grapes, halved
½ cup dried cranberries
2 dozen Marcona or blanched almonds
2 teaspoons champagne vinegar (red wine vinegar can be substituted)
2 teaspoons lemon juice
2 cups diced "bonus" chicken (pages 114 to 115)
  (turkey or duck breast can be substituted)

Kosher salt and freshly ground black pepper

For the garnish
Several mint leaves, cut into chiffonade

Stir together the mayonnaise and curry and then add everything except the chicken, salt, and pepper. Stir until well combined. Fold in the chicken and season with salt and pepper to taste. Refrigerate several hours until cold. Garnish with freshly cut mint.

Chicken Caesar Salad
. . . *with garlic croutons*
My go-to dressing is this classic Caesar, which packs a pucker. The grilled chicken and homemade garlic croutons make it a complete meal.

SERVES 4

Start to Finish: Under 1 hour

For the croutons
1 (4-ounce) loaf Italian bread, cut in half lengthwise, then in half again, then cubed into bite-size pieces (day-old bread works best)
2 garlic cloves, minced
¼ cup olive oil
1 teaspoon dried oregano

For the dressing
¼ cup white wine vinegar
1 garlic clove, grated (about 1 teaspoon)
1 heaping teaspoon Dijon mustard
1 teaspoon kosher salt
¼ teaspoon freshly ground black pepper
2 teaspoons freshly squeezed lemon juice (about half a lemon)
½ teaspoon Worcestershire sauce
1 egg yolk, optional
¼ cup plus 2 tablespoons olive oil

For the salad

2 whole hearts of romaine (about 1 pound), washed, dried, and chopped

2 cups sliced "bonus" chicken (pages 114 to 115) (turkey or duck breast can be substituted)

Preheat the oven to 400 degrees. Prepare the croutons by tossing the cubes of bread with the garlic, olive oil, and oregano. Spread in a single layer on a rimmed baking pan and bake in the preheated oven for 15 minutes. Set aside to cool.

To prepare the dressing, whisk together the vinegar, garlic, mustard, salt, pepper, lemon juice, Worcestershire sauce, and egg, if using. Let the mixture sit for about 5 minutes so the flavors marry. Slowly whisk in the olive oil. Pour the dressing into the bottom of a large wooden salad bowl and add the chopped romaine lettuce leaves. Toss the lettuce, bringing the dressing up from the bottom of the bowl. Top with the chicken strips and garlic croutons.

Feedback

Salad dressing is usually made with a ratio of 3:1 oil to vinegar, but this one has a bit more pucker. If you like a less tangy dressing you can go with that ratio, using 2 tablespoons of vinegar to 6 tablespoons (¼ cup plus 2 tablespoons) oil. To create a balanced dressing you need to emulsify the ingredients long enough for them to blend or stay in suspension. Not easy: as you might have heard, oil and vinegar don't mix. That's where strong whisking or a good shake in a tight-lidded container (a mason jar or old mayonnaise jar works well) comes in. Thickeners like mustard, mayonnaise, or an egg yolk help bind and stabilize the ingredients. When time allows, prepare the dressing in advance, refrigerate, and then let it come back to room temperature before using.

NP

A classic sprinkling of Parmesan cheese works well in this dressing. For a another creamy dairy variation, mash ¼ cup of good-quality blue cheese into the dressing before serving.

Chicken and Sausage Gumbo

BEHIND THE COUNTER:
It is important to purchase
well-seasoned sausage for this
dish from your butcher. Cajun
chicken, *merguez*, or andouille
are the best choices; otherwise, any well-spiced beef,
chicken, or turkey sausage will
work (=$).

This New Orleans favorite is definitely more than the sum of its parts. Shredded chicken, sautéed onions, peppers, celery, and spicy sausage infuse every bite with a jolt of Cajun flavor, while slow-cooked roux builds the taste and thickens the sauce. Gumbo can be thickened using any one of three methods. The name "gumbo" means okra in African and that is a common ingredient used as a thickener. But many people find okra gummy and finicky to work with. A second method is using ground sassafras leaves, also known as filé powder, but that's a hard ingredient to source. So this gumbo relies on a slow-cooked French base called a roux to build the taste and thicken the sauce.

SERVES 6 TO 8

Start to Finish: Under 2 hours

For the Cajun spice mix

1 tablespoon sweet or hot Hungarian paprika

1 tablespoon kosher salt

1 tablespoon garlic powder

2 teaspoons onion powder

1 teaspoon freshly ground black pepper

1 teaspoon cayenne pepper

2 teaspoons dried oregano

2 teaspoons dried thyme leaves

For the gumbo

1 tablespoon canola oil, plus ½ cup for the roux

2 to 3 bone-in chicken breasts (about 2 pounds)

1 pound sausage, sliced into ¼-inch-thick rounds or removed
    from casing and crumbled

½ cup all-purpose flour

1 large green bell pepper, cored, seeded, and chopped

2 celery stalks, chopped (about 1 cup)

1 large onion, chopped (about 1½ cups)

4 garlic cloves, chopped (about 2 tablespoons)

2 quarts chicken stock

2 bay leaves

Filé powder, optional

1 to 2 cups long-grain rice

In a small bowl, combine the ingredients for the Cajun spice mix. You will use it to season the chicken as well as the gumbo, and still have some left over for future use. Heat the 1 tablespoon of oil in a heavy braising pot with a tight-fitting lid and season the chicken breasts liberally with 1 to 2 teaspoons of the Cajun spice mix. Brown the chicken on all sides, then lower the heat and continue to cook uncovered until cooked through, about 20 minutes. Transfer the chicken to a plate and let it cool. Shred and reserve the chicken, discarding the bones and skin.

Brown the sausage in the pot, over medium heat, about 5 minutes. Transfer to a plate with a slotted spoon and set aside. Pour off most of the fat from the pot; you'll be cooking the gumbo in what's left. And leave those clingy brown bits: they'll join in the fun later.

To prepare the roux, heat the remaining ½ cup of oil in a large skillet over medium heat and slowly whisk in the flour. Watch the roux very carefully as it turns from light beige to chocolaty brown. Take your time, keep the heat on medium, and stir, stir, stir. If the mixture looks watery, stir in up to 2 additional tablespoons of flour to create more of a paste. The roux is done when it is just past the color of peanut butter and approaching the color and consistency of thick caramel sauce, 15 to 20 minutes. Add the pepper, celery, onion, and garlic, and sprinkle everything with 2 teaspoons of the Cajun spice mix. Cook, stirring, over medium heat, about 5 minutes.

Spoon the roux and vegetables into the pot, along with the chicken stock, bay leaves, and reserved chicken and sausage. Cook over low heat, for 45 minutes. After that time, sprinkle in 2 teaspoons of filé powder if using and 1 cup of uncooked rice (2 cups if you want less soup and more of a jambalaya) and cook 15 minutes longer, or until the rice is tender. Spoon the gumbo into deep soup bowls and serve with additional filé powder for sprinkling.

Feedback

In this version there is no okra, whose gummy texture is often used as a thickener for gumbos. Instead, the roux and the addition of filé powder thicken the gumbo. Filé is made from ground sassafras leaves and imparts a distinctive nuance that is authentically Cajun. It is available in most specialty markets and online. I scored mine from my fishmonger. If you prefer to thicken the soup with okra, add 1 pound of sliced okra to the pot.

Chicken Parts

Chicken parts can be really satisfying when smothered in a wonderful sauce, surrounded by friends such as peppers, onions, and garlic and served atop their closest acquaintances, rice or pasta. Your butcher can take the chicken apart for you or you can do it yourself. Norman Weinstein recommends using a 5-inch boning knife rather than kitchen shears to break the chicken down. It might seem like an intimidating task, but butchering your own whole chicken is easy, economical, and allows you to save the random parts like the back or neck for stock or stew. First cut along each side of the backbone. Then feel where the leg and wing joints connect, and carefully cut at those joints. They will yield to light pressure when you've found the right spot; you shouldn't have to hack them off. Now cut the whole breast, in half, right along the bone. Voilá: chicken parts! If your family prefers white meat or you only like the juicy thighs, for most recipes where a whole chicken cut up is specified, you can substitute an equal amount of your favorite parts. When using the breasts, I often suggest cutting them in half crosswise so they fit more comfortably in your pan and are easy to handle when they are eaten.

Dark meat—legs and thighs—are juicier than white meat as they contain a higher fat content, but they also take a bit longer to cook through. That's why you should start them first or place them in your pan's hot zone to get a "leg up" on the white meat. If you avoid fat, you can easily skin the parts prior to cooking. I prefer leaving the skin on so the meat remains juicy. If you like, you can remove the skin before serving.

Chicken Cacciatore

Could any dish be more classically Italian, or easier to prepare for a crowd? Grab a big pot, lots of crisp fresh peppers, onions, and mushrooms, and create a simple and delicious tomato-based stew. If you prefer eating your chicken with a fork and knife, I recommend using thighs and breasts. If you don't mind getting your hands messy, add the legs and wings. Licking the sweet and spicy sauce off your fingers is half the fun.

SIDE NOTE: Cacciatore cries out for a bed of noodles or fluffy rice. Try the rice on page 193. Studded with zucchini and tomatoes, it matches nicely with the chicken.

SERVES 4

Start to Finish: Under 1 1/2 hours

5 tablespoons olive oil
1 (4-pound) chicken, cut into 8 pieces (and then
    cut the breasts in half, or the equivalent quantity
    of your favorite chicken parts)
Kosher salt and freshly ground black pepper
1 teaspoon sweet or hot Hungarian paprika
1/2 cup all-purpose flour, for dredging
2 pounds bell peppers (an assortment of green and red works well),
    cored, seeded, and sliced into 1/2-inch strips
1 large onion, sliced
1/2 pound whole white button mushrooms
3 garlic cloves, finely minced (about 1 1/2 tablespoons)
1 (28-ounce) can whole tomatoes
1/2 cup white wine
1/2 cup chicken stock
1 bay leaf
Generous pinch of crushed red pepper flakes
Handful of fresh flat-leaf parsley, roughly chopped, optional

Heat 3 tablespoons of oil in a large braising pot. Pat the chicken dry. Lightly season both sides of the chicken with salt, pepper, and paprika. Fill a resealable plastic bag with flour, and toss the chicken pieces in the bag to completely coat. Shake off excess flour. Brown the chicken on all sides in the pot over medium to high heat, about 7 minutes, or a little longer for the dark meat. If the pot cannot hold all the pieces comfortably, brown them in batches. Transfer the chicken to a plate.

In the same pot, heat the remaining 2 tablespoons of oil. Add the peppers and onions and cook over medium heat, stirring occasionally, for 10 minutes. Add the mushrooms and continue cooking until the vegetables are soft and lightly browned. Stir in the garlic, and add the tomatoes, breaking them up with your hands or a wooden spoon, then add the wine and stock. Return the chicken to the pot, nestling the pieces in the sauce. Drop in the bay leaf and red pepper flakes (rub them between your fingers to release their heat, be sure to wash your hands thoroughly afterward). Cover and cook over low heat for 30 to 45 minutes, or until the chicken is tender and cooked through. Season to taste with salt and pepper. Remove and discard the bay leaf and sprinkle in the parsley, if using. Serve family style.

Chicken with Prunes *Tsimmes*

A *tsimmes* is a Yiddish word, which idiomatically translates as "a big fuss." In culinary terms it denotes a sweet dish that is a melting pot of flavors. This chicken *tsimmes* brings together large slices of potatoes, sweet prunes, brown sugar, and honey to create a melt-in-your-mouth meal that is sweetly satisfying.

SERVES 4

Start to Finish: Under 2½ hours

1 (3½- to 4-pound) chicken, cut into 8 pieces (and then cut the breasts
    in half, or the equivalent quantity of your favorite chicken parts)
4 tablespoons vegetable oil
Kosher salt and freshly ground black pepper
½ cup red wine (or chicken stock)
2 tablespoons brown sugar
2 tablespoons honey
2 cups pitted prunes
2 russet potatoes (about ¾ pound), peeled and cut into large chunks
    (can substitute sweet potatoes)

Pat the chicken dry with paper towels. Heat the oil in a large braising pot. Lightly season the chicken with salt and pepper, add to the pot, and brown on all sides over medium heat, about 15 minutes. Pour off the fat and add 1 cup of water, the wine (or stock), brown sugar, honey, and prunes. Season the dish with salt and pepper and bring to a boil. Reduce the heat to low, cover, and cook for 1 hour. After 1 hour, add 1 cup of hot water and the potatoes, being sure to tuck the potatoes into the sauce. Continue cooking for 45 to 60 minutes, or until the potatoes are fork-tender. Season to taste with salt and pepper and serve.

Chicken in Red Wine Sauce

Nothing could be more classically French than *coq au vin*; braised chicken in a rich red wine sauce, scattered with pearl onions and button mushrooms. This version brings together all the traditional warm aromatic flavors without complicated or time-consuming steps. To some *coq au vin* is a daylong labor of love. With this recipe you will definitely be transported to Provence—you'll just arrive sooner!

SERVES 4

Start to Finish: Under 1½ hours

1 (4-pound) chicken, cut into 8 pieces (and then cut the breasts in half, or the equivalent quantity of your favorite chicken parts)
Kosher salt and freshly ground black pepper
2 tablespoons olive oil
4 to 5 garlic cloves, peeled and smashed
12 ounces button mushrooms, wiped clean, trimmed, and halved
2 cups frozen pearl onions
2 cups red wine
Several sprigs fresh thyme
5 to 6 fresh sage leaves
1 bay leaf
1 sprig rosemary

Pat the chicken pieces dry with paper towels and season with salt and pepper. Heat the oil and garlic in a large, heavy braising pot with a tight-fitting lid. Add the chicken and brown over medium heat on all sides until the skin is golden brown, 10 to 15 minutes. Wait for the chicken to release from the pan before turning. Stand the pieces up on their sides, and use the side of the pot to balance them so that every edge is browned. You might need to do this in batches. Transfer the cooked pieces to a plate. Continue cooking until all pieces are browned, adding more oil if needed.

Remove the garlic and pour off all but 2 tablespoons of fat from the pot. Add the mushrooms and brown over medium-high heat, about 5 minutes. Add the onions and stir so the brown bits at the bottom of the pot coat the onions and mushrooms. The liquid from the onions will help deglaze the pan. Cook the onions and mushrooms, stirring occasionally, about 5 minutes. Remove with a slotted spoon, transfer to a bowl, and set aside.

Return the chicken to the pot and add the wine and herbs, wrapped in cheesecloth or tied with kitchen twine. Cover and cook on a gentle simmer for 45 to 60 minutes. Check the chicken for doneness by inserting a fork into a thick piece and seeing that it is fork-tender. You want it to be juicy, with the meat pulling away from the bone. When the chicken is done, transfer the pieces to a deep platter, and cover loosely with foil to keep warm while you prepare the sauce. Heat the sauce over medium heat, uncovered, for 5 to 10 minutes; some of the water will evaporate, leaving the sauce a little thicker. You can thicken it further by making a slurry of 1 tablespoon of cornstarch and 2 tablespoons of cold water, and stirring it into the pot. Bring the sauce to a boil and repeat until desired consistency. Add the reserved onions and mushrooms into the thickened sauce and spoon over the chicken.

Crispy Fried Chicken

No buttermilk, no problem. No deep fryer, no worries. This fried chicken comes out flavorful and perfectly crisp without either of those trappings. First the chicken goes for a quick swim in egg whites seasoned with hot sauce, then takes a dunk in a blend of flour and cornstarch. The most important step is the combination of deep-frying and steaming in a tight skillet. Generally, when you want meat or poultry to brown in a pan, you need to spread the meat out so that there is room for steam to escape and browning to occur. But for this recipe, you want the chicken to fit tightly in the pan so that it both browns in the hot oil *and* steams as a result of the cramped quarters and a tight lid. The result will be crispy, juicy chicken—no paper hat or bucket needed!

SERVES 4

Start to Finish: About 1 hour

For the soak

½ cup egg whites (from about 2 eggs)

½ teaspoon kosher salt

½ to 1 teaspoon hot sauce, or to taste

1 (3½- to 4-pound) chicken, cut into 8 pieces (and then cut each breast in half crosswise and cut away any rib meat)

For the dunk

1 cup all-purpose flour

½ cup cornstarch

1 teaspoon kosher salt

½ teaspoon freshly ground black pepper

1 teaspoon sweet or hot Hungarian paprika

1 teaspoon garlic powder

Vegetable shortening, peanut, or corn oil for frying

For the soak: Whisk together the egg whites, salt, and hot sauce and pour the mixture into a resealable plastic bag. Toss the chicken pieces in the bag and seal. Refrigerate for at least 30 minutes or up to several hours. While the chicken marinates, prepare the breading by combining all the dunk ingredients in a shallow bowl. When ready to fry, remove the chicken from the fridge and add ½ inch of oil to a heavy-bottomed or cast iron skillet, that has a cover and can hold the chicken pieces snuggly. **Heat the oil to 350 degrees.** If you do not have a cooking thermometer, do what Chinese cooks have done for centuries: take a wooden chopstick (or stem of a wooden spoon) and press down into the oil. If the oil bubbles up around the wood, it is ready.

Dredge the chicken in the flour mixture and then place the chicken in the pan skin side down, with the dark meat pieces in your pan's hot spot, since they take longer to cook. In most instances, the hot spot will be the center of the pan, but you know your stove and pan best, so for you, it might not be in the center. Cover the pan, and cook, maintaining the heat at 350 degrees, about 12 to 15 minutes, or until the skin is a golden brown. Turn the chicken over, cover, and cook an additional 10 minutes until that side is golden brown and crispy. Turn one more time so the skin side has a chance to crisp up, 2 to 3 minutes.

Drain on a rack set over a rimmed baking sheet. If you place them on paper towels or even in a paper bag, they will lose some of their crispy goodness. If you must keep the chicken warm, place the baking sheet in the oven on low until ready to serve.

Feedback

I don't have a chemistry degree, but I think the proteins in the egg whites help tenderize the chicken a little just as the buttermilk does in southern fried chicken recipes. On top of that, the egg whites are the glue that holds the flour mixture in place. Mr. Wizard would be proud. For the egg whites you can certainly crack a few eggs or buy egg whites in a container. Remember, once opened, you need to use that container within a week.

Chicken and Rice

Arroz con pollo is an authentic Latin American one-pot wonder. Juicy chicken, tender rice, and a splash of green from peas and olives make this a hearty and visually satisfying dinner. This version is based on Ruth Kohn's, a survivor of the Holocaust, whom I had the pleasure of interviewing for my first book, *Recipes Remembered*. Ruth and her family fled Germany for safe haven in Sosua, a small community located in the Dominican Republic. Her cooking style is reflective of her adopted home.

SERVES 4 TO 6
Start to Finish: Under 2 hours

1 (3½ to 4-pound) chicken, cut into 8 pieces (and then cut the breasts
    in half, or the equivalent of your favorite chicken parts)

Kosher salt and freshly ground black pepper

½ cup olive oil

2 large onions, chopped (about 2 to 3 cups)

1 clove garlic, crushed

½ teaspoon crushed red pepper flakes

2 cups converted white rice, uncooked

1 (28-ounce) can tomatoes, with their juice

1¼ cups chicken stock

1 can green chili peppers, chopped (optional)

1 cup frozen peas

½ cup pimiento-stuffed green olives, sliced

1 (4-ounce) can pimientos, drained and sliced

Preheat the oven to 325 degrees. Wipe the chicken pieces dry with paper towels. Lightly season with salt and pepper. Heat the olive oil in a heavy 6-quart braising pot. Add the chicken and brown on all sides over medium heat. You might need to do this in batches. Remove the cooked chicken with a slotted spoon, and transfer to a plate.

In the same pot, cook the onions, garlic, and red pepper flakes, stirring over medium heat until lightly browned, about 10 minutes. Stir in the rice and cook for 10 minutes longer, stirring occasionally, until everything is lightly browned. Stir in the tomatoes and their juice (breaking the tomatoes up with your hands or a wooden spoon). Then add the chicken stock and chili peppers, if using. Return the chicken to the pot and bring to a strong simmer. Season with salt and pepper. Cover the pot and place in the oven. Bake at 325 degrees for 1 hour or until the chicken is fork-tender and the rice is cooked but not mushy.

After an hour, add ½ cup of water, sprinkle in the peas, olives, and pimiento strips—do not stir, because it could make the rice mushy. Cover and continue to bake for an additional 20 minutes. The chicken should be tender and moist and cooked through. Serve family style right from the braising pot.

Peach and Ginger–Glazed Chicken

BEHIND THE COUNTER: Have your butcher remove the bones from the chicken breast, leaving the drumette portion of the wing attached. Alternate cuts: veal or lamb chops (+$), veal or lamb breast riblets (+$), or simply grilled chicken cutlets (+$), thighs, or drumsticks (−$).

This gooey and kicky glaze coats "frenched" chicken breasts to create a yummy peachy delight with a gingery bite. French style is an elegant way to serve a chicken breast, and the built in handle makes it easy to pick up and enjoy that delicious last bite. Make this dish in late spring or early summer when peaches are so ripe that they jump out of the bushel and into your shopping cart.

SERVES 4

Start to Finish: Under 1 hour

For the chicken
4 (12-ounce) chicken breasts, frenched, skin on
1 teaspoon kosher salt
½ teaspoon freshly ground black pepper

For the glaze
1 cup peach preserves
1 teaspoon grated fresh ginger
2 tablespoons low-sodium soy sauce
Pinch of freshly ground black pepper

For the peaches
2 tablespoons low-sodium soy sauce
2 tablespoons honey
1 teaspoon grated fresh ginger
4 peaches, pit removed, cut into wedges

Pat the chicken dry with paper towels. **Preheat the oven to 350 degrees.** Season the chicken with salt and pepper on both sides.

Combine the glaze ingredients in a small bowl. Reserve one-fourth of the glaze in a separate bowl to add to the peaches. Coat the chicken in the remaining glaze and place in a baking dish. Bake in the preheated oven for 30 minutes.

While the chicken cooks, prepare the peaches. Combine the soy sauce, honey, and ginger in a bowl. Toss in the sliced peaches, and let them sit while you heat a stovetop grill pan. Grill the peaches over medium heat for several minutes on each side, until the peaches have nice grill marks. Return the peaches to the bowl with the marinade. Add the reserved glaze and toss to combine. This will be the topping for the chicken.

After 30 minutes, remove the baking dish from the oven, and pour the peaches and their sauce over the chicken. Return to the oven and bake for an additional 10 to 15 minutes. For crisper skin, broil the chicken for just a minute or two right in the pan.

Moroccan Chicken

Morocco and India, although separated by land and water, both feature foods that elevate exotic spice blends. This dish is a fusion of Indian and Moroccan flavors. A *tajine,* an earthen clay pot, is traditionally used to slow bake the dish, but you can easily make this fragrant and intoxicating stew in your braising pot. This recipe uses Indian yellow curry, a pungent combination of spices including turmeric—which gives curry its yellow color—and coriander and red pepper flakes give it a pop of heat. The addition of preserved lemons (page 218) and brined green olives add a salty and tart classic Moroccan essence, while the chickpeas, an common Indian ingredient, adds an authentic element to the stew.

SIDE NOTE: The perfect landing spot for this chicken is a bed of rice. Nothing is more satisfying than basmati rice (page 192) with a hint of the preserved lemon.

SERVES 4

Start to Finish: 2 hours or up to overnight to marinate the chicken; under 1½ hours to cook

> For the chicken
> 1 (3½ to 4-pound) chicken, cut into 8 pieces (and then cut the breasts in half, or the equivalent of your favorite chicken parts)
> 3 tablespoons olive oil

For the rub

½ teaspoon ground cumin

½ teaspoon yellow curry powder

¼ teaspoon ground ginger

Pinch of ground cloves, optional

For the stew

1 large onion, diced (about 1½ cups)

3 garlic cloves, minced (about 1½ tablespoons)

Pinch of crushed red pepper flakes, add only if your curry does not have red pepper

¼ teaspoon good saffron threads

½ teaspoon ground cumin

½ teaspoon yellow curry powder

1 cup chicken stock

1 cinnamon stick

4 slices preserved lemon, rind only (homemade or look for *citrons confits* at your market)

1 cup unpitted Picholine olives or caperberries

1 (15-ounce) can chickpeas, rinsed and drained, optional

Pat the chicken dry with paper towels and place the chicken on a small baking sheet. Combine the rub ingredients in a small bowl. Coat the chicken with 1 tablespoon of olive oil and sprinkle each piece with the rub mixture. Cover the baking sheet with plastic wrap and refrigerate at least 2 hours or up to 8 hours. Heat the remaining 2 tablespoons of oil in a braising pot or tajine. Brown the chicken over medium heat for about 5 minutes per side, or until the chicken is browned; the chicken will easily release from the pan when it is ready to turn. You might need to do this in batches so you don't overcrowd the pan. Transfer the chicken to a platter and set aside.

To the same pot, add the onion, garlic, red pepper flakes if using, saffron, cumin, and curry. Cook, stirring, toasting the spices while the onions and garlic cook over medium heat, about 10 minutes. The aroma will be irresistible and the onions should have turned the color of little niblets of corn from the infusion of spices.

Return the chicken to the pot along with the stock and a cinnamon stick. Cover and cook over low heat for at least 30 minutes; the chicken should be fork-tender. Add the preserved lemon, olives, and chickpeas if using. Continue cooking covered for an additional 15 minutes over a gentle simmer until everything is heated through. Season to taste with salt and pepper. Ladle into deep dishes and serve with warmed pita bread to mop up the sauce.

Feedback

Aron notes that since most Indian, Latin, Moroccan, and even Asian foods feature many vegetables and unique spices, the trick lies in choosing a fruity wine that goes well with rich, creamy, and spicy foods. Try mineral-tinged white wines like Gewürztraminer, Riesling, or Sauvignon Blanc.

Skewered Chicken Thighs
. . . with coconut peanut dipping sauce

Grilled chicken thighs are just about foolproof. They are juicy and delicious when grilled, and do not need their fatty jackets to stay moist. They are best when prepared on an outdoor grill, but a broiler or stovetop grill pan make good second choices.

BEHIND THE COUNTER: Have your butcher prepare boneless, skinless chicken thighs. Alternate cuts: boneless white meat chicken or lamb shoulder cut into chunks and skewered (+$).

SERVES 4

Start to Finish: Under 5 minutes to prep; 2 to 6 hours to marinate; under 15 minutes to grill

For the chicken
1½ pounds skinless, boneless chicken thighs
Kosher salt and freshly ground black pepper

For the coconut milk marinade
1 teaspoon Chinese five-spice powder
¼ cup low-sodium soy sauce
¼ cup peanut or vegetable oil
¼ cup coconut milk

1 tablespoon chopped fresh cilantro

2 garlic cloves, minced (about 1 tablespoon)

1 teaspoon grated fresh ginger

2 tablespoons rice wine vinegar

For the coconut peanut dipping sauce

1/2 cup coconut milk

2 tablespoons chunky peanut butter

2 teaspoons low-sodium soy sauce

1/4 teaspoon chili oil

1 teaspoon brown sugar

1 garlic clove, finely minced

Pinch of kosher salt

1/2 teaspoon grated fresh ginger

1 teaspoon chopped fresh mint leaves

Pat the chicken dry with paper towels. Place the chicken in a resealable plastic bag. In a small bowl, combine all the marinade ingredients. Pour the marinade into the bag, reserving 1/4 cup to use as a basting sauce. Seal and refrigerate for at least 2 or up to 6 hours. While the chicken marinates, prepare the dipping sauce. Whisk all the ingredients together. If the peanut butter is stubborn, you can gently heat the mixture in a small saucepan on a gentle simmer for a minute to help combine. Reserve until ready to use.

Light the grill or preheat your broiler or stovetop grill pan. Remove the chicken from the marinade, wipe it dry, and lightly season with salt and pepper. Grill on the first side about 5 minutes, turn, and baste with the reserved marinade. Continue grilling 5 to 7 minutes longer or until nicely charred and cooked through. Serve with the dipping sauce and freshly chopped mint.

Feedback

For a satay-style presentation, you can cut the thigh meat into strips and thread them on wooden skewers that have been soaked in water for at least 30 minutes; this prevents them from catching fire on the grill.

Grilled Spice-Rubbed Chicken

Whether you light your backyard grill, or kick up the heat in the kitchen, this grilled spice-rubbed chicken will warm your mouth without burning your throat. For heat junkies, increase the rub's temperature by adding more black or cayenne pepper. The trick to grilling chicken is to cook slow and low and baste only at the end. For indoor grilling, be sure to turn the fan or vent on and get the grill pan good and sizzling hot.

BEHIND THE COUNTER: Buy a whole chicken and break it down, or buy only your favorite parts. Alternate cuts: lamb, beef, or veal skewered for kebabs (+$).

SIDE NOTE: Simply roasted corn, coated in a little of the grill rub, makes a great side (See page 207).

SERVES 4

Start to Finish: Under 30 minutes

> *For the chicken*
> 2 pounds assorted chicken parts (6 to 8 thighs or 3 to 4 breasts)
> Olive or vegetable oil
>
> *For the rub*
> 1 teaspoon cayenne pepper
> 1 teaspoon dried oregano
> 1 teaspoon ancho chili powder
> 1 teaspoon garlic powder
> 1 teaspoon kosher salt
> ½ teaspoon freshly ground black pepper (increase for more heat)
> ½ teaspoon ground cumin
>
> ½ cup barbecue sauce (page 48) or use store-bought
> 1 lime cut into wedges for serving, optional

Pat the chicken dry with paper towels. **Heat the grill**. Combine the rub ingredients in a small bowl. Toss the chicken parts in a little oil, and then sprinkle both sides with about 2 tablespoons of the rub. Mix another teaspoon of rub with ½ cup barbecue sauce. You'll use this to baste the chicken when it is grilling. Cook the chicken on indirect heat; that is, do not place it in the center of your grill's hot spot. If you do, the skin will burn and you will be left with a charred taste. You want the chicken to cook low and slow. Total grilling time will be 20 to 30 minutes, turning the chicken over at intervals and basting with the sauce in the last few minutes. Serve with a squeeze of cooling fresh lime juice.

No-Brainer Wings

Some things are just best when left simple and unfettered. These are stripped down and basic, hot and spicy, fast and easy.

SIDE NOTE: While blue cheese dressing is a classic dip to partner with wings, that wouldn't fly for a kosher carnivore, so whip up some cooling guacamole aioli to help ease the heat (page 225). They are delicious together!

MAKES 48 PIECES

Start to Finish: Under 30 minutes

For the chicken
2 dozen wings, rinsed, stray pinfeathers plucked, separated at the joint, bony tips discarded
Neutral vegetable or canola oil or peanut oil for frying

For the sauce
1/3 cup margarine, melted
1/2 cup hot sauce

Preheat the oven to 350 degrees and set a rack over a rimmed baking sheet. Dry the wings thoroughly with paper towels before frying. Heat the oil in a deep cast-iron skillet, cast-iron pot, or deep fryer; you'll need at least 4 inches of oil in the pot. If using a deep fryer, follow the manufacturer's recommendations. **Heat oil to 350 degrees.**

Carefully fry the wings for 13 minutes. This seems to be the magical cooking time to create the right crunch. While the wings fry, prepare the sauce by melting the margarine in a small saucepan or in a bowl in the microwave. Stir in the hot sauce and pour into a bowl large enough to hold the wings. You can increase the heat by upping the ratio of hot sauce to margarine.

When the wings are done, use a pair of tongs to drop them into the sauce and toss. Lift each wing out, give it a shake, and place it on the rack. Place the racked wings in the oven for 10 minutes. Remove from the oven and give them another dunk in the sauce just before serving.

Feedback

If you prefer, the wings can be baked at 450 degrees for 25 to 30 minutes, or until the skin is crisp, then tossed in the sauce.

Chicken Cutlets

A cutlet is a thin slice of meat that can be pan-fried or quickly cooked. While not always considered a glamorous main course, every culture and cuisine has its own delectable version. From Milanese to schnitzel, the cutlet has nothing to be ashamed of. Thinly sliced cutlets are not the same as pounded-thin cutlets. One is when the butcher carefully slices through a thick cutlet to present you with a thinner piece. Pounding the cutlet, however, creates a thin cutlet, but it also tenderizes the chicken for a more palatable finished result. I generally recommend cutlets be pounded to ½ to ¼ inch, unless otherwise directed. Your butcher can pound and trim the cutlets for you, or you can grab a mallet and tenderize and thin them yourself. When pounding cutlets, place them in an unsealed plastic bag, or between two pieces of plastic wrap. Smack the center of the cutlet and drag your mallet out toward the edges and repeat until you've worked all the way around the cutlet and the cutlet is the same thickness everywhere. Trim the cutlets of all fat and cartilage, and remember that the thinner the cutlets are the faster they will cook *and* the easier they will dry out, so gauge the thickness to complement the recipe. Cutlets will often have a tender, a thinner strip that's loosely attached to the main portion. These filets will cook faster than the cutlet itself, so you might want to separate them from the cutlet and save them for another use, or cook them for less time than the cutlet itself.

Chicken Piccata

There's no better trio than lemon, capers, and white wine. Together they create the basis for a classic Italian piccata sauce, which can be spooned over thinly pounded and fried chicken cutlets. If you are not a caper fan, cross the border to France and create Chicken Francese, nearly the same dish as the Italian favorite, but sans the capers.

BEHIND THE COUNTER: Have your butcher prepare cutlets about ½ to ¼ inch thick. Alternate cuts: turkey (=$) or veal(+$).

SERVES 4

Start to Finish: Under 30 minutes

4 (8-ounce) boneless chicken cutlets pounded ½
    to ¼ inch thick
1 teaspoon kosher salt
¼ teaspoon freshly ground black pepper
2 eggs, lightly beaten with a tablespoon of water
1 cup all-purpose flour, seasoned with 1 teaspoon *herbes
    de Provence*, or a combination of herbs such as chervil,
    marjoram, thyme, savory, basil, tarragon or parsley
4 tablespoons olive oil
1 cup chicken stock
½ cup white wine
Juice of 1 lemon (at least 3 tablespoons)
¼ cup freshly chopped flat-leaf parsley
1 tablespoon brine-packed capers, with 1 tablespoon
    caper liquid
Lemon wedges for serving, optional

Season the cutlets on both sides with salt and pepper. Place the eggs and water in a shallow bowl. In a separate shallow bowl, combine the flour and seasoning. **Heat the olive oil in a large skillet.** When the oil is shimmering, dredge the cutlets in the flour, then dip into the egg, then flour a second time. Repeat until all the chicken pieces are coated. Place the cutlets on a plate or baking sheet while the oil heats.

Cook the chicken over medium heat for about 3 minutes per side, until they develop a nice golden crust. You want to be sure not to burn any residual flour in the pan as it will become the basis for your sauce. Remove the chicken from the pan and set aside. To the same pan, add the stock, wine, and lemon juice, and deglaze. Stir to loosen bits stuck to the bottom of the skillet. Cook over medium heat for a couple of minutes. Add the parsley, capers, and their liquid and return the cutlets to the skillet. Cover the pan and cook for just 2 to 3 minutes, until the chicken is cooked through and the sauce has had a chance to flavor the cutlets. If the chicken has absorbed all the sauce, add a little more stock to the pan just before serving. Transfer the chicken to a serving plate and drizzle any remaining sauce on top. For extra pucker, serve with lemon wedges.

NP

For a non-pareve preparation, you can fry the chicken in a blend of oil and butter, and add an additional pat or two of butter to the skillet when preparing the sauce. Use a whisk to help it emulsify.

Panko-Crusted Chicken Cutlets

Many favor Panko, Japanese bread crumbs, because the texture is more defined and the crunch is louder and bolder than that of regular bread crumbs. The mixture of mayonnaise and mustard serve as glue for the crumbs as well as flavor enhancers.

BEHIND THE COUNTER: Have your butcher prepare cutlets about $1/2$ inch thick. Alternate cuts: turkey (=$) or veal(+$).

SERVES 4

Start to Finish: Under 30 minutes

> 4 (6- to 8- ounce) boneless, skinless chicken cutlets pounded
> $1/2$ to $1/4$ inch thick
> Kosher salt and freshly ground black pepper
> 2 tablespoons Dijon mustard
> 2 tablespoons mayonnaise
> $1/2$ cup Panko bread crumbs, seasoned with
>   2 teaspoons dried oregano
> 2 tablespoons olive oil

Preheat the oven to 350 degrees. Lightly season the chicken with salt and pepper. In a shallow dish combine the mustard and mayonnaise. In a second dish, add the Panko bread crumbs and oregano (a pie plate works well). Dredge the cutlets in the mustard and mayonnaise, coating both sides, and then dredge both sides in the panko bread crumbs, gently pressing them into the chicken so they adhere.

Heat the oil in a large skillet, then add the chicken and brown over medium heat for 3 to 4 minutes, or until the underside is golden brown. Carefully turn the cutlets over and lightly brown the second side for 2 to 3 minutes. Drizzle a little olive oil over the top of the cutlets and pop the skillet into the preheated oven. Bake at 350 degrees until the breasts are cooked through, about 10 minutes.

Grilled Chicken and Pasta Primavera

This primavera features grilled chicken mingled with roasted asparagus, zucchini, portobello mushrooms, and whole garlic cloves. Everything is then tossed with ziti pasta for a nutritious and delicious dish.

SERVES 4 TO 6

Start to Finish: Under 45 minutes

2 medium zucchini (about ¾ pound) sliced in half lengthwise
½ pound portobello mushrooms caps, stems removed,
    sliced ½ inch thick
½ pound green asparagus, ends trimmed
4 large whole garlic cloves, unpeeled
Olive oil to coat the veggies and chicken plus ¼ cup
Kosher salt and freshly ground black pepper
1 pound ziti pasta, or any other pasta
1 pound chicken cutlets pounded ½ to ¼ inch thick
Pinch of crushed red pepper flakes
1 teaspoon chopped capers
1 cup cherry tomatoes, halved
Freshly torn basil leaves (about 6) for garnish

Preheat the oven to 450 degrees. Toss the vegetables in enough olive oil to lightly coat them and then place the vegetables on a rimmed baking sheet. Lightly season with kosher salt and pepper. Roast the vegetables for 15 minutes or until the mushrooms and asparagus are lightly charred. Transfer them to a plate and set aside. Continue roasting the zucchini and garlic until the zucchini is lightly charred,

BEHIND THE COUNTER: Have your butcher prepare cutlets about ½ inch thick. Alternate cuts: turkey (=$).

SIDE NOTE: For a fiery version of this dish, toss the pasta with red pepper vinaigrette (page 227) and serve either hot or cold.

about 10 minutes longer. Place on the same plate as the mushrooms and asparagus. When the vegetables are cool enough to handle, cut them into bite-size pieces. Peel the cloves and smash the browned garlic. Set all the vegetables aside.

Bring a large pot of salted water to a rapid boil and cook the pasta according to the package directions. Reserve some pasta water for the sauce and drain the pasta. Do not rinse the pasta! While the vegetables roast and the pasta cooks, prepare the chicken. Season both sides of the chicken with salt and pepper, then coat with olive oil. Using a stovetop grill pan, or a regular skillet, cook the chicken 3 to 5 minutes per side, until lightly charred and cooked through. Transfer to a plate and set aside. Cut the chicken with a knife into strips right before the next step.

Heat 1/4 cup olive oil in a deep skillet large enough to hold all the ingredients. Cook and stir the smashed garlic, red pepper flakes, and capers over medium heat for a few minutes until very fragrant. Add the vegetables, chicken, and drained, cooked pasta to the skillet. Cook over low heat until everything is heated through, about 3 minutes, adding about 1/2 cup of the reserved pasta water to help smooth out the sauce. Spoon the pasta into a large serving bowl, toss with the cherry tomatoes, and garnish with the torn basil leaves. Serve hot or cold.

NP
For a non-pareve presentation, stir 1/4 cup Parmesan cheese into the skillet before you toss all the ingredients.

Pretzel-Crusted Chicken
. . . with honey beer mustard sauce

In college in Philadelphia I learned that you can't have pretzels without mustard. Take these friends, partner them with chicken and beer, and you have turned stadium fare into a fun adult dinner.

BEHIND THE COUNTER:
Have your butcher prepare chicken cutlets about 1/2 inch thick.

SERVES 4
Start to Finish: Under 45 minutes

For the chicken

2 eggs

4 tablespoons beer

2 teaspoons grainy mustard

1 (8-ounce bag) sourdough pretzels

4 (6- to 8-ounce) chicken cutlets

Vegetable oil for frying

For the dipping sauce

2 tablespoons beer

3 tablespoons grainy mustard

2 tablespoons honey

Preheat the oven to 350 degrees. Beat the eggs, 4 tablespoons of beer, and 2 teaspoons of mustard in a bowl large enough to dip the cutlets. Process the pretzels in a food processor, using the metal blade. Process them in two batches: grind half the bag as fine as bread crumbs, and the other half to a crumbly gravel-like texture.

Dip the cutlets in the fine pretzel crumbs, then in the egg mixture, then press them into the coarse crumbs until they adhere (it's fine if some drop off). If time allows, refrigerate the cutlets for 15 minutes to help the breading adhere better. Heat about ¼ inch of oil in a large skillet until simmering. Fry the cutlets until they are golden brown, 3 to 5 minutes per side. Remove them to a waiting baking sheet and bake in the preheated oven until the cutlets are fully cooked, 10 to 15 minutes. You might need to cut into one to check for doneness. The meat should be white with no traces of pink.

While the cutlets bake, prepare the dipping sauce by combining all 3 ingredients until well blended. You can use the sauce for dipping, or drizzle a little over each cutlet.

Feedback

The same preparation can be used for chicken tenders; this amount of cooking ingredients and sauce covers about 2 pounds of meat. If preparing the tenders for children, you can eliminate the beer and substitute water or apple juice beaten with the eggs and for the dipping sauce. Tenders love to go for a dunk!

Chicken Lettuce Cups

A fun meal in under fifteen minutes, using mainly ingredients from the vegetable bin or pantry, makes a cook a happy camper. Chicken lettuce cups fit that bill. Vibrant, colorful veggies mingle with finely minced chicken bathed in a punchy soy-based sauce and cradled in crisp lettuce leaves. It just might take you longer to read the ingredients list than it will to get this meal to the table. Mince the ingredients very fine. They can be irregular in size, but no bigger than kernels of corn. For this recipe you want to mince—not chop—the ingredients, so they are cut into teeny, tiny bits. This recipe is all about prep and using what you have available, so feel free to invent your own combinations. Don't be tempted to use a food processor, because you will end up with mushy, not minced, chicken.

BEHIND THE COUNTER: Have your butcher cut chicken cutlets, about 1 pound (2 to 3 cutlets) in total. Do not pound them out, they should be a little chunky about 1/2 inch thick. Alternate cuts: turkey cutlets (=$) or duck breasts (+$).

MAKES ABOUT 4 APPETIZER SERVINGS

Start to Finish: Under 15 minutes

For the filling

1/2 cup unsalted cashews or peanuts

1 tablespoon canola oil

1 small zucchini, minced (about 1/2 cup)

1/2 red bell pepper, cored, seeded, and minced (about 1/2 cup)

1/2 yellow bell pepper, cored, seeded, and minced (about 1/2 cup)

1 small carrot, finely minced (about 1/2 cup)

1 celery stalk, minced (about 1/2 cup)

2 to 3 garlic cloves, minced

1 pound chicken cutlets, minced (easier to do if the cutlets are very cold)

For the sauce

1/3 cup low-sodium soy sauce

2 tablespoons apricot preserves

3 tablespoons hoisin sauce

1/4 cup rice wine vinegar

1 teaspoon brown sugar

1 teaspoon toasted sesame oil

1 tablespoon chili-garlic sauce (more if you can stand the heat)

1 well-chilled head of Boston or butter lettuce for serving

In a large dry skillet, toast the cashews for a couple of minutes until fragrant. Remove the nuts to a chopping board and run your serrated knife through them to break up the large pieces. In the same skillet, heat the oil over medium-high heat and stir the vegetables and chicken until the chicken is no longer pink and the veggies just begin soften, 3 to 5 minutes. In a small bowl, mix all of the sauce ingredients together. Stir in three-quarters of the sauce and the toasted cashews, toss to coat.

To serve, spoon a teaspoon of sauce and about 2 tablespoons of the chicken and veggies into each lettuce cup, wrap, roll, and eat.

Ground Chicken

This versatile way to enjoy chicken is sometimes upstaged by ground turkey, its more famous cousin. Ground chicken is moist and delicious, healthful and economical. Look for ground white meat chicken; it has a lower fat content than a mixture of white and dark meat. It can dry out quickly if overcooked, but handled right makes a standout stand-in for ground beef, veal, or turkey.

BEHIND THE COUNTER:
Have your butcher medium grind white meat chicken. Alternate cut: ground turkey (=$).

Chicken Croquettes

In my mother's kosher home, where money was tight and cookbooks were never open, my grandmother needed creative ways to prepare chicken. Her croquettes were legendary. We called them croquettes, because they were shaped into oval patties and fried in hot oil, but you could easily form the mixture into burgers and serve on a toasted bun with interesting condiments. For a belly-filling meal, bring a canned pot of lima or butter beans to a simmer and heat the croquettes with the beans in the bean liquid.

MAKES 12 TO 15 CROQUETTES
Start to Finish: Under 30 minutes

1 small onion, grated
1½ pounds ground white meat chicken
1 egg

1 teaspoon kosher salt

¼ teaspoon freshly ground black pepper

1 teaspoon garlic powder

1 cup matzo meal or plain bread crumbs, plus extra for dredging

1 to 1½ cups vegetable oil

Grate the onion directly into a bowl, using the small or medium hole of a box grater. Add the chicken, egg, salt, pepper, and garlic powder. Using your hands, gently mix the ingredients together. Begin adding the matzo meal, until the ground chicken is no longer wet and barely sticks to your hands.

Heat ¼ inch of oil in a large skillet. Take a tablespoon of the croquette mixture for a test drive. Because you cannot check the seasonings in a raw chicken mixture, you should always fry up a little piece to be sure the seasonings are correct. If not, adjust before forming the patties. To form the croquettes, you'll need a bowl of cold water or nonstick cooking spray to coat your hands so the chicken mixture doesn't stick to them, and a flat plate with matzo meal or bread crumbs for dredging.

When the oil is shimmering, and you've tested for seasoning, begin forming the chicken into patties about 3 inches long by 2 inches wide, and about ½ inch thick. Dip the flat sides in the matzo meal or bread crumbs (for added crunch) and place in the skillet. Fry over medium heat, until golden brown, about 5 minutes per side. By the time you have all twelve in the pan, you should be ready to begin flipping the first. They are done when both sides are crusty and golden brown. Cut into one to be sure they are cooked through. Drain briefly on a paper towel–lined plate and serve hot or cold.

Chicken and Scallion Wontons
. . . with soy dipping sauce

Sometimes, it's fun to take the easy breezy way. These delicious little bites can be made with store-bought wonton wrappers. A short fry in the skillet and a dip in a soy-based pool and you've got a quick and easy small bite.

BEHIND THE COUNTER:
Have your butcher medium
grind white meat chicken.
Alternate cuts: here's the
chance to try a variety of
ground meats, from turkey
(=$) to lamb or veal (+$).

MAKES 20 TO 24 PIECES

Start to Finish: Under 30 minutes

For the filling

1 pound ground white meat chicken

2 scallions, white and green parts, minced

4 garlic cloves, grated (about 2 tablespoons)

1 teaspoon kosher salt

1 tablespoon chili-garlic sauce

1 egg, lightly beaten

For the dipping sauce

1/4 cup rice wine vinegar

Juice of 1/2 lemon

1/4 cup canola or vegetable oil

1 scallion, white and green parts, minced

1/4 cup low-sodium soy sauce

1/2 teaspoon grated fresh ginger

1 teaspoon honey

For the wontons

1 package wonton wrappers

1 egg, beaten with 1 tablespoon of water

Use your hands to gently but thoroughly combine all the filling ingredients in a small bowl. In a separate bowl, stir together all the dipping sauce ingredients and reserve. Have the wonton wrappers standing by.

Drop a teaspoon of the chicken mixture into the center of a wrapper. Dip a finger in the egg wash and run it along the border of the wrapper. Press the wrapper closed like a triangle, firmly sealing the edges. If using round wrappers, fold in half to form a half moon.

Heat 2 tablespoons of oil in a skillet, and fry a batch of the wontons until lightly browned, over medium heat; it should take just a minute or two. Pour 1/2 cup of water into the skillet, cover, and cook over medium heat for 5 minutes; this will cook the filling through. Remove the cover and cook an additional 1 to 2 minutes so the wontons become crisp. The filled wontons can be steamed instead of fried. If you have a bamboo steamer, follow the directions it came with. If you do not have a bamboo steamer, lightly oil a metal steamer basket that sits in a slightly larger saucepan. Fill the saucepan with a little water, being sure it does not touch the steamer basket. Heat the water until it reaches a strong simmer. Place about 5 wontons in the basket, cover, and steam for about 10 minutes, or until the wrappers are soft and translucent and the chicken has completely cooked through. Follow the procedure you choose for all the wontons. Serve with dipping sauce.

Feedback

For an Asian flavor variation, add 1 teaspoon grated fresh ginger, 1 tablespoon chopped cilantro or parsley, and 1 tablespoon grated lemongrass or lemon peel. If you add 1 cup of Panko bread crumbs to the ground chicken, you have the basis for a terrific mini meatball to float in soup broth. The wontons are essentially *kreplach*—Jewish dumplings—which can be filled and added to soup in place of noodles. If you do, don't fry the wontons; they'll cook in the soup, and be ready after about 8 minutes, at which time they'll float to the top.

Chicken Liver Pâté
. . . served on crostini 3 ways

Here's the offal truth. Offal is gleaned from the internal organs of an animal or are those pieces that just fall off during the butchering process. But make no pronunciation mistake, there is nothing awful about them. One of offal's best leading lights is chicken liver, the beloved centerpiece for chopped liver. This pâté is dressed-up chopped liver, with just a few extra ingredients and pulses in the processor. Not since Lucy and Ethel has there been as great a partnership as chicken fat and chicken livers, so splurge, and use a little shmaltz for the smoothest flavor and texture.

MAKES 2 CUPS PÂTÉ

Start to Finish: Under 30 minutes to prepare; plus time to chill

For the pâté
4 tablespoons chicken fat (duck fat or olive oil can substitute)

SIDE NOTE: Quince is a great partner for pâté. You can buy it as a jelly or a thickened, gelled paste called *membrillo*. The fruit, which resembles a prickly pear, is tart on its own, but when processed with sugar and other ingredients develops a mellow flavor. Spread the toast with the quince and then top with a layer of pâté. A salty garnish—maybe a small cornichon or olive—completes the crostini.

For a nod to the classic deli sandwich of pastrami and chopped liver, try taking a small dollop of Russian dressing (a mixture of mayo, ketchup, salt, and pepper) and spreading it on the crostini. Spread with a layer of pâté and top with a thin slice of pastrami. A little piece of chopped sour pickle rounds out the bite.

The seasonal juiciness of cantaloupe is also delicious when paired with this pâté. Use a vegetable peeler to make thin ribbons of peeled cantaloupe. Drizzle a little honey on the crostini, then spread the layer of pâté. Top with the cantaloupe ribbon and a small strawberry slice for a refreshing and summery note.

---

1 pound chicken livers, rinsed and cleaned of any discolored membranes, fibers, fatty deposits, or blood spots, and patted dry

1 medium onion, diced (about 1 cup)

2 large shallots, sliced

1 teaspoon chopped fresh thyme or 1/3 teaspoon dried thyme

1 tablespoon chopped fresh flat-leaf parsley

1 teaspoon kosher salt

1/2 teaspoon freshly ground black pepper

2 tablespoons Madeira or dry sherry

1 baguette

To prepare the pâté: **Heat the chicken fat in a skillet** until shimmering and cook the livers over medium heat until they are pink inside, about 5 minutes. Cover the skillet and cook several minutes longer so the livers cook through. Remove with a slotted spoon. (If you need to *kasher* the livers, join us at the next step.) Wipe out the pan and add a little more fat and cook the onions, stirring, over medium heat, about 5 minutes. Add the shallots and continue cooking until the onions and shallots are golden brown, about 10 minutes longer; reduce the heat if the shallots begin to brown too quickly. To the skillet add the thyme, parsley, salt, pepper, and Madeira. Toss the livers back into the pan and cook for several minutes. Let the mixture cool for a few minutes and then spoon it into the bowl of a food processor fitted with the metal blade. Process until smooth and creamy, adding more fat if needed. Spoon into a bowl and chill. The pâté is ready for a crisp cracker or slice of crostini.

To prepare crostini: Simply cut the baguette into slices, on the diagonal, about 1/4 inch thick. Toast the baguette slices on both sides under a broiler. Keep a watchful eye: they burn quickly. When just lightly brown on each side, remove the crostini and set aside. You can certainly stop here and spread the pâté on the toasted crostini. However, why not step it up one more level? See Side Note.

Feedback

For more traditional chopped liver, you can eliminate the Madeira or sherry, as well as the shallots, thyme, and parsley. Pulse the liver in a food processor along with 2 hard-boiled eggs that have been quartered. You can add a touch more fat or some mayonnaise to help smooth out the texture. Season to taste with salt and pepper and chill.

TURKEY

When you want to feed a large group at a reasonable cost, your best choice is the underrated and once-a-year appreciated turkey. A whole turkey can top 25 pounds and has a perfect balance of white and dark meat. "Bonus" meat is a given and a must, so when preparing a whole bird estimate 1½ pounds of turkey per person. Turkey breast is terrific to stuff, and yields wonderful cutlets, while drumsticks and wings can be barbecued or braised. Don't overlook ground turkey, which your butcher will grind, for delicious chili, spicy sausages, moist meat loaf, or turkey burgers.

Turkey with Sauerkraut

This Alsatian specialty, known in France as *dinde braisée* with *choucroute*, makes the most of its two leading players: turkey and sauerkraut. In true Alsatian cooking *choucroute* (French for sauerkraut) is a popular ingredient especially when braised with meat or poultry. The sauerkraut flavor significantly mellows in this preparation and serves as a backdrop lending a sweet note. I based this recipe on one from my friend Arlette Baker, who as a child lived near Paris and still cherishes the cooking traditions of her childhood.

SERVES 4

Start to Finish: Under 1½ hours

> 7 tablespoons vegetable oil
> 2 to 3 pounds of turkey (wing, thigh, leg, breast, or a combination)
> 2 medium onions, quartered
> 1 pound canned or packaged sauerkraut, washed and drained
> ½ cup cognac or brandy
> 1 carrot, peeled and diced (about ½ cup)
> Kosher salt and freshly ground black pepper

Heat 5 tablespoons of oil in a braising pot, and cook the turkey and onions over medium heat for 20 minutes or until both are nicely browned. (If cooking wings, separate at the joint for faster cooking and easier presentation.) In a separate skillet, lightly brown the sauerkraut in the remaining 2 tablespoons of oil. When the turkey and onions are brown, stir in the cognac, carrots, and sautéed sauerkraut. Pour in 2 cups of water and season with salt and pepper. Cover and cook on the stovetop over medium-low heat for 1 hour, or until the turkey is fork-tender and the sauerkraut is nicely browned.

Oven-Barbecued Turkey

This homemade barbecue sauce has a sweet, gentle heat that lightly dances on your tongue and bakes into the turkey as it slowly roasts in the oven. If you want the heat to tap dance on your tongue, reduce the amount of V8 and increase the amount of chili-garlic sauce.

BEHIND THE COUNTER: You can use any turkey parts you like, or a whole breast or even a whole turkey (if you use a whole turkey, double the sauce). Alternate cuts: chicken parts, (–$) or beef or veal ribs (+$).

SERVES 4

Start to Finish: 2 hours to marinate; under 2 hours to bake. You can eliminate marinating if time is crunching.

> *For the sauce*
> ½ cup ketchup
> ¼ cup chili-garlic sauce
> ½ cup V8 vegetable juice

¼ cup vegetable oil

¼ cup apple cider vinegar

1½ tablespoons Worcestershire sauce

1 tablespoon honey

¼ teaspoon dried oregano

½ teaspoon kosher salt

4 to 5 pounds turkey drumsticks, thighs, wings, or a whole breast
    (or a combination of your favorite parts)

In a small saucepan, combine all the sauce ingredients, and cook, stirring, over low heat, uncovered, about 15 minutes, until the sauce has thickened enough to coat the back of a spoon. Let the sauce cool.

Place the turkey parts in a shallow roasting pan and pour three-quarters of the barbecue sauce over the turkey, turning the pieces so they are coated on all sides. Reserve the remaining sauce to serve on the side. If time allows, cover the turkey and let it marinate in the fridge for about 2 hours. Although the marinade will not fully permeate the skin, it will help flavor the meat. When ready to bake, **preheat the oven to 325 degrees** and remove the turkey from the fridge. Place the turkey in a shallow baking pan, deep enough to catch the drippings without spilling over

Bake in the preheated oven for 30 minutes. Turn the pieces over so the undersides have a chance to brown, basting the turkey parts with the collected drippings each time you turn, and adding water to the pan if the sauce begins to dry out. Continue baking for another 30 minutes, then turn and baste the turkey parts again. Continue to bake until an instant-read thermometer inserted into the thickest part of the dark meat or center of the breast registers 160 to 165 degrees, about 30 minutes longer. Remove the turkey to a waiting plate and tent loosely with aluminum foil. Use a gravy separator to help remove the fat from the drippings. If you don't have a gravy separator, you can skim the fat using the back of a large spoon, or lightly swipe a paper towel across the surface of the gravy. In a small saucepan, heat the defatted drippings with the reserved sauce, until the drippings and sauce become fully combined and the sauce has heated through. Serve with the sauce on the side.

Turkey Roulade
...with savory stuffing

BEHIND THE COUNTER: Have
your butcher de-bone and
butterfly a whole turkey breast.
Ask your butcher to save the skin
from the breast; you will use that
to wrap the turkey for added
moistness. Alternate cuts: breast
of veal, trimmed and boned, with
a pocket for stuffing (+$).

A roulade is a thin cut of meat stuffed and rolled. When the roulade is sliced, you get that wonderfully visual pinwheel effect. This is an easy way to enjoy turkey and stuffing all year long.

SERVES 4 TO 6

Start to Finish: Under 2½ hours

For the stuffing

2 tablespoons olive oil

2 leeks, white and light green parts, thoroughly rinsed, dried,
      and chopped (about 2 cups)

¾ pound white mushrooms, chopped

1 teaspoon chopped fresh thyme leaves or ⅓ teaspoon dried thyme

1 teaspoon chopped fresh sage or ⅓ teaspoon dried ground sage

1 teaspoon chopped fresh rosemary leaves or ⅓ teaspoon dried rosemary

1 tablespoon chopped fresh flat-leaf parsley

¼ cup white wine

Kosher salt and freshly ground black pepper

¾ loaf thinly sliced white bread (Pepperidge Farm works well)

1 egg, lightly beaten

½ cup chicken stock

For the turkey

1 (2½- to 3-pound) turkey breast, de-boned and butterflied

1 teaspoon kosher salt

½ teaspoon freshly ground black pepper

Canola or vegetable oil

1 to 2 cups chicken stock

1 (15-ounce) can tomato sauce

Preheat the oven to 325 degrees and place a rack in a roasting pan. To prepare the stuffing, heat the olive oil in a large skillet, add the leeks and cook over medium heat, stirring occasionally, until they just begin to brown, about 5 minutes. Add the mushrooms to the pan, cover, and cook over medium-low heat for about 5 minutes, just until the mushrooms begin to soften and give off their juice. Stir in the thyme, sage, rosemary, parsley, and wine. Cover the skillet and simmer for about 15 minutes. Season to taste with salt and pepper, remove from the heat, and let come to room temperature.

While the vegetables cool, tear the bread, crust and all, into pieces about the size of a crouton, and place in a medium bowl. Pour the beaten egg and stock into the bowl and mash everything together using clean hands. Add the vegetables and thoroughly combine with your hands or a large spoon.

To prepare the turkey, season both sides with the salt and pepper. Lay the turkey flat and spread a $1/2$-inch layer of stuffing over it, leaving about 1 inch from edges without stuffing. Any remaining stuffing can be baked in a separate casserole while the turkey roasts. Beginning at the shorter end, roll the turkey up into a tight package. Lay the skin on top of the turkey. It might not cover it all, so center it the best you can. Using kitchen twine, or reusable cooking bands, tie the turkey into a roll, securing it every 2 inches. Sprinkle the outside of the turkey roulade with a little more salt and pepper.

Coat the bottom of a skillet with oil, add the roulade, and brown on all sides, about 10 minutes. Place the roulade, fat side down, on the rack set in the roasting pan. Pour 1 cup of chicken stock into the bottom of the pan and roast the roulade at 325 degrees for 1 hour, basting every 30 minutes with the collected drippings, and adding more stock or water if needed.

After 1 hour, turn the roulade, fat side up, add 1 cup of the tomato sauce to the pan and baste the turkey again. At this time, bake any remaining stuffing in a lightly oiled baking dish while the turkey finishes roasting. The turkey is done when an instant-read thermometer inserted into the center to test both the meat and stuffing reads 160 to 165 degrees, about 45 minutes longer. Remove the roulade from the oven, cover loosely with aluminum foil, and let it rest for at least 15 minutes. Pour the remaining tomato sauce into the roasting pan, heat on the stovetop, and serve alongside the turkey.

Country-Style Turkey Meat Loaf

How do you pack rustic flavor in a one-hour meat loaf? Simple. Combine a medley of sautéed vegetables with ground white meat turkey and glaze it with a surprising cranberry-chili sauce. The result is a moist and delicious turkey meat loaf with a nod to Thanksgiving. If you don't love the taste of cranberry, substitute tomato sauce.

BEHIND THE COUNTER: Ask your butcher to grind white meat turkey. Alternate cuts: ground chicken, veal (=$), or beef (-$).

SIDE NOTE: Thanksgiving dinner wouldn't be complete without apple cider. In quinoa with apple cider braised squash and prunes, it is used to braise the vegetables and flavor the quinoa (page 195).

SERVES 6

Start to Finish: Under 1½ hours

3 tablespoons olive oil

1 red bell pepper, cored, seeded and finely chopped (about ¾ cup)

1 green bell pepper, cored, seeded, and finely chopped (about ¾ cup)

1 medium onion, chopped (about ¾ cup)

2 garlic cloves, minced (about 1 tablespoon)

Pinch of crushed red pepper flakes

1 teaspoon kosher salt

¼ teaspoon freshly ground black pepper

1 egg

2 tablespoons Worcestershire sauce

¼ cup Heinz Chili Sauce (you can substitute ketchup)

2 pounds ground turkey

½ to ¾ cup Italian-style bread crumbs

For the glaze

½ cup Heinz Chili Sauce

½ cup cranberry sauce

½ cup chicken stock, if you want extra sauce

Preheat the oven to 350 degrees. Line a baking dish with aluminum foil (this makes cleanup easier). Heat the olive oil in a large skillet, add the peppers, onions, garlic, and red pepper flakes and cook over medium heat, stirring occasionally, until they are soft and just beginning to brown, about 10 minutes. Season with the salt and pepper and set aside to cool.

While the veggies sit, prepare the glaze by combining the chili sauce with the cranberry sauce in a small saucepan. Stir the mixture over low heat, until the two ingredients are well combined. Set aside.

Add the egg, Worcestershire sauce, chili sauce, turkey, and ½ cup of bread crumbs to the cooled vegetables. Gently work the ingredients with clean hands or a wooden spoon to combine, trying not to over-mix the turkey as it will make the meat loaf tough when it bakes. If the mixture is very sticky, add the remaining ¼ cup of bread crumbs.

Place the turkey mixture into the prepared baking dish and form into a football-shaped loaf about 12 inches long and 2 inches high. Brush the top of the loaf with the chili-cranberry glaze. Bake in the pre-heated oven for 20 minutes. Baste with the glaze and continue cooking for 40 minutes, basting one more time halfway through, until an instant-read thermometer inserted in the thickest spot registers 160 degrees. When done, let rest covered loosely with foil. While the meat loaf rests, create a sauce by combining the remaining glaze with the chicken stock. To serve, spoon the sauce over the sliced meat loaf.

Feedback

This meat loaf mixture makes great turkey burgers (about 6) that can be served with a honey-mustard sauce made of ¼ cup honey, ¼ cup Dijon mustard, and 2 tablespoons white vinegar. They can also be transformed into Swedish-style meatballs (about 2 dozen) and cooked in the chili-cranberry sauce.

Turkey Chili

Rich and lean, not a bad combination. It's a great description of ground turkey, making it a natural choice for chili. The seasoning blend provides the punch, with a great array of mild to hot spices. Cumin embodies the essence of chili while the kickier spices like cayenne and chipotle provide the heat.

BEHIND THE COUNTER: Have your butcher grind white meat turkey. Alternate cuts: ground beef (+$), ground bison (+$), or ground chicken (–$).

SERVES 8
Start to Finish: Under 1½ hours

For the chili seasoning blend
2 teaspoons chili powder
1½ teaspoons ground cumin

SIDE NOTE: Homemade guaca-mole (page 220) or salsa (page 217) make terrific toppings for the chili.

2 teaspoons sweet or hot Hungarian paprika
¼ teaspoon freshly ground black pepper
½ teaspoon cayenne pepper
1 teaspoon garlic powder
2 teaspoons kosher salt
1 teaspoon dried oregano

For the chili
2 tablespoons vegetable oil
1 medium onion, chopped (about ¾ cup)
1 red bell pepper, cored, seeded, and finely diced (about ¾ cup), optional
1 green bell pepper, cored, seeded, and finely diced (about ¾ cup), optional
1 to 1½ pounds ground white meat turkey
3 garlic cloves, finely minced
1 (28-ounce) can chopped tomatoes, drained
1 (4-ounce) can tomato sauce
2 canned chipotle chiles in adobo sauce, seeded and minced, plus 2 teaspoons of the adobo sauce from the can
1 (15.5-ounce) can vegetarian baked beans
1 (15.5-ounce) can cannellini beans, drained and rinsed
Kosher salt and freshly ground black pepper

In a small bowl, use a spoon to combine the chili seasonings, then set aside. Heat the oil in a large skillet, add the onions and peppers, and cook, stirring occasionally, over medium heat until soft, about 10 minutes. Raise the heat to medium-high and add the ground turkey and garlic. Sear the meat until it is no longer pink, breaking up any large pieces with the back of a spoon or a fork. When the meat is cooked through, after about 10 minutes, pour off most of the fat and add the tomatoes, tomato sauce, chipotle chiles, and adobo sauce. Stir in the chili seasoning blend and bring to a boil. Reduce the heat to low and cook for 20 minutes. Add the beans, cover, and simmer until the flavors have melded, about 30 minutes longer. Season to taste with salt and pepper.

NP

For non-pareve presentation, add a dollop of sour cream to each bowl and sprinkle with shredded cheese right before serving.

Turkey Sausage

. . . with orecchiette pasta and broccoli rabe

Ground turkey combines with an unusual blend of spices and herbs to create turkey sausage, a terrific add-in for pasta and a wonderful complement to the slightly bitter broccoli rabe. Orecchiette pasta—those little ear-shaped noodles—are the classic choice for this dish, as they perfectly cradle the garlic-infused, red pepper-punched anchovy-laced sauce.

BEHIND THE COUNTER: Ask your butcher for spicy Italian turkey sausage, the type that crumbles works best in this preparation. Alternate cuts: chicken, beef, or lamb sausage (=$).

SERVES 6

Start to Finish: Under 30 minutes

> 1 pound broccoli rabe, washed and thick stems trimmed
> 12 ounces orecchiette pasta, 1 cup of the pasta
>   cooking water reserved
> ¼ cup olive oil
> 1 pound turkey sausage, casings removed, crumbled
> 4 garlic cloves, sliced
> Pinch of crushed red pepper flakes
> 1 teaspoon anchovy paste
> Kosher salt and freshly ground black pepper
> Basil leaves for garnish

Bring a large pot of heavily salted water to a rapid boil (taste the water: it should really taste like the ocean). Blanch the broccoli rabe for 3 to 4 minutes. Remove with a spider or slotted spoon and plunge into an ice bath to stop the cooking process and preserve the bright green color. When cool enough to handle, drain well, then chop the leaves and stems; set aside. In the same boiling water, cook the pasta according to the package directions, about 10 minutes. Set the pasta aside.

Heat 1 tablespoon of the oil in a large skillet, add the sausage, and cook over medium-high heat until no longer pink, about 5 minutes. Remove with a slotted spoon and set aside. Add the remaining oil, garlic, red pepper flakes, and anchovy paste, reduce the heat to low, and let the mixture cook slowly. You do not want to brown the garlic, you just want to infuse the oil with flavor. Add the pasta, sausage, and broccoli rabe. Toss all the ingredients together and begin adding the reserved pasta water as needed to create a smooth sauce. Season with salt and pepper, garnish with the basil, and serve.

Feedback

For an added layer of flavor, stir in ½ cup of freshly made pesto (see page 95) right before serving. Other add-ins could include sun-dried tomatoes, artichoke hearts, and roasted red peppers.

Grilled Turkey Paillard
. . . topped with haricots verts and tomato salad

Paillards are thin cutlets that are flash-grilled and make a simple canvas for so many preparations. Because we don't want to serve the cutlets naked on the plate, this version includes a shallot tarragon vinaigrette and a crisp haricots verts and tomato salad. It's a great way to dress up a humble cut.

BEHIND THE COUNTER: Have your butcher cut turkey cutlets from the breast, about ½ to ¼ inch thick. Too thin and they'll dry out; too thick and they won't cook through quickly. Alternate cuts: chicken (=$) or veal cutlets (+$).

SERVES 4

Start to Finish: Under 1 hour to marinate; under 15 minutes to prepare

For the shallot tarragon vinaigrette
2 large shallots, sliced (about 1 cup)
⅔ cup vegetable oil
2 teaspoons minced fresh thyme leaves or ½ teaspoon dried thyme
2 tablespoons minced fresh tarragon leaves
Juice of 1 lemon
3 tablespoons red wine vinegar
1 tablespoon Dijon mustard
Kosher salt and freshly ground black pepper
4 (5- to 6-ounce) turkey cutlets

For the salad
¾ pound haricots verts, ends trimmed (If you can't get these small, thin haricots verts, you can substitute thin asparagus stalks or small young green beans; avoid those that are plump and beany.)
1 tablespoon olive oil

¾ pound grape or cherry tomatoes

3 scallions, white and green parts, sliced (reserve a handful to sprinkle on
    top of the finished dish)

Zest of ½ lemon

In a small saucepan, cook the shallots in the oil over low heat until soft but not browned, about 20 minutes. Remove from the heat and add the thyme, tarragon, lemon juice, red wine vinegar, Dijon mustard, salt and pepper to taste. Using an immersion blender, puree the dressing. It will not be perfectly smooth; there should be bits of shallot throughout. Reserve half the dressing to marinate the turkey and half to dress the bean and tomato salad.

Pound the cutlets with a mallet in a open plastic bag or between 2 pieces of plastic wrap, ½ inch to ¼ inch thick. Place them in a resealable plastic bag and marinate in the fridge for 1 hour. While the cutlets marinate, prepare the salad. Blanch the haricots verts in salted, rapidly boiling water for just a minute or two. Drain and plunge them into an ice water bath to stop the cooking process. Drain again and set aside.

Heat the oil in a skillet and sear the tomatoes and scallions over medium heat, until the tomato skins begin to develop an orange color and look as if they are going to burst. Dry the haricots verts and add them to the skillet. Cook just until the beans are heated through, about 2 to 3 minutes, then spoon everything into a bowl and set aside.

Remove the cutlets from the fridge and heat the grill or a stovetop grill pan. Dry the cutlets, then grill over medium-high heat for 2 to 3 minutes per side or until they are lightly charred and cooked through. Plate the cutlets with the salad on top, drizzle both with dressing, and garnish with the remaining chopped scallions and refreshing lemon zest.

DUCK

If chicken is sneakers, then duck is a pair of high heels: same family but way sexier. The dark meat is rich and full of woodsy flavor. The fatty skin and layer underneath, which helps keep the duck afloat, renders pure liquid gold duck fat. Once you fry potatoes in that sumptuous oil, you will never look at peanut oil the same way again. A typical duck usually reaches 4 to 5 pounds, but because there is not much meat on those bones, one duck is perfect for two people. Duck legs and breasts offer pan searing and braising options and make great "bonus" meat to elevate a composed salad or use as a savory filling for wontons (page 145).

Roast Duck
. . . with cherry port sauce

The key to great duck is crispy skin and a simple technique that allows the duck flavor to shine. The sweet tart taste of the fast and easy dried-cherry and port reduction perfectly balances the rich taste of the duck, but the duck can stand alone if you choose to go without the sauce. If your budget and oven allow, roast two birds to guarantee "bonus" duck for delicious breast of duck salad (page 165).

SERVES 2 (PLUS ½ TO 1- PINT DUCK FAT)
Start to Finish: Under 2 hours

For the duck

1 (5- to 6-pound) duck, dried inside and out

Kosher salt and freshly ground coarse black pepper

1 apple, halved (half for the duck, half for the sauce)

1 orange, halved (half for the duck, half for the sauce)

For the cherry port sauce

Remaining ½ apple, peeled and diced

4 tablespoons sugar

Remaining ½ orange, juiced (about ¼ cup)

1 piece star anise

4 tablespoons apple cider vinegar

¾ cup dried cherries

1 cup port

2 teaspoons honey

Pinch of ground cinnamon

Preheat the oven to 450 degrees. To help crisp the skin, the duck must render its fat while roasting: this allows the underlying layer of fat to melt away and it creates delectable duck fat. Scoring, or making deep slits in the duck's skin, will help accomplish both. An easy way to score the outer skin *without* piercing the meat is to pinch the fat between your fingers and run a sharp, small knife into the pinched portion of the skin, making 1-inch slits. Follow this procedure to score the entire duck, making slits in any area that has excess fat, especially the breast.

Season the duck inside and out with salt and ground black pepper. Place half the apple and half the orange in the cavity. It is not necessary to truss the bird, but tuck the wings under the back so they don't burn. Roast in the preheated oven, breast side up, on a rack placed in a roasting pan, for 30 minutes. Take the roasting pan out of the oven and close the oven door. Every time you baste you lose precious heat, about 25 degrees, so you will want to baste and siphon with your roasting pan placed on your stovetop. Be mindful that the pan and especially the duck fat will be very hot. Have a small heat-resistant bowl ready to deposit the fat that you will siphon off from the bottom of the roasting pan. Drizzle a little of the fat over the top of the duck and return the roasting pan to the oven for an additional 30 minutes. After 30 minutes take the roasting pan from the oven, siphon off the fat and baste the bird with just a little of that fat. **Reduce the oven temperature to 400 degrees** and continue roasting an additional 30 minutes or until the duck skin is crisp and a deep brown. You can test for doneness by inserting an instant-read thermometer into the thigh area; it should read about 160 degrees for medium pink.

While the duck finishes roasting, prepare the cherry port sauce. Combine all the ingredients in a saucepan and bring to a boil. Reduce the heat, cover, and simmer for 15 minutes. Remove the star anise.

Remove the duck from the oven, and place on a serving plate. Remove all but 2 tablespoons of the collected duck fat, add it to what you've already collected, and refrigerate or freeze for later use. The fat can hold for months in the fridge or freezer. Drizzle one-fourth of the cherry sauce over the duck. Cover the duck with aluminum foil. Place the roasting pan directly on the stove over low heat and pour the remaining cherry sauce into the roasting pan, stirring it into the pan drippings and being sure to scrape up any brown bits that collected in the bottom of the pan.

Duck is not easy to carve; the frame is different from a chicken or turkey. For most people, the breast is the prize, along with the crispy fat. The duck legs are also delicious and should be removed at the joint. I would suggest you remove the breast as a whole, rather than trying to carve slices from the frame. Plate the duck with a leg and one half of the breast with a drizzle of sauce over the breast meat. If you have additional crispy fat, shred that with a sharp knife and serve alongside the meat. Drizzle the sauce over each duck portion just before serving.

Feedback

Port is a sweet, fortified red wine from the Douro Valley in Portugal. Just as the only true champagne comes from French champagne grapes, the only authentic port comes from Portugal. If you cannot locate port at your local wine store, you can substitute similar wines from other regions, such as Madeira, which comes from an island off the coast of Africa; Marsala, a Sicilian fortified wine; or sherry, Spain's answer to port.

Pan-Seared Duck Breasts
. . . with fig, apricot, and Madeira sauce

BEHIND THE COUNTER:
Have your butcher prepare the
duck breasts with the bone
removed but skin on. Alternate cut: frenched chicken
breasts (–$).

The gamy flavor of the duck pairs perfectly with the sweet taste of the
figs and apricots to create a sinfully simple and delicious dish. You
could actually forgo the sauce and spoon some of the collected fat over
the sliced breasts and be very happy, but why stop at very happy when
you can be full-out delirious.

SERVES 4

Start to Finish: Under 30 minutes

> 10 dried Mission figs, stems removed
> 10 dried Turkish apricots
> 2 cups chicken stock
> 3 tablespoons Madeira wine or dry sherry
> Several sprigs thyme
> 1 sprig rosemary
> 4 (½- to ¾- pound) duck breasts
> Kosher salt and freshly ground black pepper

In a medium saucepan, combine the figs, apricots, and stock. Bring to
a boil, then reduce the heat and simmer, covered, for about 15 minutes
or until the sauce has thickened. Remove the fruit from the sauce with
a slotted spoon, chop into small pieces, and set aside. To the pot of
stock, add the Madeira, thyme, and rosemary, and cook, uncovered,
over low heat for 10 minutes.

While the sauce cooks, prepare the duck breasts by patting the meat
dry and then scoring the fat in a cross-hatch pattern, being careful not
to pierce the meat. You will be able to gauge how deep you can make
the slits by looking at the two layers of fat that you need to pierce before
touching the actual meat on the breast. Sprinkle the duck with kosher
salt and pepper and let them rest for a few minutes on a paper towel
while your pan heats to be sure they are nice and dry.

Heat a grill pan or cast-iron skillet on the stove until sizzling hot,
and lay the breasts skin side down in the pan. Cook over medium heat,
until the skin is nicely browned, 5 to 7 minutes. Using a turkey baster
or large spoon, remove the excess duck fat as it collects in the pan. Reserve the fat. Turn the breasts over and cook for 3 to 5 minutes on the

second side until the meat color changes from red to medium brown. Turn them once more, skin side down, and cook for just a couple of minutes to crisp up the skin. For rare, remove the breasts to rest, covered loosely with foil, for at least 5 minutes. For medium, continue to cook the breasts until desired doneness, or pop the pan into a preheated 350 degrees oven for 5 to 10 minutes.

Heat the sauce in a small saucepan. It should be slightly syrupy. If you want it thicker, make a slurry by mixing 1 teaspoon of cornstarch with 2 teaspoons of cold water, stir back into the pan, bring to a boil, and repeat until desired consistency. Add the reserved fruit and heat through. You can serve the breasts whole or slice on the diagonal with the sauce spooned over the meat.

Feedback

Not only is it delicious, but duck fat is actually healthful, with properties similar to olive oil. Because it is nondairy, it makes a great substitute for the taste and texture of butter. Potatoes are especially delicious when fried or mashed with duck fat. The mild, rustic goodness of the fat has a high smoking point, and infuses fried food with its rich flavor.

Breast of Duck Salad
. . . with raspberries and candied walnuts

This refreshing salad is perfect for any "bonus" duck you might be lucky enough to have. A sprinkling of candied walnuts and the addition of fresh raspberries give this salad a sweet yet tart taste. If you can, shred or slice the duck while it's still warm, trimming the excess fat. If you cannot find beautiful red raspberries, substitute sliced strawberries, orange segments, or grapes.

SERVES 6
Start to Finish: Under 30 minutes

> *For the walnuts*
> 1 cup walnut halves
> 1 tablespoon light corn syrup

1 tablespoon honey
1 tablespoon maple syrup
¼ teaspoon salt
Pinch of cayenne pepper
1 tablespoon brown sugar

For the champagne vinaigrette
¼ cup champagne vinegar
½ teaspoon kosher salt
1 tablespoon chopped fresh soft herbs, such as chervil, tarragon, or parsley
Freshly ground black pepper
1 tablespoon water
Juice of 1 orange (about 2 to 3 tablespoons)
1 shallot, minced (about 1 tablespoon)
¼ cup walnut oil
2 tablespoons canola oil

For the salad
6 cups loosely packed baby spinach leaves
1 medium red onion, thinly sliced
1 pint raspberries
2 cups sliced or shredded "bonus" duck (turkey or chicken can be substituted.)

Preheat the oven to 325 degrees and spray a small, rimmed baking sheet with a nonstick cooking spray. Toss the walnuts with the corn syrup, honey, and maple syrup. When the walnuts are completely coated, spread them out on a plate and sprinkle them with the salt, pepper, and brown sugar. Spread them out evenly on the prepared baking sheet. Bake in the preheated oven for 7 to 8 minutes. Using a spoon, toss the walnuts on the baking sheet, then continue to bake for another 5 to 7 minutes. Remove from the oven and cool.

Put all the vinaigrette ingredients except the oils into a bowl and whisk to combine. Slowly whisk in the walnut oil, and then the canola oil. To build the salad, toss the spinach, red onions, and raspberries with the vinaigrette. Divide the salad equally among individual salad plates and lay the sliced or shredded duck on top of the salad, and sprinkle each serving with the cooled candied walnuts. Pass any extra vinaigrette to top the duck.

SOUP AND STOCK

Nothing warms, soothes, or nourishes like a hearty bowl of steaming soup. If you did nothing more than take a pot of cold water and add a chicken to that pot, you would have a wholesome dish. This section builds on good homemade stock and features delicious soups brimming with chunks of meat or ribbons of chicken, sure to fill your house with an intoxicating aroma and your belly with a satisfying one-bowl meal.

Homemade Stock

Many recipes in this book rely on good stock, and while you can buy good-quality boxed or canned stock or broth, it's easy and you will always get a better result if you make your own. Here are a few things to consider when making chicken or beef stock.

TO MAKE STOCK

1. To lock in flavor, always begin with cold water.

2. Stockpile odds and ends, bones and meat from chicken, turkey, veal, and beef to enrich the stock.

3. Use a stockpot, which, Norman Kornbleuth explains, is specifically designed with equal height and diameter to mitigate evaporation. A 12- or 16-quart pot will allow you to make a big batch.

4. The meat and bones are the stars, so don't go overboard with aromatics.

5. Skim the surface of the soup to remove any scum that collects. There will be more at the start, less as it simmers.

6. Don't salt the stock until ready to use. As the stock concentrates and intensifies, so will any salt in the broth.

7. Cook your stock low and slow. One of Chef David's most ardent tips is "nothing should boil in your kitchen, except water." That is particularly true when preparing stock. When you boil stock, the fat and impurities cook into and taint the soup. A stock or soup cooked at a low simmer builds the most flavor. Read a book, watch a movie, learn bridge, but don't take that stock off the stove until it has cooked at least 4 hours.

8. Once the stock is done, strain it using a fine-mesh sieve or a standard strainer lined with cheesecloth or a coffee filter, pressing on the solids to extract all their goodness.

9. Don't invite bacteria to the party by leaving the stock out to slowly cool. Instead, place the pot in a sink filled with cold water to bring down the temperature quickly so you can ladle it into containers and get it in the fridge or freezer.

10. If using the stock immediately, run a paper towel across the top to remove the fat that rises to the surface. Otherwise, refrigerate the stock until ready to use, and then remove any solidified fat. The stock will hold about 3 days in the fridge or up to a week if you boil it every few days. If you are freezing the stock, the fat will serve as an added seal from freezer burn, you can scrape it off before using. The stock can hold up to 3 months in your freezer.

Chicken Stock

My father says there are two types of chicken broth: one that favors the chicken, and one that favors the broth. Stock definitely favors the broth: when it's done, the chicken will have sacrificed itself for your rich, chickeny stock that can be used as the foundation for other soups and recipes.

MAKES ABOUT 5 QUARTS

Start to Finish: Under 15 minutes to prep; at least 4 hours to cook

½ pound giblets
1 pound chicken wings
4 to 5 pounds chicken bones (frame, backbone, neck)
   or 1 (4 - to 5-pound) pullet or "soup chicken," cut into 8 pieces,
   with ½ pound giblets and 1 pound wings
3 carrots, rinsed, ends trimmed
2 large celery stalks with their leaves, washed and cut into pieces
½ pound yellow onions, halved, stem and root removed,
   skins left on
4 unpeeled garlic cloves, smashed
2 bay leaves
12 whole black peppercorns
12 sprigs flat-leaf parsley
12 sprigs dill

To a large stockpot add all the ingredients except the parsley and dill. Fill the pot with enough cold water to cover everything by several inches, about 16 cups. **Bring the stock to a strong simmer over medium heat,** skimming off any foam that rises to the top. Lower the heat to a low simmer, add the parsley and dill, and cook, uncovered, for at least 4 hours. Cool, strain, and reserve the stock as directed on page 168.

Creamy Mushroom Soup

This earthy mushroom soup is a good chance to show off your freshly brewed stock. It's flavored with an abundance of mushrooms, thyme, and aromatics such as onions and leeks, which bring out the goodness in the homemade broth. When I prepared this soup for my daughter, she was surprised to learn that there was no cream or butter in the recipe. The creaminess comes from the potato that cooks in the broth and is then pureed to achieve the velvety texture.

MAKES ABOUT 6 CUPS

Start to Finish: Under 1 hour

2 tablespoons olive oil

1 medium onion, diced (about 1 cup)

2 medium leeks, thoroughly rinsed and sliced into $\frac{1}{4}$-inch pieces (about 1 cup)

2 garlic cloves, minced (about 1 tablespoon)

1 pound mushrooms, white, cremini, or an assortment, roughly chopped

1 teaspoon fresh thyme leaves

1 teaspoon kosher salt

$\frac{1}{4}$ teaspoon freshly ground black pepper

1 quart chicken stock

$\frac{1}{2}$ to $\frac{3}{4}$ pound Yukon gold potatoes, peeled and quartered

Splash of sherry, Marsala or dry white vermouth, optional

Splash of hot sauce, optional

Croutons and freshly snipped chives for garnish, optional

Heat the olive oil in a large heavy-bottomed saucepan, add the onions, leeks, and garlic, and cook, stirring, over medium heat until translucent, about 10 minutes. Add the mushrooms, thyme, salt, and pepper, cover, and sweat the mushrooms until they have cooked down, or released their liquid, about 10 minutes. Add the chicken stock and potatoes and cook, covered, over low heat for about 45 minutes, or until the potatoes are very tender. Let the soup cool, then puree in batches in a blender or use an immersion blender right in the pot. You can rev up the flavor by adding a splash of sherry, Marsala, dry white vermouth, or even hot sauce. Season to taste with salt and pepper. Serve garnished with croutons and freshly snipped chives, if desired.

NP

For a non-pareve presentation, a little butter and a quarter cup of light cream can be added in the pureeing stage. They will make the soup a little sweeter and lighten the texture.

Martha's Excellent Matzo Ball Soup

There might not be a more iconic use of chicken than in "Jewish penicillin," homemade chicken soup. There's actually some scientific explanation of why chicken soup has medicinal powers, but for me, it's all about the taste. One of the best bowls of chicken soup you can find in New York is served nightly at Blue Ribbon, Eric and Bruce Bromberg's wonderful restaurant. Their Grandma Martha's soup is a mainstay on their menu, and her ethereal matzo balls are legendary. The Bromberg brothers write that her soup and matzo balls are "a return to simpler things, simple things that if done just so can transform life and lead to so much more." With that introduction, we present Grandma Martha's Excellent Soup and Matzo Ball recipe.

SERVES 8 TO 10

Start to Finish: Under 2½ hours

For the broth
1 whole (3- to 4-pound) hen
1 tablespoon kosher salt
4 celery stalks, with leaves, cleaned and chopped
3 carrots, cleaned and chopped
1 onion, chopped
2 leeks, cleaned and chopped
3 whole unpeeled garlic cloves
4 sprigs flat-leaf parsley

3 sprigs dill
½ teaspoon whole black peppercorns
2 dried bay leaves

For the garnish
Carrot rounds (blanched until soft)
Chopped fresh dill
Kosher salt and freshly ground black pepper

For the matzo balls
1 cup matzo meal
4 eggs
1 ounce rendered chicken fat (schmaltz)
½ ounce kosher salt
½ teaspoon double-acting baking powder
2 ounces seltzer

For the broth: Rub chicken with kosher salt, inside and out. Let stand 15 minutes. Rinse *well* under cold water. Pat dry with paper towel. Put chicken in a large pot and cover with cold water by 3 inches. **Bring to a boil.** Impurities will rise to the top; skim them off and discard. Add the rest of the broth ingredients. Bring back to a boil, skim again, then reduce to a simmer. After simmering for 45 minutes (or until chicken is cooked) remove chicken from the pot. Take the meat off of the bone (save meat for another meal) and put bones back in pot and cook for 1 hour more. Strain the broth though a fine-mesh sieve lined with cheese-cloth. Cool in the refrigerator. When cool, the fat will rise to the top and solidify, making it easy to remove.

For the matzo balls: In a large mixing bowl combine all ingredients ex-cept the seltzer and mix well. Add seltzer and set the mixture aside, covered, in the refrigerator, for 1 hour. Fill a large-diameter pot three-quarters full with water and bring to a simmer. With wet hands roll the matzo mixture into 1-ounce balls. Lower balls into water on a slotted spoon. Cook until the matzo balls are tender, 45 to 60 minutes (test with toothpick or do what Eric Bromberg does and cut in half). The balls should be light and fluffy in the center. Let the matzo balls cool.

For soup: Bring the broth to a boil with the carrot rounds, the dill, and the matzo balls. Season to taste. The soup is ready to serve when the matzo balls are warm in the center.

Abundant Asian Noodle Soup

I like to think of this recipe as a salad bar in a soup bowl, where everyone can add their own favorite vegetables to the sublime flavor of the sweet-and-sour broth.

SERVES 4

Start to Finish: Under 30 minutes

> 1 quart chicken stock
> ¾ pound bok choy, rinsed, white part chopped, leafy portion cut into strips
> ½ pound Napa cabbage, leafy part only, chopped
> 6 ounces white mushrooms, sliced very thin, caps only
> 1 (7-ounce) jar baby corn, drained
> 1 garlic clove, smashed
> 3 tablespoons low-sodium soy sauce
> 1 tablespoon mirin
> 1 tablespoon rice wine vinegar
> Pinch of ground ginger
> 1 (3-ounce) package ramen, shirataki, or udon noodles, prepared as directed on the package
> 2 cups shredded chicken (see pages 114 to 115 to prepare freshly roasted breasts or use "bonus" chicken)
> Kosher salt and freshly ground black pepper
>
> *For the garnish*
> 2 scallions, white and green parts, chopped
> Chili-garlic sauce

In a large soup pot heat the stock just until simmering. Add the white portion of the chopped bok choy, chopped Napa cabbage, sliced mushrooms, baby corn, and garlic to the stock. In a small bowl, mix together the soy sauce, mirin, vinegar, and ground ginger, and add to the simmering stock. Heat for about 15 minutes, over low heat, or until the vegetables are tender and the flavor is developed.

Add the chicken pieces and strips of the bok choy leaves to the soup and cook until everything is heated through, about 5 minutes. Season to taste with salt and pepper and adjust the soy sauce (for salty), mirin (for sweet), and vinegar (for sour) to balance the taste. Evenly divide the prepared noodles among the soup bowls and ladle the hot soup over them. Sprinkle with the chopped scallions and—for those who like it spicy—top with a shot of chili-garlic sauce to taste.

Feedback

The mixture of vegetables you could use in this soup is endless, and you can easily add more veggies to this pot. You'll have a lower broth-to-solid ratio, but that's OK. Straw mushrooms, water chestnuts, and bamboo shoots can all be added after being drained and rinsed. Fresh vegetable options include snow peas, green peas, thinly sliced carrots, and fresh bean sprouts. Use your imagination and your family's personal favorites to create the perfect abundance.

Tuscan Ribollita Soup

. . . with ground sausage

BEHIND THE COUNTER:
Good flavorful Italian beef sausage that can be crumbled works great. Alternate cuts: veal, lamb, or turkey sausage or diced smoked turkey (=$).

There are three must-have ingredients for this hearty Italian peasant soup: good stock, cannellini beans, and crusty bread. This variation on minestrone is filled with vegetables, herbs, and tomatoes that blend with the beans and bread to create a thick, stick-to-your-ribs soup that tastes like you've cooked it all day. Traditionally the dish starts with rendered bacon or pancetta, but for this version sausage adds the fat you need to build the soup.

SERVES 6

Start to Finish: About 1 hour

¼ cup olive oil

½ pound ground Italian-style sausage, removed from the casings
   and crumbled

2 large onions, diced (about 2 cups)

3 carrots, chopped (about 1 cup)

2 celery stalks, chopped (about 1 cup)

5 large garlic cloves, finely chopped (about 3 tablespoons)

Generous pinch of crushed red pepper flakes

1 (28-ounce) can whole tomatoes, broken up, with their juice

2 (15.5-ounce) cans cannellini beans, one drained and rinsed,
   one with the liquid

6 cups chicken stock

1 pound fresh spinach or kale leaves, any tough stems removed

½ cup fresh basil leaves, roughly chopped

½ cup flat-leaf parsley, roughly chopped

Kosher salt and freshly ground black pepper

3 cups Italian bread cubed into 1-inch pieces

Heat the oil in a large soup pot over medium-low heat. Add the sausage and onions and cook, stirring occasionally, until the onions begin to soften and the meat browns, about 10 minutes. Add the carrots, celery, garlic, and red pepper flakes and continue to cook for another 5 to 7 minutes, until the vegetables are just softened. Add the tomatoes and the one can of drained beans to the pot. Cook for 10 minutes, until the ingredients are melded.

While the soup cooks, puree the second can of beans with its liquid. Add the pureed beans, chicken stock, spinach or kale, basil, and parsley to the pot and stir to combine. Bring the soup to a boil, reduce the heat to low, cover, and cook for 20 to 30 minutes. Season the soup to taste with salt and pepper and drop the bread into the soup. Heat for 10 minutes until the bread absorbs some of the soup. Serve piping hot.

Hungarian Bean Soup
. . . *with smoked turkey*

BEHIND THE COUNTER:
Smoked turkey is available in
most markets; it comes
pre-packaged in a small
chunk. Alternate cut: smoked
turkey or beef sausage or hot
dog (=$).

This soup is bountiful, incorporating a variety of vegetables and legumes. But it's the turkey that adds a hint of smoky intrigue, giving this soup its bold character.

SERVES 8 TO 10

Start to Finish: Under 4 hours

2 cups dried beans (kidney, black-eyed, navy, or mixed)
5 tablespoons vegetable oil
2 large onions, diced (about 2 cups)
5 tablespoons all-purpose flour
4 carrots, peeled and diced (about 2 cups)
1 pound smoked turkey
4 teaspoons kosher salt
1 teaspoon freshly ground black pepper
2 tablespoons sweet Hungarian paprika
2 tablespoons finely chopped flat-leaf parsley
2 teaspoons garlic powder
1 quart chicken stock
1 quart water

Rinse the beans and check for any foreign matter and pick out. Place the beans in a large pot and add at least three times their volume in cold water. Bring to a boil and cook for 2 to 3 minutes. Remove the pot from the heat and let the beans sit for 1 hour. This is a quick soak method (see Feedback on the next page). While the beans soak, prepare the remaining ingredients.

Heat the oil in a large soup pot, add the onion, and cook over medium-low heat, until soft and translucent, about 10 minutes. Stir in the flour, being sure to coat all the onions. Cook several minutes, until the onions are golden. Add the beans, carrots, turkey, salt, pepper, paprika, parsley, garlic powder, stock, and water. Bring to a boil, then reduce the heat to low, cover, and simmer for 1½ to 2 hours, or until the beans are tender, adding boiling water as needed if the soup becomes too thick. Remove the meat and cut it into bite-size pieces, return to the pot and heat through. Serve.

You no longer need a day's notice to prepare bean soup or any dish with dried beans. The quick-soak method replaces the overnight soak, which can actually cause beans to ferment. The whole idea behind soaking beans is to allow the dry beans to absorb water, which begins to dissolve some of the starches that give beans their legendary reputation. Soaking also lessens their cook time and reduces the amount of splitting. The quick-soak method accomplishes all this in just about an hour. You should include this important step anytime you cook dried beans, other than split peas or lentils—they do not require a soak. When adding dried beans to soup or a recipe, don't let the small quantity fool you, 1 cup of dry beans swells to 2½ cups cooked.

Lentil Soup

This thick and satisfying soup, based on a recipe my friend Rachel Cohen shared with me, is spiked with spicy sausage and finished with a zing of balsamic vinegar. Rachel says that the addition of tomato paste and vinegar is a very Greek cooking tradition. Every spoonful is packed with flavor and nutrition.

SERVES 6 TO 8

Start to Finish: Under 1½ hours

¾ pound spicy beef, veal, lamb, or turkey sausage, removed
  from the casings and crumbled (hot dogs sliced ¼ inch thick
  can be substituted)
1 tablespoon olive oil
1 medium onion, chopped (about ¾ cup)
2 garlic cloves, chopped
2 celery stalks, diced (about 1 cup)
2 carrots, peeled and diced (about 1 cup)
1 (6-ounce) can tomato paste
1 quart chicken stock
1 pound green or brown lentils, rinsed
2 bay leaves

> 2 cups water
> Kosher salt and freshly ground black pepper
> Balsamic vinegar, for serving

In a large soup pot, brown the crumbled sausage over medium heat, about 5 minutes. (If using hot dogs, skip this step and add at the end.) Remove from the pot with a slotted spoon, but leave the released fat in the pot. Add 1 tablespoon olive oil (2 tablespoons if you did not start with crumbled sausage) and the onions, garlic, celery, and carrots and cook, stirring, over medium heat, about 10 minutes until the vegetables pick up some color and soften. Spoon in the tomato paste and stir to coat the vegetables, and cook an additional 5 minutes. Stir in the chicken stock, lentils, bay leaves, browned sausage, and water. Cover and cook over low heat for about 1 hour. If the soup becomes too thick, add boiling water as needed. Always add boiling rather than cold water when you are cooking soup so you do not bring down the temperature and slow the cooking process. If using hot dogs in place of sausage, add them during the last 15 minutes of cooking. Season to taste with salt and pepper. Remove and discard the bay leaves. Drizzle a few drops of balsamic vinegar into each soup bowl right before serving. I like to spoon the vinegar into the bottom of the bowl and then top with the soup. You will see the rich balsamic come up the sides and create an appetizing visual presentation.

Beef Stock

BEHIND THE COUNTER:
Most butchers sell beef and veal soup bones; they generally come from the shin and neck. Look for those with some meat on them and marrow-filled centers for the most flavor.

Making homemade beef stock requires a little more attention than making chicken stock, but with just a little effort you'll have something much better than boxed stock and demi-glace to add depth of flavor and beefy essence to soups, stews, and sauces. By roasting the bones you'll add an even richer taste to the stock.

MAKES 2 QUARTS STOCK OR 2 CUPS DEMI-GLACE
Start to Finish: At least 4 hours

> 4 pounds beef shin and neck bones
> 2 pounds veal bones

3 tablespoons tomato paste

2 tablespoons olive oil

2 carrots, washed, roughly chopped

2 celery stalks (the inside leafy ribs are best), washed and
    roughly chopped

2 onions, unpeeled and quartered

2 tablespoons Worcestershire sauce

3 whole cloves or a pinch of ground cloves

24 whole black peppercorns

2 bay leaves

12 sprigs parsley

Preheat the oven to 425 degrees. Rinse and dry the bones and place them in a large roasting pan. Roast in the preheated oven for 30 minutes. After that time, baste the bones with the tomato paste diluted with 2 tablespoons of water. **Reduce the heat to 400 degrees** and continue roasting for 30 minutes, until the bones are a rich brown and the aroma is very strong.

While the bones finish roasting, heat the oil in the stockpot and add the carrots, celery, and onions. Cook over medium-low heat, stirring occasionally, until they lightly brown. When the bones are done, remove them from the oven and pour off all the fat. Add the bones to the stockpot and place the defatted roasting pan on the stovetop. Pour 1 cup of cold water into the pan and, over low heat, begin scraping up any bits that have clung to the bottom of the pan; this should take just a couple of minutes. Pour the liquid and collected bits into the stockpot along with the remaining ingredients and 16 to 18 cups of cold water; the bones should be covered by about 2 inches. If you did not roast the bones first, simply add all the ingredients to the stockpot along with the cold water.

Bring the soup to a strong simmer over medium heat, skimming off any foam that rises to the top. Reduce the heat to low and simmer the stock for at least 4 hours, checking the pot periodically to add hot water if needed to cover the contents. When the stock is done, use a small spoon to push out any softened marrow from the bones: it will enrich the soup's flavor. Cool, strain, and reserve the stock, as directed on page 168.

Feedback

You can turn your stock into demi-glace, a concentrated wiggly reduction that can be used in many recipes to enhance and amplify flavor. It might break your heart to see all your soup concentrated down to a very small amount, but that focused flavor is extra robust and full-bodied, and adds dimension to stews, gravies, and soup. After the fat and solids have been removed, heat the stock over medium-high heat in a saucepan (you can add wine, herbs, or tomato paste for even more flavor). When it begins to bubble, lower the heat to a strong simmer and cook until the stock has reduced considerably, and is thick enough to coat the back of a spoon. While this is not true Escoffier-worthy demi-glace, it is a reasonable and easy substitute. To freeze, pour the demi-glace into an ice cube tray or small containers, cover, and freeze for several months, thaw before using, or refrigerate for up to 1 week.

Grandma Rose's Cabbage Soup

BEHIND THE COUNTER:
Have your butcher cut the flanken short rib–style into 2-inch-long riblets. I wouldn't think of substituting any other meat in this recipe. For the hot dogs, the thicker the better.

My grandmother Rose would cook up a pot of this Russian-inspired soup all year long, with thick pieces of flanken flavoring the soup and hot dogs swimming happily in the broth. Some of us preferred bowls ladled with more meat and cabbage, while others dunked chunks of bread in the beefy broth. We never knew whether to eat Grandma Rose's cabbage soup with a spoon or a fork, so I put both out and let my guests choose.

SERVES 8 TO 10

Start to Finish: Under 2½ hours

1 large head green cabbage, cored and shredded
1 (28-ounce) can whole tomatoes, with ½ cup of their juice
3 to 4 pounds short ribs, cut into 2-inch pieces
1 (15-ounce) can sauerkraut, rinsed and drained
2 quarts beef stock
8 jumbo hot dogs, sliced into ¼-inch-thick slices
Juice of 1 lemon (more or less to taste)
Kosher salt and freshly ground black pepper

Place the shredded cabbage in a very large soup pot. Add the tomatoes, crushing them over the pot with your hands, allowing the juices to stream in. Add ½ cup of the juice from the can. Tuck the ribs into the cabbage and top with the sauerkraut. Pour the stock into the pot and bring to a strong simmer. Reduce the heat to low, cover, and cook for 1½ to 2 hours. If the meat is not falling off the bone, cook an additional 30 minutes. When the meat is cooked, remove it from the pot, cut it into large chunks, and reserve. Add the hot dogs and the lemon juice and cook for 15 minutes. Season to taste with salt and pepper. If time allows, refrigerate the soup overnight, and remove any solidified fat before serving. Reheat the soup, adding the meat back, and cook over medium-low heat until heated through. Serve the soup with a piece of short rib in each bowl, plenty of hot dogs, and extra lemon for your guests to squeeze to taste.

Beef and Barley Soup

This iconic American dish walks a fine line between a soup and a stew. Thick and rich, laden with beef bits, chewy mushrooms, and tender pearl barley, this soup is a meal in itself.

SERVES 8

Start to Finish: Under 1½ hours

3 tablespoons olive oil
1 pound beef stew meat cut into ½-inch pieces
1 large onion, chopped (about 1 cup)
3 to 4 garlic cloves, chopped
2 celery stalks, chopped (about 1 cup)
1 large carrot, peeled and chopped (about ½ cup)
2 quarts beef stock
2 bay leaves
1 pound cremini mushrooms, cleaned and chopped
1 cup pearl barley
Kosher salt and freshly ground black pepper

BEHIND THE COUNTER:
Have your butcher cut stew meat from the chuck or shin. If you can score some bones, toss them in for added flavor. Alternate cut: lamb cut from the shoulder (+$).

Heat 1 tablespoon of olive oil in a large soup pot, and add the stew meat until nicely browned, 5 to 7 minutes. Remove the meat with a slotted spoon, transfer to a plate, and pour off the fat from the pot. Heat the remaining 2 tablespoons of oil in the pot, add the onions, garlic, celery, and carrots, and cook over medium heat, until they begin to soften, about 15 minutes. Add the stock, bay leaves, mushrooms, barley, and reserved beef and any collected juices on the plate. Season with salt and a generous sprinkling of pepper. Bring to a strong simmer, then reduce the heat, cover, and simmer for 1 hour, adding boiling water if the soup becomes too thick. Season to taste with salt and pepper. Remove and discard the bay leaves. Serve.

GOOD CARBS

Aside dish is not the focus of a carnivorous meal; it is there to balance and complement the protein. Like a good accessory, it should complete the picture, but never steal the show. The best supporting players are carbs, those often-maligned sides that feature filling potatoes, fluffy rice, and nutritious legumes. It takes a confident potato to share the plate with a grilled steak, or the boldest rice dish to cozy up beside the perfect chop, but these good carbs are up to the challenge.

Potato and Zucchini Pancakes

Potatoes play nicely with a variety of ingredients, so why not add vibrant green zucchini for a burst of color and a sweet note for an otherwise traditional latke.

MAKES ABOUT 18 PANCAKES

Start to Finish: Under 30 minutes

2 medium russet potatoes (about 1 pound), peeled and shredded

1 medium zucchini, shredded

1 small onion, peeled and grated

2 eggs

1½ teaspoons kosher salt
¼ to ½ teaspoon freshly ground black pepper
½ cup matzo meal
½ cup vegetable oil for frying

In a food processor using the shredding disk or on the large hole of a box grater, shred the potatoes. Immediately plunge them in a bowl of cold water, and let them sit while you prepare the remaining ingredients. Shred the zucchini and place it in a colander so the liquid can drain out. Take the potatoes and wring them dry, using an old dish towel or your hands, and discard the brownish water. Place the completely drained potatoes in a bowl, along with the drained and squeezed dry zucchini. Grate the onion right over the bowl so you capture the juice as well as the onion.

Stir the eggs, salt, and pepper into the potato-zucchini mixture. Begin adding the matzo meal until the mixture is semi-firm, with no visible liquid. Let the mixture rest while you heat the oil in a 12-inch skillet. The pan should be able to comfortably hold 6 pancakes at a time, so you'll need to make the pancakes in 3 batches. When the oil is shimmering, drop a very tiny amount of potato batter into the pan: this way you can taste the mini pancake and correct the seasoning if necessary. Once you have, it's time to fry them all.

Take a generous tablespoon of batter and flatten it in your hand so it is about ¼ inch thick. You can make the pancakes as large or small as you like, but if they are too thick they won't cook through. Keep the heat at medium-high, turning and flattening the pancakes after 3 to 4 minutes. Continue cooking until nicely browned and cooked through on the second side. Remove with a slotted spatula (so the oil drips back into the skillet) and let the pancakes hang out on a wire rack set over a baking sheet. If you notice any liquid collecting in the bottom of the bowl, add a little more matzo meal a tablespoon at a time before beginning your next batch. The subsequent batches usually cook a little faster than the first one, so don't walk away from the stove. Add more oil to the pan if needed; just be sure to bring the oil up to temperature before you add more pancakes. Serve hot or reheat on the wire rack in the oven for a few minutes.

Roasted Rosemary Potatoes

These simple little bites go well with almost any main dish with their garlic and herb flavor and crispy brown exterior.

SERVES 4

Start to Finish: Under 1 hour

1½ pounds small red potatoes, washed and quartered

¼ cup olive oil

1 tablespoon chopped fresh rosemary leaves or 1 teaspoon dried rosemary

About 6 sprigs fresh thyme or 1 teaspoon dried thyme leaves

1 teaspoon kosher salt

3 garlic cloves, smashed and roughly chopped

Preheat the oven to 425 degrees. In a small bowl combine all the ingredients and toss (your hands work best) to coat all the potatoes. Spread the potatoes out in a rimmed baking sheet and roast in the preheated oven for 20 minutes, or until they begin to develop a crust. **Reduce the oven temperature to 375 degrees,** stir the potatoes, to prevent them from sticking to the pan, and continue roasting for 20 minutes longer, until hot and crispy.

Herbed Potato Salad

It's not a BBQ without potato salad. This one is a cross between deli-style mayo-based and German vinegar. The Dutch yellow potatoes have a buttery taste and a waxy texture, perfect for this dish. If you cannot find them at your market, substitute red new potatoes, small Yukon gold, or fingerling.

SERVES 4

Start to Finish: Under 30 minutes to prepare; then several hours to chill

1½ pounds baby Dutch yellow potatoes, scrubbed and halved, cut larger ones in thirds

1½ teaspoons kosher salt

1/4 teaspoon freshly ground black pepper

1/2 cup good-quality mayonnaise (for homemade, see page 223)

2 teaspoons Dijon or grainy mustard

1/2 teaspoon chopped fresh thyme leaves

1/2 teaspoon chopped fresh rosemary leaves

3 scallions, white and green parts, chopped

Juice of 1/2 lemon (1 to 2 tablespoons)

4 tablespoons red wine vinegar (more or less to taste)

Place the potatoes in a medium pot and add 3 cups of cold water and a teaspoon of kosher salt. Bring to a boil, and cook for 15 to 20 minutes or until the potatoes are fork-tender. Drain and set aside. Try to coat the potatoes with the dressing while the potatoes are still warm, they will absorb the dressing better.

In a medium bowl, whisk together the mayonnaise, mustard, thyme, rosemary, scallions, lemon juice, vinegar, 1/2 teaspoon of salt, and pepper. Gently toss the warm potatoes in the dressing and stir to combine. Refrigerate until completely chilled, at least 2 hours.

Twice-Fried Potatoes

The key to perfect French fries is to soak the potatoes first to draw out the starch, then fry them twice, once to soften the inside, the second to crisp up the outside. If you happen to have any duck fat in the fridge, use it instead of oil and you'll achieve French fry nirvana.

SERVES 4

Start to Finish: 1 hour to soak the potatoes; under 30 minutes to fry twice

4 russet potatoes, washed thoroughly and sliced into even sticks about 1/2 inch thick by 2 to 3 inches long. Try to keep the size consistent so they cook evenly.

About 2 cups of shortening, vegetable, or peanut oil (1 pint of duck fat can be substituted for a richer taste)

Kosher salt

Soak the potatoes for at least 1 hour in cold water to draw out the starch. You can do this hours in advance; keep the bowl in the fridge. Before frying, roll them in an absorbent towel to remove all the water.

Heat the fat in a large skillet or deep fryer. If using a skillet, there should be several inches of oil in the pan. If you have a cooking thermometer, it should read 325 degrees. When the oil is ready for frying, fry the potatoes in batches until they are light blonde and limp, about 7 minutes. Transfer them with a slotted spoon and let them rest on a parchment paper–lined baking sheet. They should be pliable and bend at the waist when handled. They can hang out like this up to 1 hour until you are ready for them.

Reheat the oil to about 360 degrees. This second fry at a higher temperature makes them crispy. Fry the potatoes for a second time, for just about 3 minutes, until golden brown. Drain, salt, and serve immediately.

Feedback

For French fries or any food that needs to be uniformly cut, you might want to try cutting them into *bâtons*—culinary speak for consistent planks. For fries, you would leave them in planks, but for other preparations this technique will help you create a perfect cube, dice, or julienne, if you don't own a mandolin. There are lots of how-to videos online, take a peek to learn this method.

Creamy Mashed Potatoes

Here's the challenge. Creamy mashed potatoes without butter or cream. The solution? Amplify the taste by simmering the potatoes in chicken stock and then add fresh herbs and roasted garlic. Trust me, you won't miss the dairy.

SERVES 6

Start to Finish: Under 1½ hours

2½ pounds Yukon gold potatoes, quartered

1 quart chicken stock

6 sprigs thyme

1 head garlic, unpeeled

Kosher salt and freshly ground black pepper

1 tablespoon freshly snipped chives

Preheat the oven to 400 degrees.

Rinse, but do not peel the potatoes, and place in a pot along with the chicken stock and thyme sprigs. Bring to a boil and cook over medium-low heat until the potatoes are very tender, 20 to 25 minutes. When done, transfer the potatoes to a large bowl, reserve the broth, and discard the thyme.

Roast the garlic while the potatoes boil. Place the head of garlic on a piece of aluminum foil and roast in the preheated oven for about 25 minutes. Squeeze the roasted garlic from the cloves and set aside. The potatoes and garlic should be done at about the same time. Smash the potatoes while still hot along with the roasted garlic and about a third of the cooking broth. You don't want the potatoes to be soupy, so add the broth slowly as needed, until they reach a creamy consistency. Season to taste with salt and pepper and stir in the chopped chives.

Vegetable Fried Rice

Don't know what to do with that container of white rice leftover from Chinese take-out? Try this recipe and you'll never toss extra rice out again.

SERVES 4

Start to Finish: Under 45 minutes

3 cups cooked white long-grain rice (brown can be substituted)

4 tablespoons low-sodium soy sauce

3 teaspoons rice wine vinegar

1½ teaspoons toasted sesame oil

Pinch of sugar

2 tablespoons peanut or vegetable oil

4 ounces (about 5 medium) cremini mushrooms, sliced

1 small carrot, peeled and diced (about ¼ cup)

2 large eggs, lightly beaten

1 scallion, thinly sliced

Kosher salt and freshly ground black pepper

Cook the rice according to the package instructions and set aside, or use leftover rice brought to room temperature. Prepare the sauce by whisking together the soy sauce, vinegar, sesame oil, and sugar; set aside.

Heat the oil in a large skillet. Add the mushrooms and carrots over medium heat and cook, stirring occasionally until lightly, browned, about 5 minutes. Add the eggs to the skillet and scramble until the egg is dry. Stir in the rice, scallions, and sauce and cook until all the ingredients have combined and the rice is heated through and completely coated with the sauce. Season to taste with salt and pepper.

Feedback

Fried rice is a great stand-alone dish, especially when you add diced cooked chicken or any other "bonus" diced meat. You can embellish the rice with chopped bok choy, frozen peas (thawed), water chestnuts, or just about any vegetable you enjoy. The key is not to overcook the dish; you want the rice to pick up flavor, color, and a slight crunch. It's always best to start out with leftover rice or rice you just prepared and have allowed to come to room temperature. The texture and lack of moisture helps the rice brown better. A similar rice dish called *nasi goreng* is enjoyed in Indonesian culture as a filling and nutritious breakfast. For an authentic *nasi goreng,* add to this dish some indigenous spices such as cumin, ginger, and coriander.

Black Beans and Rice

This Latin staple is nourishing, economical, and so easy to prepare. It is perfect with *picadillo,* but is also great with any chicken, beef, or veal dish.

SERVES 4

Start to Finish: Under 2 hours if using dried beans; under 30 minutes if using canned

3 cups cooked white rice

2 (15.5-ounce) cans black beans, drained

½ cup tomato sauce

¼ teaspoon ground cumin

¼ teaspoon cayenne pepper

2 tablespoons sofrito (see recipe page 225) or jarred

Kosher salt and freshly ground black pepper

Prepare the rice according to the package directions. Stir the beans into the cooked rice along with the tomato sauce, cumin, cayenne, and sofrito. You will probably not need to add salt and pepper, but adjust seasonings to your taste.

Porcini Mushroom Risotto

This creamy rice dish needs no butter or cream to create a wonderfully smooth and earthy taste and texture. Dried porcini mushrooms and their intense liquid provide a burst of concentrated flavor.

MAKES 3 CUPS RISOTTO

Start to Finish: Under 45 minutes

1 (1-ounce) package of dried porcini mushrooms

3 to 4 cups chicken stock, warmed

3 tablespoons olive oil

1 medium onion, chopped (about ¾ cup)

1 cup raw Arborio rice

½ cup dry vermouth or white wine

Kosher salt and freshly ground black pepper

Soak the dried mushrooms in 1 cup of hot water, right in a glass measuring cup. Allow the mushrooms to soak at least 15 minutes, until they are very soft. Squeeze the mushrooms to extract all their liquid, rinse, to remove any remaining grit, chop, and reserve. Strain the porcini water through a fine-mesh sieve, cheesecloth, a lightly dampened paper towel, or a coffee filter placed in a strainer over a bowl. You should have about 1 cup porcini water. Pour half the strained liquid into a saucepan and add the chicken stock. Warm over a low heat and keep at a simmer. If pairing this recipe with a roasted meat dish, add the remaining half cup of porcini water to the roasting pan or gravy.

Heat the oil in a large skillet, add the onion, and cook, stirring occasionally, over medium heat, until translucent, 5 to 7 minutes. Add the rice, and cook, stirring, over medium heat, for 5 minutes until the onions have coated all the grains. Add the vermouth or white wine and cook until the liquid has been absorbed, about 3 minutes. Begin ladling the warm stock into the skillet, a ladle at a time, stirring over medium heat, until the stock is absorbed. The first couple of ladles will be soaked right up; the next few will take a little longer. Continue ladling and stirring until you have about 2 ladlefuls left. Add the chopped porcini mushrooms. Continue adding stock and stirring until the rice is al dente, firm to the bite but not crunchy. Season with salt and pepper.

NP

For a non-pareve preparation, use butter in place of the oil, and stir in about ¼ cup of grated Parmesan cheese and a pat of extra butter before serving.

Wild Rice
. . . *with dried cranberries*
Wild rice has a nutty distinctive flavor and a nice crunch. The addition of dried cranberries gives this dish a subtle tartness and a welcome burst of color.

SERVES 4

Start to Finish: Under 45 minutes

> 1 cup wild rice, prepared according to package directions,
>   substituting chicken stock for the water, and eliminating the salt
>   and margarine, if called for
> 2 tablespoons olive oil

1 large shallot, chopped
½ cup dried cranberries
1 tablespoon chopped fresh flat-leaf parsley
½ cup pecans, optional
Kosher salt and freshly ground black pepper

While the rice cooks, heat the olive oil in a small skillet. Add the shallots and cook over medium heat until they just begin to pick up color, 2 to 3 minutes. Remove the shallots using a slotted spoon, and reserve. Pour the shallot oil from the pan into the rice while it finishes cooking. When the rice is done, stir in the shallots, cranberries, parsley, and pecans if using. Season to taste with salt and pepper. Cover and keep warm or gently reheat, adding a touch of stock, before serving.

Basmati Rice

I had an illuminating cab ride one day on my way to Kalustyan's, New York's premier spice shop. I engaged the driver in conversation as I often do, and invariably the conversation led to food. I learned that the driver, Abdul, was a native of Afghanistan, educated in Kabul, a naturalized American citizen, and an avid cook. His best piece of advice related to his favorite side dish, basmati rice. Abdul explained that unlike Chinese-style rice, basmati is less sticky and has a nuttier taste. He strongly advises using brown basmati rice and letting it soak for at least 2 to 3 hours or even overnight to help release the starch and open the grain. I tried Abdul's method and compared it to cooking the rice without the long soak, and I have to agree that it helps the rice retain its individual grains and improves its texture. You can add almost anything you like to the cooked rice, from sweet currants to sautéed onions and garlic. This dish uses the wonderful salty and tart flavor of preserved lemons, which balances nicely with Middle Eastern flavors.

SERVES 4
Start to Finish: 3 hours to soak the rice; 40 minutes to cook

1 cup brown or white basmati rice

2 cups water

2 tablespoons minced preserved lemon, rinsed

1 tablespoon chopped fresh mint leaves

1 tablespoon chopped fresh cilantro or parsley leaves

Soak the rice for at least 3 hours before cooking, changing the water several times to remove the excess starch. Drain the rice. Combine the rice with the 2 cups water, and bring to a boil. Cover, reduce the heat, and cook until the rice is tender, about 40 minutes. Fluff the rice with a fork and add the lemon, mint, and cilantro.

Feedback

A general ratio when preparing rice is 1 cup of rice to 2 cups liquid. Any time you substitute stock for the water or infuse the cooking liquid with herbs, you amplify the flavor. You can also try the "Italian" method of cooking rice. They approach rice as they do pasta, and fill a large pot with salted cold water. When the water comes to a full boil, drop the amount of rice you want to prepare (1 cup serves about 4 people, 1½ cups about 6, and 2 cups about 8) into the pot. Boil the rice about 15 minutes, and then drain as you would pasta.

Tomatoey Rice
...with zucchini

My Sephardic great grandmother cooked a dish that she called Spanish rice, which we thought got its subtle reddish pink color from the grain itself. Who knew it was the addition of stewed tomatoes that created the pleasing color and authentic flavor? Here's an updated rendition of Grandma Esther's Spanish-*style* rice.

SERVES 4

Start to Finish: Under 30 minutes

2 cups cooked rice, prepared according to package directions

2 tablespoons olive oil

> 2 medium zucchini, cut into 1-inch pieces
> 1 small red onion, roughly chopped into 1-inch pieces
> 2 large garlic cloves, chopped
> 1 (14.4-ounce) can stewed tomatoes
> Kosher salt and freshly ground black pepper
> 2 tablespoons sofrito (see recipe page 225 or jarred), optional

Heat the oil in a large skillet, add the zucchini, red onion, and garlic and cook over medium heat, stirring occasionally, until brown, about 10 minutes. Stir in the stewed tomatoes and simmer, uncovered, to reduce the liquid by half and season to taste with salt and pepper. When the rice is ready, add it to the vegetables. For an added kick, stir in 2 tablespoons sofrito before serving.

Tuscan Beans

There's probably no more rustic and wholesome side than a steaming pot of slowly braised beans. In Italy, these make the perfect accompaniment to almost any main dish or can become a meal in itself when fresh greens such as spinach or kale or chunks of beef or sausage are added to the pot.

SERVES 4 TO 6

Start to Finish: Under 3 hours

> 1 pound dried white cannellini beans, giant lima beans,
>   or your choice of dried beans
> 2 tablespoons olive oil
> 1 large onion, chopped (about 1½ cups)
> 2 celery stalks, finely minced (about 1 cup)
> 2 carrots, peeled and diced (about 1 cup)
> 2 large garlic cloves, chopped (about 1 tablespoon)
> Pinch of crushed red pepper flakes
> 1 (28-ounce) can whole tomatoes
> 3 cups chicken stock

1 bay leaf

3 sprigs rosemary

Kosher salt and freshly ground black pepper

Rinse the beans to remove any foreign matter. Add the beans to a pot with about 3 times their volume in cold water and bring to a boil. Cook for 2 to 3 minutes and then remove the pot from the stove and allow the beans to soak for 1 hour. Drain and set aside (see Feedback on page 177)

While the beans soak, heat the oil in a heavy braising pot with a lid. Add the onions, celery, carrots, garlic, and red pepper flakes and cook over medium heat, until the vegetables begin to pick up some color and soften. Remove from heat.

After the beans have soaked, drain them and add them to the braising pot. Add the tomatoes, crushing them with your hands as you add them to the pot. Add the chicken stock, bay leaf, and 2 sprigs of the rosemary. If the liquid does not cover the beans, add an additional cup of stock or water. Bring the beans to a boil, reduce the heat, cover, and simmer until the beans are tender, about $1\frac{1}{2}$ to 2 hours. Season with salt and pepper and remove and discard the bay leaf and rosemary sprigs (the leaves will have fallen off and melded with the stew). If the stew has not thickened, you can cook it a little longer with the lid off. Garnish with the remaining rosemary sprig and serve.

Quinoa

. . . with apple cider–braised squash and prunes

Quinoa is an ancient food with its roots in the Peruvian Inca culture. Once considered sacred in the South American Andes, this protein-rich grain has been rediscovered and introduced to American markets. It has a nutty flavor and makes a great substitute for rice or couscous. It is easy to prepare, filling, and nutritious. The flavor-packed partners in this recipe bring out quinoa's natural goodness. After trying it, I'm sure you'll describe it as interestingly delicious.

SERVES 4 TO 6

Start to Finish: Under 30 minutes

> 3 cups cooked quinoa, prepared according to package directions
> 2 tablespoons vegetable oil
> 2 large shallots, sliced (about ½ cup)
> 1 cup (about 15 bite-size) pitted prunes, cut into ½-inch pieces
> 1 pound butternut squash, peeled and cut into ½-inch pieces
> 1½ cups apple cider
> ½ teaspoon ground cinnamon
> Pinch of freshly grated nutmeg
> Kosher salt and freshly ground black pepper

You can substitute chicken stock for the water to add more flavor to the quinoa. While the quinoa cooks, prepare the squash and prunes.

Heat the oil in a large skillet. Add the shallots and prunes and cook over medium heat, stirring occasionally, until the shallots begin to soften, 7 to 10 minutes. Stir in the squash and cook for several minutes or until the squash develops a light brown crust. Add the cider, cinnamon, and nutmeg. Cover and cook over medium heat until the squash is tender but not mushy, 15 to 20 minutes, adding more cider or stock to the pan if needed. Spoon the cooked quinoa into the pan and cook for several minutes until all heated through and flavors have combined, adding more cider or stock if the mixture is dry. Season to taste with salt and pepper.

Kasha Varnishkes

If we called this dish pasta with toasted grains and sautéed onions, it could easily appear on the menu of a trendy restaurant. Kasha is a nutritious and delicious grain, especially when toasted to bring out its nutty goodness. I learned this recipe from my dear friend Chana Wiesenfeld, a traditional Eastern European cook. This dish is the perfect accompaniment to brisket or any dish with a rich gravy.

Start to Finish: Under 1 hour

> 12 ounces bow-tie pasta
> 3 tablespoons vegetable oil or chicken fat
> 2 medium onions, chopped (about 2 cups)
> 1 egg, beaten
> 1 cup kasha (buckwheat groats)
> 2 cups beef stock
> Kosher salt and freshly ground black pepper

Bring a large pot of salted water to a rapid boil, add the bow-tie pasta, and cook according to the package directions. Drain and set aside. While the pasta cooks, heat the oil in a large skillet, add the onions and cook over medium heat, until they are very brown but not burnt, about 20 minutes. Using a slotted spoon, transfer them to a bowl and set aside. In a small bowl, mix together the egg and kasha. Using the same pan you used for the onions, spread the kasha and egg mixture in a thin layer and cook, over medium heat, until the egg has dried and the kasha has lightly browned, about 3 minutes. This step will help develop the kasha's nutty, toasty flavor.

In a small saucepan, bring the stock to boil. Slowly pour the liquid into the skillet with the kasha and simmer, covered, for 15 minutes. Stir to completely break up any hardened bits of kasha until the egg has basically disappeared. When the kasha is tender, combine it with the reserved pasta and onions. Generously season to taste with salt and pepper. If the mixture is too firm, add a touch more fat or liquid to loosen.

Chickpea and White Bean Hummus

Hummus is a blank canvas that can take on so many different flavors, incorporating the elements you enjoy. This hummus is a blend of white beans, chickpeas, and tahini, which is a sesame paste often used in Middle Eastern cooking. It adds a subtle, smooth nutty note to the hummus.

MAKES ABOUT 2 CUPS
Start to Finish: Under 15 minutes

> 1 (15.5-ounce) can chickpeas (garbanzo beans), liquid reserved
> 1 (15.5-ounce) can white cannellini beans, drained
> ¼ cup tahini paste
> 2 garlic cloves, roughly chopped
> ½ cup loosely packed flat-leaf parsley or cilantro leaves
> Juice of 2 lemons
> ¼ cup plus 1 to 2 tablespoons olive oil
> Salt and freshly ground black pepper

In the bowl of a food processor fitted with the metal blade, process the chickpeas, with about 2 tablespoons of their liquid, the cannellini beans, tahini paste, garlic, parsley, and lemon juice. Slowly drizzle in the olive oil and continue blending until smooth and creamy, adding more chickpea liquid or oil if needed. Season to taste with salt and pepper. Serve cold topped with chopped garlic, parsley, a squeeze of lemon or a drizzle of olive oil.

DOUGH

Combine all-purpose flour, eggs, salt, and water in varying amounts and you have dough. The following recipes build on these simple cornerstones of ingredients to create classic staples that will round out your meal. If you've never rolled your own pasta or kneaded your own dough, give it a whirl. The tactile sensation is well worth the effort and the results are better than anything you can get in a box or from a twist-tied bag.

Egg Barley
. . . with mushrooms and onions

Egg barley has more in common with orzo or Israeli couscous than it does with barley. While it is shaped like tiny barley pellets, it is really an egg pasta that makes a great side or a terrific stand-in for noodles in soup. This traditional Eastern European dish that can be found at almost every deli counter is elevated with the addition of sweet red onion, shallots, and fresh herbs.

SERVES 6

Start to Finish: Under 30 minutes

2 tablespoons olive oil

1 medium red onion, diced (about ¾ cup)

1 medium yellow onion, diced (about ¾ cup)

2 garlic cloves, chopped (about 1 tablespoon)

2 large shallots, minced (about 2 tablespoons)

1 celery stalk, minced (about ½ cup)

¾ pound button or cremini mushrooms, sliced

½ to 1 cup chicken stock

12 ounces uncooked egg barley, prepared according to
   package directions

Kosher salt and freshly ground black pepper

Garlic powder, to taste

1 tablespoon chopped fresh dill leaves, optional

1 tablespoon chopped fresh flat-leaf parsley, optional

Heat the olive oil in a medium skillet, add the red and yellow onions, and cook over medium heat, stirring occasionally, for 5 minutes until they are lightly browned. Add the garlic, shallots, and celery and cook 5 to 10 minutes longer until the onions are very soft and begin to lightly brown. Add the mushrooms. Cook and stir the mixture over medium-high so that the mushrooms and onions develop a medium-brown color. Add the stock, turn off the heat, and cover.

Add the barley to the mushrooms and onions. Season to taste with salt, plenty of black pepper, and garlic powder. The egg barley can be served hot or cold, garnished with the dill and parsley.

Israeli Couscous

...with mint courtesy of Flatiron Kitchen

Israeli couscous has a lighter more pasta-like texture than regular couscous, making it a cross between pasta and rice.

SERVES 4 TO 6

Start to Finish: Under 30 minutes

⅓ cup pine nuts

2 shallots, minced

3 tablespoons olive oil

2 cups Israeli couscous

3 cups chicken stock (water or vegetable stock can also be used)

Kosher salt and pepper to taste

½ cup fresh mint leaves, chopped

Juice of ½ lemon

Toast the pine nuts in a dry skillet over medium heat, stirring or swirling them around in the pan frequently to avoid burning. After a couple minutes, when they start to turn golden, remove from heat and set aside. In a large pot, sauté the shallots in olive oil until they just start to brown. Stir in the couscous and continue to cook over medium heat for about 5 minutes, or until it begins to brown slightly as well. Add the stock or water, bring to a boil, then reduce to a simmer. Season with salt and pepper to taste and cook, covered, for about 10 minutes. Most of the liquid should be absorbed by the time the couscous is finished cooking. Transfer to a bowl, stir in the chopped mint, lemon juice, and pine nuts, and serve.

Homemade Egg Noodles

While it is so easy to open a box, there is something incredibly satisfying about making your own noodles. Here is a basic egg noodle recipe that can be turned into any type of pasta. If you have a pasta machine or attachment for your standing mixer, it makes the rolling and cutting much easier.

MAKES 1 POUND NOODLES

Start to Finish: Under 1 hour

2 cups all-purpose flour

3 eggs

½ teaspoon table salt

Water

Scoop the flour out onto a clean, dry countertop and create a well in the center. Crack the eggs into the center of the well and lightly beat with a fork, then season with salt. Slowly begin bringing the flour into the well, using the fork or your hands. (You can do this step in a food processor, using the pulse feature to incorporate, but do not overprocess the ingredients.) Once the ingredients are combined, begin kneading the dough, by hand, on a lightly floured surface, for about 10 minutes, adding a drop or two of water or a pinch of flour as needed. The dough will go from crumbly to smooth and elastic with a pale yellow color. When ready, push it in: like the "Pillsbury dough-boy," it should bounce back. Wrap the dough tightly in plastic wrap and let it rest for 30 minutes.

After the dough has rested, divide it into manageable pieces that you can easily roll. If you have a pasta attachment, use it to stretch and roll the dough. Otherwise, roll each piece of dough out on a lightly floured board, using a large rolling pin. Do not tug at the dough, or it will resist and pull back. Use the rolling pin, turning the dough after each roll and flouring your surface to prevent it from sticking to the board. Roll the dough to about ⅛-inch thick (you should be able to see your hands through the pasta). Let the pasta rest for a few minutes before cutting.

Cut the pasta into ribbons, thick or thin, depending on how you want to use them, with a pizza wheel or sharp knife. A good trick is to fold the pasta into a sheet about 3 inches wide to make cutting easier. Toss the cut noodles with a little flour or cornmeal and let the cut noodles rest on a pan lined with a towel or a drying rack while you bring a large pot of salted water to a rapid boil.

Fresh pasta cooks quickly, usually in just 3 to 5 minutes. When done, quickly toss the pasta with your sauce or gravy and enjoy. If you are not using the pasta immediately, you can roll the uncooked strands into loose balls, cover, and refrigerate up to a day on an aluminum foil–lined pan. To preserve the pasta for several days, allow it to dry out completely (if you don't it will get moldy), then seal in a resealable plastic bag and freeze; no need to thaw before cooking.

Dumplings and Spaetzle

These simple and easy dumplings provide a pillowy foundation for just about any sauce or stew. You can easily take these Hungarian dumplings across the border to create spaetzle, a Austrian-German variation.

SERVES 4

Start to Finish: Under 30 minutes

1 cup all-purpose flour
2 eggs, beaten
Kosher salt and freshly ground black pepper
1 tablespoon water

Bring a large pot of salted water to a boil. Stir the flour into the beaten eggs, season with salt and pepper, and mix with a fork until the dough is crumbly. Begin adding the water, 1 teaspoon at a time, until you have a ball of dough. If the dough does not come together, add a drop more water; if it is too sticky handle, add a touch more flour.

Flour your hands and your work surface and take the dough out of the bowl to knead it. Kneading is done to help develop the gluten (the glue) in the flour, which gives the dough its structure. To properly knead the dough, flour your work surface and your hands and press the dough with the saddle of your hand, folding the dough in half. Repeat this for several minutes until the dough is smooth and pliable and feels like Play-Doh.

Divide the dough into 4 equal pieces and roll each between your hands to form a long rope, about 1/2 inch in diameter. If you try to stretch the dough, it will resist and pull back, so you need to roll it. Let the dough rest on a plate or cutting board until the water is rapidly boiling. Using a spoon or dull knife, cut the dough into 1/2-inch pieces and push them into the water. When the water returns to a boil, reduce the heat to a gentle simmer and cook until the dumplings float to the top and are no longer doughy inside (check by cutting into one), about 10 minutes. Drain the dumplings and serve hot with gravy spooned on top.

Feedback

The Austrian-German specialty spaetzle is prepared with the same ingredients, just different proportions. You'll want to add more liquid so the dough will be thinner, a cross between elastic dough and pancake batter. Let the batter rest while you bring a pot of salted water to a rapid boil. Take a ladleful of batter at a time and pour it into a sieve that you hold over the boiling water. Push the batter through the holes into the boiling water to create little flutters of dough (*spätzle* means "little sparrow" as the dough seems to flap its wings in the water). Boil until they float to the top, just a few minutes, drain, and serve. Cooked spaetzle can also be fried in a little oil for a crispier finish.

Yorkshire Pudding

When this recipe emerged from the oven, my daughter re-titled them pop-unders instead of popovers because the center portion of the pudding inverts, while the outside forms a light, airy crust. The British custom is to cook the pudding using drippings from the beef you are roasting. If that's your plan, while the meats rests, the Yorkshire pudding will bake and provide the perfect accompaniment to a very solid English meal.

SERVES 6

Start to Finish: Under 30 minutes

3 eggs
¾ cup cold water
¾ cup all-purpose flour
½ teaspoon table salt
1 teaspoon minced fresh chives, optional
1 teaspoon minced fresh thyme leaves, optional

Beat the eggs with the cold water in a medium bowl. In a separate bowl, combine the flour and salt. Whisk the flour mixture into the egg mixture until the lumps disappear and it resembles a thin pancake batter. Stir in the herbs, if using, and let the batter rest 15 to 30 minutes. If preparing the pudding with a roast beef, siphon off several tablespoons of the beef drippings.

Preheat the oven to 450 degrees. Pour the drippings into a 9-inch cake, popover, or muffin tin, adding drippings in each well, and pop the pan in the oven for a couple of minutes. You want the drippings to be searing hot, but not burned. Pour the batter into the pan, filling each cup about ½ full, and bake for about 20 minutes; do not open the oven door. After 20 minutes, you can check for doneness. If the center seems eggy, cook for several minutes longer until the pudding is cooked through. Serve alongside the beef, with a bit of gravy ladled over the pudding, and a dollop of horseradish cream (page 224).

NP

For a non-pareve preparation, substitute milk for the water.

Grilled Pizza Flatbread

Shortcut alert! Most markets—and just about every pizzeria—will sell you pizza dough to use at home. One terrific way to use the dough is to grill it right alongside whatever meat you are cooking. It is so easy and the result is crisp, delicious flatbread in just a few minutes. You can, of course, make the pizza dough from scratch, but this is one cheat I highly recommend.

MAKES 4 MINI FLATBREADS

Start to Finish: Under 15 minutes

> 1 pound pizza dough
> Canola or olive oil

Divide the dough into 4 equal pieces and roll or stretch each into a 3- to 4-inch circle. (No problem if the shape is a little funky.) Brush the dough with the oil. Throw the dough onto the grill, oiled side down. Grill for a couple of minutes, over medium-high heat. You want nice char marks, not a burned crust. While the underside grills, brush the top with more of the oil. Use tongs to flip the pizza over and grill a couple of minutes on the reverse side. Remove the flatbread from the grill and dip it into hummus, spread it with pesto, or use it to create a street food–style sandwich.

VEGGIES

Unless you are preparing a vegetarian feast—unthinkable!—vegetables should complement but not dominate your meal. There are a couple of good veggie rules present to help you prepare perfect vegetables every time. Chef David stresses that only pasta should be eaten al dente, not vegetables. So while you want them crisp and fresh, you don't want cooked vegetables to be *too* crunchy. Blanching is one of the best ways to achieve the perfect balance. Bring a large pot of salted water to a boil, add the vegetable, and cook for just several minutes (they should be slightly crisp and retain their vibrant color), then plunge into an ice water bath. The cold water stops the cooking process and preserves the color. Buy local and organic vegetables if those features are important to you, but most important buy seasonal and you'll have a vegetable that tastes as it should.

Roasted Corn on the Cob

You don't need a grill or a checkered tablecloth to serve this roasted corn.

SERVES 4

Start to Finish: Under 45 minutes

1 teaspoon spice rub (pages 135–136)

1 tablespoon olive oil

4 ears of corn, husks pulled down and corn thoroughly cleaned
   of all silky threads

1 lime, quartered, for serving

Preheat the oven to 350 degrees. In a small bowl, mix 1 tablespoon of oil with 1 teaspoon grill rub. Rub the resulting paste on the ears of corn. Pull the husks up to cover the corn and roast in the preheated oven directly on the oven rack for 30 minutes. Serve with a squeeze of lime.

Oven-Roasted Plum Tomatoes

Take the goodness of a tomato and concentrate it by slow roasting it in the oven with the simple addition of olive oil, garlic, and herbs. The result is a mouthwatering tomato that can be served as a side dish, pureed for sauce, or chopped and added to just about anything. The longer you roast them, the drier the tomatoes become and the more the flavor intensifies.

SERVES 4 TO 6

Start to Finish: Under 2½ hours

1½ pounds ripe plum (Roma) tomatoes, halved lengthwise and seeded

2 to 3 garlic cloves, minced (about 1 tablespoon)

3 tablespoons olive oil

1 teaspoon dried oregano

½ teaspoon kosher salt

¼ teaspoon sugar

1 tablespoon chopped fresh basil

Preheat the oven to 250 degrees and line a rimmed baking sheet with aluminum foil.

Seed the tomatoes by running your finger or a spoon on either side of the rib, and gently squeeze to release any hidden juice. Place the tomato halves cut side up on the prepared baking sheet. In a small bowl combine the remaining ingredients. Brush a dollop of the oil and herb mixture on each tomato half. Roast in the preheated oven for about 2 hours to retain a little juiciness, or up to 4 hours if you want the tomatoes to be completely dried. Serve at once or place in a airtight container and cover with olive oil. The cooked tomatoes will keep for weeks in the fridge.

Lemon and Garlic Broccoli

This broccoli recipe is a perfect example of letting the vegetable's fresh goodness come through. This same preparation can be used with just about any green vegetable.

SERVES 4 TO 6

Start to Finish: Under 30 minutes

> 1 head crisp broccoli (be sure the stems are not rubbery,
>   they should snap when bent)
> Olive oil
> 2 to 3 garlic cloves, sliced
> Juice of ½ lemon
> Kosher salt

Prepare the broccoli by cutting off the florets from the stems. Try to cut them into consistent sizes for even cooking. Trim the stems with a vegetable peeler to remove the tough outer layer. When you have whittled the stems down to reveal the pale green portion, slice the stems into 1-inch rounds.

Bring a large pot of salted water to a rapid boil. Drop in the broccoli florets and trimmed stems and blanch for about 3 minutes. Using a wire strainer (spider), lift the broccoli out of the boiling water and plunge into an ice water bath. Drain and dry thoroughly before the next step.

Heat a tablespoon of olive oil in a large skillet, add the garlic, and cook for 1 minute, then toss in the broccoli. Cook and stir over medium heat for a minute or two until the broccoli is fork-tender and heated through. Squeeze the lemon juice over the broccoli right before serving—if you do it earlier, it will cause the broccoli to turn an unappealing brownish color. Sprinkle with kosher salt to taste and drizzle with a bit more olive oil.

Lemony Cauliflower Fritters

These zesty cauliflower fritters have been in my father's repertoire for as long as I can remember. The recipe hails from the Greek Isle of Rhodes, where my father's family is from. The batter creates a crispy and eggy exterior that protects and enhances the cauliflower as it bakes. A hearty amount of lemon insures a strong pucker and fresh flavor.

SERVES 4 TO 6

Start to Finish: Under 1½ hours

> 3 eggs, beaten
> Juice of 2 lemons
> 1 cup all-purpose flour for dredging, seasoned with 2 teaspoons kosher salt
>   and ½ teaspoon freshly ground black pepper
> 1 head cauliflower
> Vegetable oil for frying (about ½ cup)
> Kosher salt and freshly ground black pepper for sprinkling

Preheat the oven to 300 degrees. Beat the egg in a shallow bowl and squeeze the juice of half a lemon into the egg. Place the seasoned flour in a second shallow dish for dredging. After trimming the cauliflower of the outer green leaves, stand it up on its core to make it easier to slice. Slice the cauliflower into ½-inch-thick slices. Some florets will fall off, especially as you trim away some of the hard core. At the end, you can gather those little pieces, dredge, coat, fry, and bake them along with the larger slices to enjoy as small bites.

Heat ¼ cup of the oil in a large skillet. To help the egg adhere better, lightly press the cauliflower pieces in the seasoned flour, shaking off any excess. Using a tapping motion, dip the cauliflower in the beaten egg, making sure it is fully coated. Do not shake off the excess. Fry the cauliflower in batches over medium-high heat until golden brown on both sides, about 3 minutes per side. If the oil in the pan begins to have too many browned flour bits, wipe it clean in between batches and add fresh oil and bring the oil back up to temperature. Transfer the fried cauliflower to a waiting baking pan or glass baking dish.

When all the pieces have been fried, squeeze the juice of half a lemon over the cauliflower and bake in the preheated oven until fork-tender, about 20 to 30 minutes. Remove from the oven, sprinkle with kosher salt and pepper to taste, and the juice of the remaining lemon. This cauliflower is delicious hot right from the oven or cold from the fridge, even the next day.

Roasted Eggplant and Tomato Salad

Every Romanian household serves a version of this classic dish. Some insist you chop the eggplant with the side of a ceramic plate, others argue that only wood can come in contact with the temperamental vegetable. Truth is, chop as you please and add the garlic and herbs to your taste.

SERVES 4 TO 6

Start to Finish: Under 45 minutes

1 large eggplant, about 1¼ to 1½ pounds, cut in half lengthwise,
   stems and ends removed
3 tablespoons olive oil
2 tablespoons finely minced garlic
1 cup drained diced canned tomatoes
1 teaspoon sweet or hot Hungarian paprika
¼ teaspoon ground cumin
¼ teaspoon dried oregano
1 teaspoon kosher salt
¼ teaspoon freshly ground black pepper

> 1 tablespoon chopped fresh flat-leaf parsley
> 1 tablespoon chopped fresh basil leaves
> Juice of ½ lemon

Preheat the broiler and lightly oil a small rimmed baking sheet. Place the eggplant halves, skin side up, on the baking sheet and broil 4 to 5 inches from the heat source until the skin begins to crisp, 20 to 25 minutes. Remove the eggplant from the baking sheet and place in a colander to drain. When the eggplant is cool enough to handle, remove any large seeds, pull out the eggplant meat, and discard the skin; set aside.

Heat the olive oil in a large skillet, add the garlic and cook for 1 minute. Add the tomatoes, paprika, cumin, oregano, and salt and pepper, and cook over medium heat, until everything is heated through and fully incorporated, about 5 minutes. Toss in the eggplant and stir to combine set aside cool. When the mixture is cool, chop by hand using a hak-messer (mezzaluna), or pulse in the bowl of a food processor fitted with the metal blade. You don't want to over process and lose the texture or cause the mixture to become thin and runny. Stir in the parsley, basil, and lemon juice. Serve hot or cold.

Creamed Spinach

Everyone loves creamed spinach, especially when it is lighter and healthier than the usual cream and butter version. This preparation delivers the flavor without the fat and makes a great side for any meat and potatoes dinner.

SERVES 4

Start to Finish: Under 15 minutes

> 2 tablespoons olive oil
> ½ small onion, diced (about ¼ cup)
> 2 tablespoons all-purpose flour
> 1 (10-ounce) package chopped frozen spinach, thawed but not drained
> Pinch of freshly grated or ground nutmeg
> Kosher salt and freshly ground black pepper

Heat the oil in a small skillet, add the onion, and cook over medium heat until just translucent, about 5 minutes. Stir in the flour, cook, stirring, until the flour and onions create a blonde paste (for more about roux see Feedback pages 116–117).

Squeeze the water out of the thawed spinach and reserve the liquid. Add the drained spinach to the skillet with the roux and cook until the spinach and onions are well combined. Begin pouring the spinach water into the pan, a little at a time, stirring until you reach the desired consistency. Season with nutmeg, salt, and pepper to taste.

One person's chutney is another's salsa. Many of us relish *anything* pickled. Whether incorporating avocados to create silky cream, or roasting pineapple to balance a spicy chicken, these sweet and savory concoctions combine complex and often unexpected flavors into a brand-new taste. Serve these condiments alongside meat and poultry and bring color and flavor to your plate.

Cranberry Raisin Apple Chutney
Tart, sweet, chunky, cinnamon—deliciously easy and fast.

MAKES ABOUT 1 QUART CHUTNEY
Start to Finish: Under 1 hour

4 crisp apples, any variety (a combination of apples and pears
   works well too)
Zest and juice of 1 orange
1 cup apple juice or apple cider
1 teaspoon ground cinnamon
1 cup plump raisins, black, golden, or a combination
1 bag whole fresh cranberries (12 oz.)
3 tablespoons light brown sugar

Peel, core, and dice the apples (they don't need to be uniform in size, it's nice to have some pieces larger and chunkier). Place the diced fruit in a large saucepan. Stir in the orange zest, orange juice, apple juice or cider, and cinnamon. Cook over medium heat for 15 minutes, or until the apples have begun to soften. Stir in the raisins, cranberries, and sugar. Continue cooking, over low heat, until the cranberries have mostly burst and melted into the sauce and the apples and raisins are very soft, about 20 minutes. Serve hot or cold. The natural pectin in the apples will thicken the sauce as it stands.

Pineapple Mango Chutney
Sweet but not cloying, with a salty Asian accent.

MAKES ABOUT 3 CUPS CHUTNEY

Start to Finish: Under 30 minutes to prep, plus time to chill

1 whole pineapple, peeled, cored, and cut into 1-inch pieces
¼ cup thinly sliced red onion
1 tablespoon brown sugar
1 teaspoon grated fresh ginger
¼ cup water
1 tablespoon honey
1 tablespoon low-sodium soy sauce
1 teaspoon toasted sesame oil
Pinch of kosher salt
A few grinds of black pepper
½ cup golden raisins, optional
1 mango, diced
1 small jicama, peeled and shredded (about 1 cup)

Cook the pineapple, red onion, and brown sugar in a saucepan over medium heat, until the onions become translucent and the pineapple begins to lightly brown (caramelize), about 10 minutes. Add the ginger, water, honey, soy sauce, sesame oil, salt, pepper, and raisins if using. Cover the pot and cook, over low heat, about 10 minutes. Spoon the chutney into a bowl and chill. When ready to serve, stir in the mango and jicama.

Plum Tomato and Tomatillo Salsa

Tomatillos look a lot like small, hard green tomatoes and have a tart taste. Maybe that's why they hide behind thin light green husks. To prepare them, pull away the husk and enjoy them raw, or blanch or roast them to change their texture and flavor. Traditionally cilantro is added to salsa, but if you are a cilantrophobe, feel free to substitute parsley or fresh oregano.

SERVES 4 TO 6

Start to Finish: Under 30 minutes to prepare, plus time to chill

½ pound tomatillos, husks removed
1 pound plum (Roma) tomatoes, seeded and chopped into small
    bite-size pieces
1 small red onion, chopped (about ½ cup)
2 garlic cloves, finely minced (about 1 tablespoon)
1 teaspoon chopped jalapeño pepper, seeds removed
    (more or less to taste)
2 tablespoons red wine vinegar
1 tablespoon olive oil
1 teaspoon honey
Juice of 1 lime
1 heaping tablespoon chopped fresh cilantro leaves
1 teaspoon kosher salt
¼ teaspoon freshly ground black pepper

Bring a medium pot of salted water to a boil, and blanch the tomatillos at a gentle simmer for about 5 minutes. You don't want to cook them, just soften them slightly. Drain and set aside to cool.

To seed the plum tomatoes, cut them in half lengthwise and use your finger or a spoon to push out the seeds and rib. Use a serrated knife to cut the tomatoes into small pieces (a regular knife will tear at the flesh and be less efficient). Add the tomatoes and all the remaining ingredients to a bowl. When the tomatillos are cool, finely chop them, add them to the bowl with the other ingredients, and toss gently. Refrigerate for at least several hours to incorporate all the flavors.

Preserved Lemons

Meyer lemons are small, yellow-orangish lemons that are less tart than conventional lemons and have an almost tangerine flavor. Because they are thin-skinned, they take very well to pickling, and their rinds become soft and deliciously edible. Preserved lemons are often used in Moroccan dishes, such as *tajines,* and add a sweet, tart, and salty layer to almost anything they are added to. It can be difficult to find preserved lemons, also called *citrons confits,* at your grocer, but they are so easy to make at home. They will hold in your fridge for up to 6 months . . . but you'll find a million reasons to use them long before then. If you cannot find Meyer lemons, substitute yellow lemons. They might be a bit more tart, but they're still delicious.

MAKES 1 PINT PRESERVED LEMONS
Start to Finish: 5 minutes to prepare; 3 weeks to preserve

6 to 7 Meyer lemons
¼ cup kosher salt

Slice 5 of the lemons in a shallow bowl so that you don't lose any of their juices. Cut them in quarters, then quarter again. Remove all the seeds, and the small nub at each end of the rind. Sprinkle the lemons with the salt. Pack everything into a sterilized pint-size canning jar that can hold them snugly, pushing down on the lemons to release their juices. Squeeze the juice from the remaining lemons into the jar and then toss in 1 of the remaining lemons. Tightly close the jar and leave it out on your counter for 1 day. After one day, refrigerate, remembering to shake the jar daily, until the lemons are very soft to the bite, about 3 weeks.

The preserved lemons will be very salty. You can use them as is, dice them, or make them into a paste. If adding them to a recipe that contains salt, you might want to omit or cut down the quantity of salt in that recipe. You can rinse the lemons before adding them to a dish; you'll lose some of the salty goodness, but it makes them more palatable if you prefer a sweeter bite. You can add additional spices to the jar for another layer of flavor. Middle Eastern ingredients such as a cardamom pod, a cinnamon stick, or coriander seeds complement the lemon nicely. It might be fun to try one jar as directed above, and another with some of these more exotic spices, and compare the tastes.

Quick Pickled Cucumber Salad

This simple and quick pickled salad can feature just about any thinly sliced vegetable. For tougher veggies like cauliflower or broccoli, a quick blanching is helpful. The flavors intensify the longer they pickle.

SERVES 4 TO 6

Start to Finish: Under 15 minutes to prepare, plus at least 1 hour or up to 1 week to marinate

2 cucumbers, peeled and seeded
1 medium red onion, thinly sliced
   (a mandolin works very well for consistently thin slices)
2 teaspoons kosher salt
1/2 teaspoon white or freshly ground black pepper
1/2 cup apple cider vinegar
1/2 cup white vinegar
Juice of 1 lemon
Chopped fresh dill, optional

To seed the cucumbers, cut them in half lengthwise and then run a teaspoon along the seed path, gently scoop them out, and discard. You can skip this step (and the peeling) if you don't mind the seeds. Cut the cucumber into 1/4-inch thick slices, and place in a bowl. Add the remaining ingredients, cover, and chill. If the pickling is too sour, you can add a little sugar for balance.

Celery Root–Apple Slaw

I first discovered celery root (aka celeriac) while writing my first book, which featured many German and Eastern European recipes. I soon learned that this funny-looking root vegetable has a crunchy texture and a sweet hint of celery taste. It stands up to pickling and can be the foundation for a very healthful salad. I am reprinting the recipe here because it pairs very well with so many of the meat and poultry dishes we are presenting. If you like a lot of crunch, shred or thinly slice the celery root as you would jicama and eat it raw; if you prefer it tender to the bite, blanch the celery root before adding to the salad. Either way, it is refreshing and flavorful.

MAKES ABOUT 6 CUPS SLAW
Start to Finish: Under 15 minutes

1 celery root (about 1½ pounds), peeled and cut into matchstick
     pieces or grated on the large holes of a box grater
½ cup mayonnaise
4 teaspoons Dijon mustard
1 tablespoon apple cider vinegar
2 tablespoons freshly squeezed lemon juice
2 tablespoons minced shallot
½ cup finely chopped cornichons or sour pickles
1 tablespoon *herbes de Provence,* or a combination of dried herbs
     such as chervil, tarragon, and thyme
1 Granny Smith apple, peeled, cored, and cut into matchstick pieces
Kosher salt and freshly ground black pepper

Bring a medium pot of water to a boil and blanch the julienned celery root for 2 to 3 minutes (you can skip this step for a crunchier salad). Drain and place the blanched celery root in a bowl filled with ice water. While the celery cools, prepare the dressing by whisking together the mayonnaise, mustard, vinegar, lemon juice, shallots, and cornichons or pickles, and herbs. Drain and then spoon the celery root into the bowl and combine until all the pieces are coated with the dressing. Stir in the apples. Season to taste with salt and pepper. Cover and chill in the fridge until nice and cold for several hours or up to 1 week.

Traditional Guacamole

Chef Fermin Ortega of New York's Mañana restaurant and lounge makes some of the city's best guacamole. After I sampled several bowls at a recent Cinco de Mayo sangria-fueled lunch, he graciously shared the recipe with me.

SERVES 2

Start to Finish: Under 15 minutes

1 ripe avocado
¼ tablespoon lime juice from 1 lime
½ tablespoon chopped fresh cilantro
1 tablespoon chopped Vidalia onion
1 tablespoon chopped tomatoes, seeded
½ tablespoon chopped jalapeños (more or less depending on taste)
¼ teaspoon kosher salt

Cut the avocado in half lengthwise and remove seed. Scoop out the avocado flesh and mash in a mixing bowl to preferred consistency. Add the remaining ingredients and mix thoroughly with wooden spoon. Serve with chips, vegetables, or as a spread.

DRESSING UP

There to highlight the main or accessorize a side dish, these little inspirations dress up whatever you prepare. While it is so easy to open a jar or reach for that familiar bottle of salad dressing, with just a few simple ingredients and a quick shake, stir, or spin you can create a homemade version that is sure to be fresher, healthier, and more economical than anything with a label and a lid.

Homemade Mayonnaise

There's nothing wrong with reaching into the fridge for the iconic yellow and blue jar. But until you've tasted homemade mayonnaise, you won't know what you're missing. If the mayonnaise is a featured ingredient in a recipe, why not start with pure homemade goodness?

MAKES ABOUT 1 CUP MAYONNAISE
Start to Finish: Under 15 minutes

1 egg yolk
Juice of 1 lemon (about 2 teaspoons)
½ teaspoon Dijon mustard
½ teaspoon kosher salt
2 tablespoons plus ¾ cup canola or other neutral-tasting oil

In a small bowl, combine the egg yolk (pasteurized eggs carry very little risk of harmful bacteria), lemon juice, Dijon mustard, and salt. Slowly whisk in (use an electric mixer or immersion blender with a whisk attachment) 1 to 2 tablespoons of canola oil. This small amount of oil, beaten in slowly, will start the emulsion. Then continue whisking in, ever so slowly, drop by drop, about ¾ cup of canola oil until you have a creamy, light yellow, rich-tasting mayonnaise. Do not rush the whisking, or you will end up with a separated gloppy mess. You can use the mayo as is, or flavor it with fresh herbs. Fresh mayonnaise will hold up to 1 week in the fridge.

Feedback

To turn this mayo into its culinary cousin, aioli, use good-quality olive oil in place of canola and pump it up with garlic.

Horseradish Cream

This sharp condiment features jarred horseradish, but you can use fresh if you are game. Be sure to wear a pair of swimming goggles or protective eye gear, as fresh horseradish fumes are pungent and can sting your eyes. The cream is a wonderful complement for roast beef, or a terrific spread on next-day sandwiches.

MAKES ABOUT ½ CUP HORSERADISH CREAM
Start to Finish: Under 15 minutes

½ cup good-quality mayonnaise (for homemade, see pages 223–224)
2 tablespoons jarred or freshly grated horseradish
1 clove garlic, peeled and grated
Pinch of wasabi powder, optional
1 tablespoon freshly squeezed lemon juice
Kosher salt and freshly ground black pepper

In a small bowl, whisk the mayonnaise with the horseradish. Grate the garlic clove over the bowl and combine. Stir in the wasabi powder, if using, and lemon juice. Season to taste with salt and pepper. Chill until ready to use.

Guacamole Cream Aioli

This guacamole aioli is perfect when your hot and spicy wings want to take a refreshing plunge. It's also great to spread on grilled chicken or a toasted bun before it is closed around a juicy burger.

MAKES ½ CUP AIOLI
Start to Finish: Under 15 minutes

1 avocado, pitted and scooped out
1 large garlic clove, peeled and chopped
Juice of 1 lime (about 1½ tablespoons)
¼ cup mayonnaise (or homemade, see pages 223–224)
¼ cup loosely packed cilantro or parsley leaves
Kosher salt and freshly ground black pepper

Combine all the ingredients in the bowl of a food processor fitted with a metal blade. Blend until smooth and creamy.

Sofrito

Sofrito is to Latin and Caribbean cooking what pesto is to Italian. It's a party of onions, bell peppers, and garlic that boosts the flavor of anything it touches. It can be added to salad dressing, stews, and sauce. Try sofrito as a seasoning any time you want to wake up a dish.

MAKES 1 QUART SOFRITO
Start to Finish: Under 15 minutes

1 Spanish onion, roughly chopped
1 green bell pepper, cored, seeded, and roughly chopped
1 red bell pepper, cored, seeded, and roughly chopped
1 head of garlic (about 10 cloves), peeled and roughly chopped
1 bunch cilantro (about ¼ pound), leaves only, roughly chopped
2 plum tomatoes, roughly chopped
½ bunch flat-leaf parsley (about 2 ounces), roughly chopped

Combine all the ingredients in the bowl of a food processor fitted with the metal blade. Pulse until combined and all the ingredients are finely minced, but not watery. You can add a drop of olive oil to help the process along. You can add salt and pepper to the sofrito, but I prefer to season it when I use it. The sofrito freezes well in an ice cube tray or ziplock freezer bags. It will hold in the fridge for 3 days or in the freezer for months.

Tomato Jam

In one mouthful you get so many tastes: savory, sweet, tart, and a subtle heat that warms the palate. The plum tomatoes and spices cook down, concentrating the surprisingly harmonious flavors to create a delectable jam. If you know how to make preserves, make a large batch for the whole season. Otherwise, refrigerate and use within a week.

MAKES ABOUT 1½ CUPS JAM
Start to Finish: Under 1½ hours

1½ pounds plum tomatoes, cored, seeded, and diced
1 cup sugar
1 tablespoon freshly squeezed lime juice, from 1 to 2 limes
1 tablespoon freshly squeezed lemon juice, from ½ lemon
1 teaspoon grated fresh ginger
1 teaspoon ground cumin
¼ teaspoon ground cinnamon
1 teaspoon kosher salt
Pinch of cayenne pepper, optional

Combine all the ingredients in a saucepan and bring to a boil over medium heat. Reduce the heat to low and simmer, covered, for about 45 minutes, stirring occasionally. Remove the cover and cook until the jam has thickened, about 15 to 30 minutes longer.

Red Pepper Vinaigrette

This simple dressing is great with any salad or tossed with pasta. You can fire-roast your own peppers by charring them over an open flame, but the process is labor intensive. This is one cheat you can easily get away with by purchasing fire-roasted red peppers at your grocer. Only buy those in a clear jar so you can see if the peppers have a charred exterior; you want that for a true smoky experience.

MAKES ABOUT ¾ CUP DRESSING
Start to Finish: Under 15 minutes

> ¼ cup red wine vinegar
> ½ teaspoon kosher salt
> Freshly ground black pepper, about ¼ teaspoon
> 1 teaspoon dried oregano
> ¼ cup plus 2 tablespoons olive oil
> ½ cup chopped jarred fire-roasted red peppers
> ¼ teaspoon sugar

Combine all ingredients in the bowl of a food processor fitted with the metal blade. Process until smooth.

INDEX

Abundant Asian Noodle Soup, 173–74
Acids, in marinades, 11
Aioli, Guacamole Cream, 225
Alvarez, Ivan, 33
Animals acceptable for human consumption, 1–2
Apple(s)
    Celery Root-Apple Slaw, 48, 219–20
    Cranberry Raisin Apple Chutney, 215–16
Apricots, Pan Seared Duck Breasts with, 164–65
Arroz con pollo, 128–29
Asian Noodle Soup, Abundant, 173–74
Avocado(es)
    Guacamole Cream Aioli, 225
    Traditional Guacamole, 220–21

Baby back ribs, 24
Baker, Arlette, 149
Banschik, Karen, 47
Barbecue
    Oven-Barbecued Turkey, 150–51
    Simpler BBQ Ribs, 44–46
    Slow-Day BBQ Brisket, 47–49
Barley, Egg, 199–200
Bases, in marinades, 11–12
Basil, 13
Basmati Rice, 192–93
Bâtons, 187
BBQ

Oven-Barbecued Turkey, 150–51
Simpler BBQ Ribs, 44–46
Slow-Day BBQ Brisket, 47–49
Bean(s)
Black Beans and Rice, 189–90
    Chickpea and White Bean Hummus, 198
    Hungarian Bean Soup, 176–77
    Lentil Soup, 177–78
    Tuscan Beans, 194–95
Beef
    Beef and Barley Soup, 181–82
    Beef Braciole in Sunday Sauce, 36–39
    Beef Stew Provençal, 41–42
    Beef Stock, 178–80
    Best Burger, The, 56
    Breakfast Burrito, 66
    Chicken–Fried Steak, 30–31
    Classic Brisket, 49–51
    Classic Pot Roast, 26–27
    Coffee-Crusted Hanger Steak, 34–35
    Corned Beef Hash, 53–54
    Crispy Orange Beef and Broccoli, 39–40
    cuts of, 19–22
    Grilled Steak Chimichurri, 32–34
    Grilled Steak Salad, 35–36
    Matzo Meat Cakes, 60–62
    New England Boiled Dinner, 51–53
    overview of, 19–23, 55

Picadillo, 59–60
Pushcart Puppies, 63–64
Rib Steak Florentine, 28–29
Roasted Beef, 24–25
Sausage, 62–63
Sausage and Peppers, 64–65
Simple Oven-Braised Short Ribs,
    43–44
Simpler BBQ Ribs, 44–46
Simplest Korean *Kalbi* Ribs, 46–47
Slow-Day BBQ Brisket, 47–49
Spaghetti Bolognese, 56–58
Spicy Grilled *Mititei*, 58–59
Standing Rib Roast, 23–24
Steak and Eggs, 31–32
Steak Pizzaiola, 27–28
Beer
    Pretzel-crusted Chicken, 141–42
    Simpler Beer-basted Chicken,
        109–10
Best Burger, The, 56
Bison, 21–22
Black Beans and Rice, 189–90
Blue Ribbon, 171
Boiled Dinner, New England, 51–53
"Bonus" Chicken, 114–15
"Bonus" meat, 114–15, 149, 161
Braciole (Beef) in Sunday Sauce, 36–39
Braising, method overview, 7–8
Breakfast Burrito, 66
Breast of Duck Salad, 165–66
Breast of lamb, 87, 88
Brisket
    Classic Brisket, 49–51
    Slow-Day BBQ Brisket, 47–49
    Veal Brisket, 81–82
Brisket cut, 21, 46
Broccoli
    Crispy Orange Beef and Broccoli,
        39–40
    Lemon and Garlic Broccoli, 209–10
    Turkey Sausage with, 157–58

Broiling, method overview, 9
Bromberg, Eric and Bruce, 171
Brown sugar, 13
Buca Lapi, 28–29
Burgers
    The Best Burger, 56
    Lamb Sliders, 102–03
Burrito, Breakfast, 66
Butchering
    of chickens, 122
    knives for, 22
    rules for, 2–3
Butcher's surprise, 24

Cabbage Soup, Grandma Rose's,
    180–81
Cacciatore, Chicken, 122–24
Caesar Salad, Chicken, 118–19
Cage-free poultry, 105
Cajun spice, 120–21
Calf's Liver, 83–84
Carbs
    Basmati Rice, 192–93
    Black Beans and Rice, 189–90
    Chickpea and White Bean Hummus,
        197–98
    Creamy Mashed Potatoes, 187–88
    Herbed Potato Salad, 185–86
    Homemade Egg Noodles, 201–2
    Kasha Varnishkes, 196–97
    Porcini Mushroom Risotto, 190–91
    Potato and Zucchini Pancakes,
        183–84
    Quinoa, 195–96
    Roasted Rosemary Potatoes, 185
    Tomatoey Rice, 193–94
    Tuscan Beans, 194–95
    Twice-Fried Potatoes, 186–87
    Vegetable Fried Rice, 188–89
    Wild Rice with Dried Cranberries,
        191–92

Carrots, 44
Cauliflower Fritters, Lemony, 210–11
Celeriac, 219–20
Celery Root–Apple Slaw, 48, 219–20
Chicken
    "Bonus" Chicken 114–15
    Chicken Cacciatore, 122–24
    Chicken Caesar Salad, 118–19
    Chicken Croquettes, 144–45
    Chicken-Fried Steak 30–31
    Chicken Lettuce Cups, 143–44
    Chicken Liver Pâté, 147–48
    Chicken Piccata, 137–39
    Chicken with Prunes *Tsimmes,*
      124–25
    Chicken in Red Wine Sauce, 124–25
    Chicken and Rice, 128–29
    Chicken and Sausage Gumbo,
      120–21
    Chicken and Scallion Wontons,
      145–47
    Chicken Stock, 169
    Crispy Fried Chicken, 126–28
    Curried Chicken Salad, 117–18
    cutlets, 137
    Grilled Chicken and Pasta Primav-
      era, 140–41
    Grilled Spice-Rubbed Chicken, 135
    ground, 144
    Moroccan Chicken, 131–33
    No-Brainer Wings, 136
    overview of, 105–6
    Panko-Crusted Chicken Cutlets,
      139–40
    Peach and Ginger-Glazed Chicken,
      130–31
    Pretzel-Crusted Chicken, 141–42
    Roasted Cornish Hen, 112–14
    Simple Spatchcocked Chicken,
      107–9
    Simpler Beer-Basted Chicken,
      109–10
    Simplest Roast Chicken, 111–12
    Skewered Chicken Thighs, 133–34
    Topless Chicken Potpie, 115–17
Chicken Fried Steak, 30–31
Chickpea and White Bean Hummus,
    197–98
Chiffonade, 13
Chili, Turkey, 155–56
Chimichurri, Grilled Steak, 32–34
Chinese five spice powder, 14
Choucroute, 149
Chuck cut, 20
Chutneys, Salsas, and Relish
    Celery Root–Apple Slaw, 48, 219–20
    Cranberry Raisin Apple Chutney,
      215–16
    Pineapple Mango Chutney, 216
    Plum Tomato and Tomatillo Salsa,
      217
    Preserved Lemons, 218
    Quick Pickled Cucumber Salad, 219
    Traditional Guacamole, 220–21
Citrons confits, 218
Classic Brisket, 49–51
Classic Pot Roast, 26–27
Coconut, Skewered Chicken Thighs,
    133–34
Coffee-Crusted Hanger Steak, 34–35
Cohen, Rachel, 177
Cooking methods
    braising/pot roasting/stewing, 7–8
    broiling, 9
    dry roasting, 8–9
    grilling, 9–10
    pan searing, 10
    rules for kosher, 1–3
Coq au vin, 126–27
Corn on the Cob, Roasted, 207–8
Corned beef
    Corned Beef Hash, 53–54
    New England Boiled Dinner, 51–53
Country-Style Turkey Meat Loaf, 154–55

Couscous, Israeli, 200–201
Cranberry(ies)
    Cranberry Raisin Apple Chutney,
        215–16
    Wild Rice with Cranberries, 191–92
Creamed Spinach, 212–13
Creamy Mashed Potatoes, 187–88
Creamy Mushroom Soup, 170–71
Cremini mushrooms, 82
Crescent steak, 24
Crispy Fried Chicken, 126–28
Crispy Orange Beef and Broccoli,
    39–40
Croquettes, Chicken, 144–45
Crostini, Chicken Liver Pâté on,
    147–48
Cucumber Salad, Quick Pickled, 219
Curried Chicken Salad, 117–18
Curry powder, yellow, 14
Cutlets
    overview of, 137
    Panko-Crusted Chicken Cutlets,
        139–40
Cuts
    of beef, 19–22
    of lamb, 87–88
    of veal, 67–68

Dairy, meat and, 3
Damant, Irving, 44
Demi-glace, 180
Dinde braisée, 149–50
Dough
    Dumplings and Spaetzle, 203–4
    Egg Barley, 199–200
    Grilled Pizza Flatbread, 205
    Homemade Egg Noodles, 201–2
    Israeli Couscous, 200–201
    Yorkshire Pudding, 204–5
Dressings
    Guacamole Cream Aioli, 225

Homemade Mayonnaise, 223–24
    Horseradish Cream, 224
    Red Pepper Vinaigrette, 226
    Sofrito, 225–26
    Tomato Jam, 226
Dry aged steak, 29
Dry roasting, method overview, 8–9
Duck
    Breast of Duck Salad, 165–66
    overview of, 161
    Pan-Seared Duck Breasts, 164–65
    Roast Duck, 161–63

Eco-kosher movement, 3, 105
Eggplant (Roasted) and Tomato Salad,
    211–12
Egg(s)
    Egg Barley, 199–200
    Homemade Egg Noodles, 201–2
    Poached Egg, 54–55
    Steak and Eggs, 31–32
Emulsifiers, in marinades, 12

Figs, Pan-Seared Duck Breasts with,
    164–65
Filé powder, 121–22
Flanken, Beef Stew Provençal, 42
Flatbread, Grilled Pizza, 205
Flatiron Kitchen, 90, 200
Flatiron steak, 37
Flavor
    marinades for, 11–13
    rubs for, 13
    spices and herbs for, 13–15
Forequarter
    beef, 19–22
    veal, 67
Foresaddle, 87
Foreshank
    lamb, 87, 88

veal, 67–68

Fowl, forbidden species, 2

Franks, Pushcart Puppies, 63–64

Fried Chicken, Crispy, 126–28

Fritters, Lemony Cauliflower, 210–11

Fruit, supreming and, 35

Galbi Ribs (Korean), Simplest, 46–47

Garber, Carl, 21–22

Gastrique, 84

Ghinassi, Luciano, 28–29

Ginger (and Peach) -Glazed Chicken,
    130–31

Glatt kosher, 2

Glazes
    Oaky Bourbon glaze, 45
    Peach and Ginger-Glazed Chicken
        and, 130–31
    Teriyaki-Glazed Shoulder Lamb
        Chops, 93–94

Grandma Rose's Cabbage Soup,
    180–81

Grass-fed beef, 21

Gravy separators, 9

Gremolata, Mediterranean Osso Buco,
    71–73

Grilled Chicken and Pasta Primavera,
    140–41

Grilled Lamb Riblets, 92–93

Grilled Pizza Flatbread, 205

Grilled Spice-Rubbed Chicken, 135

Grilled Steak Chimichurri, 32–34

Grilled Steak Salad, 35–36

Grilled Turkey Paillard, 158–59

Grilled Veal Chops, 74

Grilling, method overview, 9–10

Ground beef
    Best Burger, The, 56
    Breakfast Burrito, 66
    Matzo Meat Cakes, 60–62
    overview of, 55
    Picadillo, 59–60
    Pushcart Puppies, 63–64

Sausage and Peppers, 64–65
    Spaghetti Bolognese, 56–58
    Spicy Grilled *Mititei*, 58–59

Ground chicken, 144

Guacamole
    Guacamole Cream Aioli, 225
    Traditional Guacamole, 220–21

Gumbo, Chicken and Sausage, 120–21

Hanger steak, 39

Hash, Corned Beef Hash, 53–54

Herb-Crusted Rib Lamb Chops, 89–91

Herbed Potato Salad, 185–86

Herbes de Provence, overview of, 14

Herbs and spices
    in marinades, 12
    overview of, 13–15
    za'atar, 92–93

Homemade Mayonnaise, 223–24

Honey, in marinades, 12

Horseradish Cream, 224

Hot dogs. *See* Franks

Hummus, Chickpea and White Bean,
    198

Hungarian Bean Soup, 176–77

Hungarian paprika, 14

Italian herb, overview of, 14

Jam, Tomato, 57, 226

Kalbi Ribs (Korean), Simplest, 46–47

Kasha Varnishkes, 196–97

Klarberg, Eddie, 92

Knives, for butchering, 22

Kohn, Ruth, 128

Korean *Kalbi* Ribs, Simplest, 46–47

Kornbleuth, Norman, 7–8, 10

Kosher, criteria for, 2–3

LaFrieda Meat Purveyors, 56
Lamb
    Grilled Lamb Riblets, 92–93
    Herb-crusted Rib Lamb Chops,
        89–91
    Lamb Sliders, 102–3
    Lamb and Spinach Spanakopita,
        99–102
    Lamb Tagine, 98–99
    Mediterranean Rack of Lamb,
        90–91
    Moroccan Lamb Shanks with
        Pomegranate Sauce, 96–98
    overview of, 87–88
    Pesto-Crusted Roasted Lamb
        Shoulder, 94–96
    Teriyaki-Glazed Shoulder Lamb
        Chops, 93–94
Lemon(s)
    Lemon and Garlic Broccoli, 209–10
    Lemony Cauliflower Fritters, 210–11
    Lemon zest, 90
    Preserved Lemons, 218
Lentil Soup, 177–78
Lettuce Cups, Chicken, 143–44
Liver
    Calf's Liver, 83–84
    Chicken Liver Pâté, 147–48
London broil cut steak, 33

Madeira sauce, Pan-Seared Duck
    Breasts with, 164–65
Mañana restaurant, 33, 220
Mango Pineapple Chutney, 216
Marango, Veal, 78–79
Marinades
    overview of, 11–13
    Teriyaki-Glazed Shoulder Lamb
        Chops and, 92–93

Martha's Excellent Matzo Ball Soup,
    171–73
Mashed Potatoes, Creamy, 187–88
Matzo
    Martha's Excellent Matzo Ball Soup,
        171–73
    Matzo Meat Cakes, 60–62
Mayonnaise, Homemade, 223–24
Meat Cakes, Matzo, 60–62
Meatballs, Veal, 76–77
Meatloaf, Country-Style Turkey,
    154–55
Mediterranean Osso Buco, 71–73
Mediterranean Rack of Lamb, 90–91
Membrillo, 148
Methods. *See* Cooking methods
Meyer lemons, 218
Milanese, Veal, 79–81
Mititei, Spicy Grilled, 58–59
Moroccan Chicken, 131–33
Moroccan Lamb Shanks with Pome-
    granate Sauce, 96–98
Mushroom(s)
    Creamy Mushroom Soup, 170–71
    Mushrooms Egg Barley, 199–200
    overview of, 82
    Roasted Veal Shoulder, 69–71
    Stuffed Mushroom Caps with Asian
        or Italian Filling, 75–76
    Veal Brisket and, 81–82
Mustard, Pretzel-Crusted Chicken,
    141–42

Nasi goreng, 189
New England Boiled Dinner, 51–53
No-Brainer Wings, 136
Noodle(s)
    Abundant Asian Noodle Soup,
        173–74
    Homemade Egg Noodles, 201–02
NP symbol, defined, 18

Oaky Bourbon glaze, 45
Offal, 147
Okra, 120
Olive oil, in marinades, 11–12
Orange Beef (Crispy) and Broccoli, 39–40
Orecchiette pasta, Turkey Sausage with, 157–58
Oregano, 103
Ortega, Fermin, 220
Osso buco
    Mediterranean Osso Buco, 70–72
    overview of, 68
Oven-Barbecued Turkey, 150–51
Oven-Roasted Plum Tomatoes, 208–9
overview of, 55

Paillard, Grilled Turkey, 158–59
Pan-Seared Duck Breasts, 164–65
Pan searing, method overview, 10
Pancakes, Potato and Zucchini, 183–84
Panko-Crusted Chicken Cutlets, 139–40
Papaya, tenderizing and, 11
Paprika, 14, 34–35
Pareve
    defined, 3
    NP symbol in recipes and, 18
    Worcestershire sauce as, 12
Parsley, overview of, 13
Pasta
    Abundant Asian Noodle Soup, 173–74
    Egg Barley, 199–200
    Grilled Chicken and Pasta Primavera, 140–41
    Homemade Egg Noodles, 201–2
    Israeli Couscous, 200–201
    Kasha Varnishkes, 196–97
    Turkey Sausage with, 157–58
Pastore, Mark, 56
Pasture-raised poultry, 105
Pâté, Chicken Liver, 147–48

Peach and Ginger-Glazed Chicken, 130–31
Peanut dipping sauce, Skewered Chicken Thighs and, 133–34
Pepper, overview of, 14
Peppers
    Red Pepper Vinaigrette, 226
    Sausage and Peppers, 64–65
Pesto-Crusted Roasted Lamb Shoulder, 94–96
Phyllo dough, 100–102
Picadillo, 59–60, 189
Piccata, Chicken, 137–39
Pickling spice, 53
Pimentón, 35
Pine nuts, 96
Pineapple
    Pineapple Mango Chutney, 216
    tenderizing and, 11
Pita, Patricia, 59–60
Pizza Flatbread, Grilled, 205
Pizzaiola, Steak, 27–28
Plate cut, overview of, 20–21
Plum Tomato and Tomatillo Salsa, 217
Pomegranate Sauce, Moroccan Lamb Shanks with, 96–98
Porcini mushroom(s)
    Porcini Mushroom Risotto, 190–91
    Roasted Beef and, 24–25
    Roasted Veal Shoulder, 69–71
Port sauce, Roast Duck with, 161–63
Pot Roast, Classic, 26–27
Pot roasting, method overview, 7–8
Potato(es)
    Creamy Mashed Potatoes, 187–88
    Herbed Potato Salad, 185–86
    Potato and Zucchini Pancakes, 183–84
    Roasted Rosemary Potatoes, 184–85
    Twice-Fried Potatoes, 186–87
Potpie, Topless Chicken, 114–17
Poultry, marinating, 12. *See also* Chicken; Duck; Turkey
Preserved Lemons, 218

Pretzel-Crusted Chicken, 141–42
Pricing, 17
Primavera (Pasta), Grilled Chicken
    and, 140–41
Prunes
    Chicken with Prunes *Tsimmes*,
        124–25
    Quinoa with, 195–96
Pudding, Yorkshire Pudding, 204–5
Pushcart Puppies, 63–64

Quick Pickled Cucumber Salad, 219
Quince, 148
Quinoa, 195–96

Rack, 68. *See also* Rib cut
Rack of Lamb, Mediterranean, 90–91
Ragout, 50–51
Raspberries, Breast of Duck Salad with,
    165–66
Reback, Ariella, 105
Red Pepper Vinaigrette, 226
Red Wine Sauce, Chicken in, 125–26
Relish. *See* Chutneys, Salsas, and Relish
Rib cut
    Herb-Crusted Rib Lamb Chops,
        89–91
    lamb, 87, 88
    overview of, 20
    Rib Steak Florentine, 28–29
    Standing Rib Roast, 23–24
Riblets, Grilled Lamb, 92–93
Ribollita Soup, Tuscan, 174–75
Ribs
    Baby back ribs, 24
    Grilled Lamb Riblets, 92–93
    Simple Oven-Braised Short Ribs,
        43–44
    Simpler BBQ Ribs, 44–46
    Simplest Korean *Kalbi* Ribs, 46–47

Rice
    Basmati Rice, 192–93
    Black Beans and Rice, 189–90
    Chicken and Rice, 128–29
    Israeli Couscous, 200–201
    Mediterranean Osso Buco and, 73
    Porcini Mushroom Risotto, 190–91
    Tomatoey Rice, 193–94
    Vegetable Fried Rice, 188–189
    Wild Rice, 191–92
Risotto, porcini-studded, 69
Roast Duck, 161–63
Roasted Beef, 24–25
Roasted Corn on the Cob, 207–8
Roasted Cornish Hen, 112–14
Roasted Eggplant and Tomato Salad,
    211–12
Roasted Rosemary Potatoes, 185
Roasted Veal Shoulder, 69–71
Roasting, method overview, 8–9
Roasts
    Classic Pot Roast, 26–27
    defined, 22
    Roasted Cornish Hen, 112–14
    Simple Spatchcocked Chicken,
        106–9
    Simpler Beer-basted Chicken,
        109–10
    Simplest Roast Chicken, 111–12
Rosemary
    overview of, 13
    Roasted Rosemary Potatoes, 184–85
Rotter, Aron, 14–15
Roulade, Turkey, 152–153
Roux, 116–117
Rubbed Chicken, Grilled Spice-,
    135–36
Rubs, overview of, 13

Sage, 13
Salad dressing, as marinade, 13

Salad(s)
  Breast of Duck Salad, 165–66
  Chicken Caesar Salad, 118–19
  Curried Chicken Salad, 117–18
  Grilled Steak Salad, 35–36
  Herbed Potato Salad, 185–86
  Quick Pickled Cucumber Salad, 219
  Roasted Eggplant and Tomato
    Salad, 211–12
Salsas. *See* Chutneys, Salsas, and Relish
Salt, in rubs, 13
Sangria, 33
Sauerkraut, Turkey with, 149–50
Sausage 62–63
  Chicken and Sausage Gumbo,
    120–21
  Sausage and Peppers, 64–65
  Turkey Sausage, 157–58
  Tuscan Ribollita Soup with, 174–75
Schlaff, Norman, 10, 21
Searing. *See* Broiling; Pan searing
Serving size, 17
Shallots Bistro, 98
Shin meat, 21, 68
Short ribs
  overview of, 42
  Simple Oven-Braised Short Ribs,
    42–44
Shoulder, 67, 87–88
Shoulder, Pesto-Crusted Roasted
    Lamb, 94–96
Shoulder Lamb Chops, Teriyaki-
    Glazed, 93–94
Silver tip cuts, 26, 35
Simple Oven-Braised Short Ribs, 43–44
Simple Spatchcocked Chicken, 107–9
Simpler BBQ Ribs, 44–46
Simpler Beer-Basted Chicken, 109–10
Simplest Korean *Kalbi* Ribs, 46–47
Simplest Roast Chicken, 111–12
Skewered Chicken Thighs, 133–34
Skirt steak, 33

Slaughtering, rules for, 2
Slaw, Celery Root-Apple, 48, 219–20
Sliders, Lamb, 102–03
Slow-Day BBQ Brisket, 47–49
Slurry, 78
Smoked turkey, Hungarian Bean Soup
    with, 176–77
Sochets, 2
Sofrito, 225–26
Soup and stock
  Abundant Asian Noodle Soup,
    173–74
  Beef and Barley Soup, 181–82
  Beef Stock, 178–80
  Chicken Stock, 169
  Creamy Mushroom Soup, 170–71
  Grandma Rose's Cabbage Soup,
    180–81
  homemade, 167–68, 178–79
  Hungarian Bean Soup, 176–77
  Lentil Soup, 177–78
  Martha's Excellent Matzo Ball Soup,
    171–73
  Tuscan Ribollita Soup, 174–75
Southern Fried Sweetbreads, 84–85
Spaetzle, Dumplings and, 202–4
Spaghetti Bolognese, 56–58
Spanakopita (Spinach), Lamb and,
    99–102
Spanish paprika, 35
Spatchcocked Chicken, Simple, 106–9
Spice-Rubbed Chicken, Grilled, 135–36
Spices and herbs
  in marinades, 12
  overview of, 13–15
  za'atar, 92–93
Spicy Grilled *Mititei,* 58–59
Spinach
Creamed Spinach, 212–13
Lamb and Spinach Spanakopita,
    99–102
Standing Rib Roast, 23–24

Steak
  Chicken-Fried Steak, 30–31
  Coffee-Crusted Hanger Steak,
    34–35
  defined, 22
  Grilled Steak Chimichurri, 32–34
  Grilled Steak Salad, 35–36
  Rib Steak Florentine, 28–29
  Steak and Eggs, 31–32
  Steak Pizzaiola, 27–28
Stew
  Beef Stew Provençal, 41–42
  defined, 22
  Veal Marengo, 78–79
Stewing, method overview, 7–8
Stir fry
  Crispy Orange Beef and Broccoli,
    39–40
  defined, 22
Stock. *See* Soup and stock
Stuffed Mushroom Caps with Asian or
    Italian Filling, 75–76
Stuffing, Turkey Roulade with, 152–53
Sugar in marinades and rubs, 12, 13
Sunday Sauce, Beef Braciole in, 36–39
Supreming, 35
Sweetbreads, Southern Fried, 84–85
Sweeteners and rubs, 12, 13
Syrah, Grilled Veal Chops, 74

Tagine, Lamb, 98–99
Tajines, 130, 218
Tenderizing
  marinades for, 11–12
  rubs for, 13
Teriyaki-Glazed Shoulder Lamb Chops,
    93–94
Thyme, overview of, 13
Timing, 17–18
Tomato(es)
  Oven-Roasted Plum Tomatoes,
    208–9

Plum Tomato and Tomatillo Salsa,
  217
  Roasted Eggplant and Tomato
    Salad, 211–12
  Tomatoey Rice, 193–94
  Tomato Jam, 57, 226
Topless Chicken Potpie, 115–17
Traditional Guacamole, 220–21
Treif, defined, 2
Tsimmes, Chicken with Prunes, 125–26
Turkey
  Country-Style Turkey Meat Loaf,
    154–55
  Grilled Turkey Paillard, 158–59
  Hungarian Bean Soup with,
    176–77
  Oven-Barbecued Turkey, 150–51
  overview of, 149
  Turkey Chili, 155–56
  Turkey Roulade, 152–53
  Turkey Sausage, 157–58
  Turkey with Sauerkraut, 149–50
Tuscan Beans, 194–95
Tuscan Ribollita Soup, 174–75
Twice-Fried Potatoes, 186–87

Umami, in marinades, 12

Varnishkes, Kasha, 197
Veal
  Calf's Liver, 83–84
  Grilled Veal Chops, 74
  Mediterranean Osso Buco, 71–73
  Mushroom Caps, 75–76
  overview of, 67–68
  Roasted Veal Shoulder, 69–71
  Southern-Fried Sweetbreads, 84–85
  Veal Brisket, 81–82
  Veal Marango, 78–79
  Veal Meatballs, 76–77
  Veal Milanese, 79–81

Vegetables
    Black Beans and Rice, 189–90
    Celery Root–Apple Slaw, 48, 219–20
    Chickpea and White Bean Hummus,
       197–98
    Creamed Spinach, 212–13
    Creamy Mashed Potatoes, 187–88
    Creamy Mushroom Soup, 170–71
    Crispy Orange Beef and Broccoli,
       39–40
    with Egg Barley, 199–200
    Grandma Rose's Cabbage Soup,
       180–81
    Guacamole Cream Aioli, 225
    Herbed Potato Salad, 185–86
    Hungarian Bean Soup, 176–77
    Lamb and Spinach Spanakopita,
       99–102
    Lemon and Garlic Broccoli,
       209–210
    Lemony Cauliflower Fritters, 210–11
    Lentil Soup, 177–78
    Mushroom Caps, 75–76
    Oven-Roasted Plum Tomatoes,
       208–9
    overview of, 207
    Plum Tomato and Tomatillo Salsa,
       217
    Potato and Zucchini Pancakes,
       183–84
    Red Pepper Vinaigrette, 226
    Roasted Corn on the Cob, 207–8
    Roasted Eggplant and Tomato
       Salad, 211–12
    Roasted Rosemary Potatoes, 185
    Roasted Veal Shoulder, 69–71
    Sausage and Peppers, 64–65
    Simple Spatchcocked Chicken and,
       107–9
    Tomato Jam, 57, 226
    Tomatoey Rice, 193–94
    Traditional Guacamole, 220–21
    Tuscan Beans, 194–95

    Twice-Fried Potatoes, 186–87
    Veal Brisket and, 81–82
    Vegetable Fried Rice, 188–89
Venison, 21
Vermouth, 70
Vinaigrette, Red Pepper, 226

Walnuts (candied), Breast of Duck
    Salad with, 165–66
Weinstein, Norman, 22, 122
Wiener schnitzel, 81
Wiesenfeld, Chana, 197
Wild Rice, 191–92
Wines
    Chicken in Red Wine Sauce, 124–25
    flavor and, 14–15
    with Grilled Steak Chimichurri, 33
    Grilled Veal Chops and, 74
    with Moroccan Chicken, 133
    Pan Seared Duck Breasts with,
       164–65
    Roast Duck with, 161–63
    with Roasted Beef, 25
    Roasted Veal Shoulder and, 70
    with Steak Pizzaiola, 25
Wings, No-Brainer, 136
Wontons, Chicken and Scallion, 145–47
Worcestershire sauce, whether pareve,
    12

Yellow curry powder, 14
Yield, 17
Yorkshire pudding, 23, 204–5

Za'atar, 92–93
Zucchini
    Potato and Zucchini Pancakes,
       183–84
    Tomatoey Rice with, 193–94